The Art of Drama,

Hamlet

PERIPETEIA PRESS

Published by Peripeteia Press Ltd.

First published May 2020

ISBN: 978-1-9997376-9-6

Check out our A-level English Literature website, peripeteia.webs.com

Contents

With thanks to our families for their patience and support and to Rosa for her help and creativity.

Introduction to *The Art of Drama* series

The philosopher Nietzsche described his work as 'the greatest gift that [mankind] has ever been given' while the Elizabethan poet Edmund Spenser hoped his book *The Faerie Queene* [1590] would magically transform readers into noblemen. Two hundred years later Wordsworth and Coleridge hoped their *Lyrical Ballads* [1798] would radically improve English sensibilities. In comparison, our aims for *The Art of Drama* series of books are a little more modest. Fundamentally we aim to provide books that will be of maximum interest and usefulness to students of English and to their teachers.

In this new series of books, we aim to reproduce the success of our *The Art of Poetry* series by providing fine-grained, well-informed, lively and engaging material on the key issues in key drama set texts. In the first book in the series, we focused on J. B. Priestley's popular old stager, *An Inspector Calls*. In the second, we turned our critical attention to Shakespeare's notoriously dark and troubling Scottish play, *Macbeth*, and in this edition we explore perhaps the bard's most famous play, *Hamlet*.

As with all our poetry books, we hope this new series will appeal to English teachers as well as students of Literature. There is a plethora of material already available on both *Macbeth* and *Hamlet* on the market. However, many books aimed at GCSE pupils present information in condensed, broken up or broken down, note and bullet pointed formats. A distinguishing feature of our critical guides is that they are, fundamentally, comprised of a series of short essays. We may ask GCSE students to write essays, yet rarely do we encourage them to read literary essays, not least because there's a paucity of this sort of material pitched at this age group. Although there is academic material on *Hamlet*, little of this is written specifically for A-level students. Hence we have tried to fill this significant gap with essays modelling how to engage critically with Literary texts.

With the ever-increasing demands and importance of terminal exams, there's a great pressure on students and teachers to reach top grades. One way to attempt to do this is to drill students with exam technique and fill their heads with information in the hope that they will be able to regurgitate it accurately. In our opinion, that sort of production-line approach to learning cuts out an absolutely essential part of the experience of reading and writing about literature, perhaps the most rewarding and richest part, i.e. the forming of our own critical views.

Good critical writing about poems, novels and plays does not merely repeat somebody else's ideas uncritically. Rather it expresses the critical opinions of the writer, informed, of course, by their experiences in the classroom. No two essays on any Literary text should be exactly the same. Ideally teaching should nurture pupils' ability to express their own critical thinking about texts in their own emerging critical voices, informed by discussion with peers and the expertise of teachers.

Our essays in this collection do not follow any specific framework or aim to hit specific assessment objectives. We are not trying to get in 12.5% of context or to make sure we always finish with a telling quote. Rather the writers of this guide have been given free rein to write about what they find most interesting about their chosen topics, whether this be a central theme, character or scene. It is our conviction that when we write about the things that most interest us we write our best work.

This new *Hamlet* guide is aimed primarily at A-level English Literature students as well as their teachers and lecturers. We expect, however, that it will also be useful for undergraduates too. Our material seeks to stimulate a critical response, which might include fervent agreement or strong disagreement. We aim to make students think critically, to reflect, compare and evaluate different critical views as part of the process of formulating their own.

Writing about plays

The play and the novel

Plays and novels have several significant features in common, such as characters, dialogue, plots and settings. In addition, students read plays in lessons, often sitting at desks in the same way as they read novels. So it's not surprising that many students treat these two related, but distinct, literary art forms as if they were indistinguishable. Time and again, teachers and examiners come across sentences such as 'In the novel *Hamlet...*' Though sometimes this can be just a slip of the pen, often this error is a good indicator of a weak grasp of the nature of the text. Stronger responses fully appreciate the fact that *Hamlet* is a play, written for the stage by a playwright and realise the implications of the writer's choice of the dramatic form.

Characterisation

Imagine you're a novelist writing a scene introducing a major character. Sit back and survey the rich variety of means at your disposal: You could begin with a quick pen portrait of their appearance using your narrative voice, or you could have your characters say or do something significant. Alternatively, you could utilise your narrator to provide comments about, and background on, the character. Then again, you might take us into the character's thoughts and reveal what's really going on inside their head. If you're trying to convey thought as it happens you could even use a stream of consciousness.

Now imagine that you're a playwright introducing a major character. Sit up and survey the far more limited means at your disposal. Though you could describe a character's appearance, you'd have to communicate this through stage directions, which, of course, a theatre audience would not be able to read or hear. The same holds true for background information and narratorial style comments about the character; none of which would an audience be able to read. And unless you are going to use the dramatic devices known as the aside and the soliloquy, as Shakespeare famously used in his great tragedies, you will struggle to find a direct way to show what your character's really thinking. As a playwright, action and dialogue, however, are your meat and drink. While for a novelist being able to write cracking dialogue is a useful part of the repertoire, for a dramatist it's absolutely essential.

In general, drama focuses our attention on the outward behaviour of characters. Skilfully done, this can, of course, also reveal their interior thoughts. Nevertheless, novels more easily give access to the workings of the mind. You may have noticed this when novels are adapted into films and directors have to make the decision about whether to use a voiceover to convey the narrator or characters' thoughts. Rarely does this work uncheesily well.

Settings

With a swish of his or her fountain pen or deft fingers running over a keyboard, a novelist can move quickly and painlessly from one setting to another. One chapter of a novel could be set in Medieval York, the next on a far distant planet in the far distant future. The only limitation is the novelist's skill in rendering these worlds. What is true for geographical settings is also true for temporal ones. A novelist can write 'One thousand years later...' or track a character from cradle to grave. A novelist can also play around with narrative time, using flashbacks and flashforwards.

Though a little more restricted, a modern film director can also move fairly easily between geographical and temporal settings and can cross-cut between them. But not so a playwright. Why? Because plays are written for an actual physical stage and radically changing a stage set during the action of a play is a tricky, potentially cumbersome business. Imagine your Medieval York village, with its ramshackle thatched huts, pig pens and dirty streets. How are you going to transform this stage set to the dizzyingly futuristic world of Planet Zog in 2188 A.D. without the audience really noticing?

Possibly you could get your stage technicians to dismantle and construct the different stage sets while the audience waits patiently for the action to restart. But wouldn't that be clumsy and rather break the spell you'd hope your play was weaving? More likely you'd use a break, perhaps between the scenes or, better, during the interval for the major re-arrangement of stage scenery. Practically speaking, how many different stage sets could you create for a single play? Minimalistic stage designs might allow you to employ more settings, but you'd still be far more restricted than a film director or a novelist. And then there's the expense of building elaborate sets. Theatres aren't usually flush with money and complex stage sets are likely to be expensive. Another way out of this problem would be to have a pretty much bare and unchanging stage set and convey changes in scenes through the dialogue, a technique Shakespeare had to use for The Globe stage. Think, for instance, of the start of *The Tempest*, where the action of the opening scene takes place on a boat out a sea.

Here's our version of this sort of minimalist, setting-through-dialogue technique:

Stage direction: Two characters meet on a bare stage.
Character 1: What is this strange, futuristic place with extraordinary buildings?
Character 2: Why, this is the capital city of the Planet Zog.
Character 1: Aha! And, unless I'm mistaken, the year is now 2188 A.D.

etc.

As we'll see, Shakespeare tends to do this with a little more subtlety.

The action in plays also tends to take place in chronological order, with time always moving forward in a linear direction. Partly this is because as we watch plays in real time, it's difficult to convey to an audience that a particular scene is actually a flashback. There are exceptions, of course, to the chronological trend. Notably Harold Pinter's *Betrayal*, for instance, in which the action of the play unfolds backwards from the present to past.

The time frame of a play also tends to be limited – days, weeks, perhaps even months, but very rarely years, decades or centuries. After all, it's not easy for an actor, or series of actors, to convincingly present characters aging over a prolonged period.

The stage and the page

Physicists and chemists have many things in common, as do rugby and football players. So too, vets and doctors. Novelists and playwrights also have many things in common, but they work in distinctly different fields. You wouldn't want a chemist teaching you physics or depend on a rugby player to score a crucial FA cup goal. Nor would you want a vet to operate on you if you were ill, or for your GP to treat your darling pet. And, with only a few exceptions, nor would you want to read a novel written by a playwright or witness a play written by a novelist. Precious few writers excel in both literary forms [Samuel Beckett, Anton Chekhov and Michael Frayn come to mind, but few others] which underlines the point about the different demands of writing for the stage and for the page.

Novels take place in the reader's mind or ear; plays take place in an actual physical space on an actual stage. For the latter to happen a whole load of people other than the writer have to be involved – directors, actors, designers, producers, technicians and so forth. This takes us to the heart of another crucial difference between reading a play, reading a novel and seeing a play on a stage. When we're reading a novel, the novelist can fill in the details of what is happening around the dialogue, such as gestures made by the characters:

'Did they even have pig-pens in medieval York?' asked Mikey, cocking his left eyebrow in a typically quizzical manner.

When we **read** a play, sometimes these details are apparent from stage directions. However, on the page we cannot see what characters are doing while other characters are speaking. So it's easy for us to forget that silent characters are present in a scene and that their presence significantly affects the action. When we **watch** a play, however, the actors on stage reveal how their characters are reacting to the scene and these reactions often convey crucial information about relationships, feelings and atmosphere. We can anticipate, for instance, how Hamlet might be feeling about his uncle becoming the new Danish king even before the Prince says anything because he is on stage while Claudius delivers his first long speech in Act II, Scene 1.

In addition, we have seen him entering the court at the back of a line of dignitaries and Shakespeare has already drawn the audience's attention to him, visually, by making Hamlet's costume out-of-tune with the celebratory atmosphere of the scene. Hence, as we listen and watch Claudius half our attention is also drawn to Hamlet.

Without this visual dimension it is all too easily for readers to ignore the things that are supposed to be happening in the narrative background while each character is speaking. If a play on a page is similar to a musical score awaiting performance, a play on the stage is like the concert itself.

Greater appreciation of the differences between a novel and a play, helps students to notice the key skills of the playwright. And focusing on the dramatic devices used by a playwright has a double benefit: Firstly, all good analytical literary essays concentrate on the writer's craft; secondly, such a focus emphasises to the examiner that students understand the nature of the type of text they are exploring, viz. a play, and distinguishes them from many other readers who don't really appreciate this fact. In the next section we'll focus our attention on the playwright's craft by concentrating in on stagecraft.

Stagecraft

When you're writing about a novel it's always productive to focus on narration. Narration includes narrative perspective, such as first and third person, types of narrator, such as naïve and unreliable, as well as narrative techniques, such as the use of dialogue, cross-cuts and flashbacks. Narration is worth focusing your attention on because it's an absolutely integral feature of all novels and short stories. In plays, the equivalent of narration is stagecraft. Examining stagecraft is an incisive and revealing way to explore the writer at work. Some playwrights are able to use all the craft and resources of the theatre [namely stage set, props, costumes, lighting and music] while for various reasons [technical, artistic, budgetary] other playwrights may be more restricted.

Shakespeare, for instance, doesn't really use lighting in his plays, except notably in *The Winter's Tale* [1611], because most of his plays were performed at the Globe theatre and in broad daylight. However, as we will go on to explore, often Shakespeare set scenes at night, in darkness, the first scene of *Hamlet* being a prime example. Of course, all theatre is an illusion, a pretence willingly shared by the audience. The stage is not the real world and the people on it are not who they say there are; they are actors, playing parts. They are also not speaking verbatim, but in carefully worked verse. But we accept them as real for the duration of the play. For the Globe audience, the disjuncture between what they could see on stage and what they could hear in Shakespeare's words was even more acute. By engaging the audience's imaginations through the power of his words Shakespeare could make them feel darkness and night-time if they couldn't actually see it.

Shakespeare's instructions on costume are also limited, usually embedded within the texts, rather than stated separately in stage directions. Think, for example, of Malvolio's yellow cross-gartered stockings or Hamlet's inky suit of woe. On the other hand, the importance of costumes is underlined repeatedly in Shakespeare's plays by characters who disguise themselves by changing their clothes. For instance, Viola becoming Cesario in *Twelfth Night* [1602] Kent and Edmund disguising themselves in *King Lear* [1606] and Macbeth wearing borrowed clothes. Repeatedly too, villainy in Shakespeare's plays tries to remain hidden under a layer of polished manners and fine clothes. Lady Macbeth's famous injunction to her husband in *Macbeth* [1606] is to look 'like the innocent flower/ But be the serpent under't'. In *Hamlet*, the main villain is, of course, the King, and while Shakespeare doesn't specify Claudius' costume, directors usually dress him in resplendent royal attire.

The general sparsity of information about costumes has, however, allowed directors over the years to relocate Shakespeare's plays to all sorts of settings with a huge variety of matching costumes. In a recent RSC production of *Antony and Cleopatra* [1607], for instance, the designs for the Egyptian queen's costumes were inspired by powerful contemporary female celebrities such as Beyoncé.

When a playwright is restricted in the range of stagecraft he or she can utilise, not only do the devices they employ made more more prominent, but other integral aspects of stage business also become more significant. In *Hamlet*, as in *Macbeth*, exits and entrances are particularly important. Consider, for instance, Hamlet's first entrance into the play. Indeed the managing of exits and entrances is at the core of all plays. Exits facilitate changes in costume and allow actors to recover from, or prepare for, major scenes. Tracking these seemingly simple instructions always uncovers interesting and significant patterns, particularly in terms of which characters know what information at crucial points in the action.

Stage sets

As we mentioned in our discussion of the key differences between novels and plays, the latter invariably have fewer settings due to the fact that dramatic texts have to be physically realised in stage designs. And, as we also noted, changing from one elaborate stage set to another presents problems for directors and, potentially for the finances of a production. What sort of choices does a stage designer have to make when creating a set? Firstly, a lot depends on the nature of the play, as well as the playwright, the director and the budget. Some playwrights are very particular about the settings of their plays and describe them in tremendous detail.

The American playwright Tennessee Williams, for instance, wrote particularly lyrical stage directions, such as those that open his play *A Streetcar Named Desire*: 'First dark of an evening in May' and the 'sky is a peculiarly tender blue, almost turquoise, which invests the scene with a kind of lyricism and gracefully attenuates the atmosphere of decay'. If that isn't enough to get a stage designer to shake and scratch their head, Williams finishes with a synesthetic poetic flourish - 'you can almost feel the warm breath of the brown river'. Imagine being asked to create that effect on stage.

Other playwrights will sketch out far more minimalistic sets. Samuel Beckett in *Waiting for Godot*, for instance, describes the stage set in the sparest way possible, using just six simple words: 'A country road. A tree. Evening'. [Despite the skeletal detail, in production, Beckett was notoriously specific and exacting about how he wanted the stage to be arranged.] Even if the playwright doesn't provide a great deal of information about the exact setting, a director is likely to have an overall concept for a play and insist, albeit to varying degrees, that the set design fit with this. If, for instance, a director wishes to bring out the contemporary political resonances of a play such as *Julius Caesar* she or he might dress the characters like well-known American politicians and set the play in a place looking a little like the modern White House. Similarly, Shakespeare's *Richard III* has often been relocated to an imagined modern fascistic state. Many recent productions of *Hamlet* have imagined Elsinore as the epicentre of a surveillance state, with security cameras and screens in almost every scene.

Given free rein, a stage designer has to decide how realistic, fantastical, symbolic and/or expressionist their stage set will be. The attempt to represent what looks like the real world on stage, as if the audience are looking in through an invisible fourth wall, is called verisimilitude and is the equivalent of photographic realism in fine art.

Stage sets for *Hamlet*

What are the various spaces that directors and stage designers have to create for a production of *Hamlet*? The castle battlements; a number of rooms within the royal palace - including the state room and the 'hall' where public spectacles, such as the celebratory scene in Act I and the duel in Act V can take place as well as other more private rooms where secret conversations such as that between Claudius and Laertes in Act V can happen; the place where Hamlet sees the Ghost; various other private chambers, including Hamlet's and Polonius' [although in some editions the stage directions refer to a 'room in Polonius' house']; Gertrude's private closet; the 'plain' at the edge of Denmark where Hamlet encounters Fortinbras' troops; the graveyard where Ophelia is buried. Additionally, essential to any stage design for this play is the requirement for specific places where characters can hide unseen by other characters, such as when Polonius and Claudius spy on Ophelia and Hamlet in the nunnery scene and when Polonius watches Gertrude and Hamlet in the closet scene.

Of course, all of these spaces are much more easily created in realistic ways on film or even on a modern stage compared with the much more limited space and resources of the Globe theatre. Consider, for example, how, if you were directing the play for the Globe stage you might try to generate a sense of Gertrude's closest, the most private of all female spaces, transgressed in this scene by both Hamlet and Polonius. Gertrude's costume plus a few props, perhaps, could be used on the bare stage to create the sense of the closet, but there'd be little else to distinguish this supposedly most intimate of spaces

 from any other in the play. For obvious reasons, in many film versions the set for this scene features prominently the royal bed. But such a large item would be hard to wheel on to the Globe stage without distracting the audience's attention. In addition, Shakespeare's stage directions indicate that Polonius should be hiding behind an 'arras' [a large, hung tapestry] which might also be hard to get onto the stage unnoticed. As with lighting, the lack of verisimilitude on the Globe stage meant that these spaces had to be generated in the audience's imaginations mostly through the evocative power of Shakespeare's words.

The Ghost also enters this scene, and this would have posed a dilemma for contemporary productions. Specifically, from where does this ghost come? The Globe stage was split into three sections: The balcony and above represented the heavens, the stage represented the earthly realm and below stage, entered by a trap door, represented hell. Hamlet's description of the Ghost as an 'old mole' in Act I, Scene 5 suggests that it should come and go via the trapdoor, but, for Elizabethans this would have implied the Ghost must be diabolical [as we will go on to discuss elsewhere, Elizabethan Protestants and Catholics had very different attitudes to ghosts]. When it re-enters during the closest scene does the Ghost appear upon the balcony, from the back of the stage or from underneath it? Each of these entrances would signal a different meaning for the Ghost.

Creating a sense of the graveyard for the start of Act V would be also be challenging and raises a similar significant staging issue, this time about Ophelia's grave; where should her grave be placed? It would make sense for the gravediggers to mime digging into the trapdoor, as if digging into the ground. But that would imply Ophelia's grave is in hell, in turn suggesting that

 she has been damned for committing suicide. According to the critics Gurr and Ichikawa[1], Hamlet and Laertes leaping down into the grave through the trap door, as they did in Elizabethan stagings of the play, indicated to a contemporary audience that the two avengers were damning themselves by this action. If this is correct, then it implies that Ophelia was already damned.

Famously cutting Fortinbras entirely from the story, Laurence Olivier's 1948 film version of the play concentrated on Hamlet's psychological anguish. With its twisty staircases, giddy upper reaches, shadowy, maze-like corridors, bare walls and stark contrasts of black and white, the stage set of the castle of Elsinore became a macrocosmic symbol for Hamlet's tormented mind. In contrast, modern productions of *Hamlet* often interpret the play more politically, in a dystopian fashion, with Hamlet cast as the alienated citizen trapped within some sort of totalitarian state. In this sort of reading, evidence of the surveillance state is everywhere, signalled on the stage set by the use of cameras, microphones, screens and other types of recording equipment. Notable examples include modern productions with David Tennant [RSC, 2009] and Andrew Scott [BBC, 2018] playing the lead.

Many productions have found ways to use the stage or film set to reflect one of the play's most distinguishing tropes, doubling. In Kenneth Branagh's 1996 film of the play, for instance, the main state room where the major scenes take place is lined on each side with mirrored walls giving way to private rooms. When Branagh delivers the 'To be or not to be' soliloquy he looks directly at himself in one of these mirrors. And, in further doubling, as Hamlet raises his dagger and talks of killing, we see Claudius and Polonius hiding in one of these rooms, watching the Prince unseen through a two-way mirror. The design of this set is also noticeably symmetrical, with a line of mirrors down each side of the oblong space.

A similar design idea is evident in many of the scenes in the Tennant version.

---

[1] Gurr and Ichikawa, *Staging in Shakespeare's Theatres.*

Not only is the throne room symmetrical in design, but a repeated motif of the film's camera shots is the careful balancing of symmetrical images. The use of dark, highly polished surfaces in this production generates more doubling, with ghostly doubles caught in various reflections.

Other stage directions

Most playwrights include stage directions within their scripts. By convention often written in italics, these directions usually establish the setting of a scene, outline lighting or music, convey physical action and sometimes also indicate to the actors how lines should be spoken. In *Who's Afraid of Virginia Woolf*, for example, the playwright, Edward Albee provides lots of extra information alongside the actual words his characters say. Here's a short extract that illustrates the point [in this scene a middle-aged, married woman, Martha, is flirting outrageously with a much younger married man, Nick, in front of both his wife, Honey, and Martha's own husband, George]:

MARTHA: [*to George...still staring at Nick, though*]: SHUT UP! [*Now, back to Nick*] Well, have you? Have you kept your body?

NICK: [*unselfconscious... almost encouraging her*]: It's still pretty good. I work out.

MARTHA: [*with a half-smile*]: Do you!

NICK: Yeah.

HONEY: Oh, yes...he has a very...firm body.

MARTHA: [*still with that smile... a private communication with Nick*] Have you! Oh, I think that's very nice.

Through the stage directions, Albee indicates to the actors where characters are looking, who they are at addressing at different moments, the tone they should adopt and even the facial expression the actors should put on. Additionally, he uses capital letters as well as punctuation to convey tone and volume.

In contrast, Shakespeare's stage directions are minimalistic. As we've noted, at the start of scenes he establishes the setting with a just a few quick strokes of his quill. Take the opening scene's stage directions:

Elsinore. A platform before the castle.
FRANCISCO at his post. Enter to him BERNARDO

Just a 'platform' and a 'castle', no adjectives to give specificity and colour. Other than various entrances, exits and exeunts [the exits of multiple characters] relatively speaking, there are few other stage direction in the play. This relative lack of stage directions makes the ones used more prominent and significant. So, for example, during the murder of Gonzago, Shakespeare writes an exact stage direction for the actor playing an actor playing Lucianus to carry out:

Pours the poison into the sleeper's ears.

It's important too, that the choreography of some scenes is clear. A good example is the closet scene from Act III. In this scene Shakespeare uses an unusually high number of stage directions:

- POLONIUS *hides behind the arras*
- [Hamlet] *makes a pass through the arras*
- [Hamlet] *lifts up the array and discovers POLONIUS*
- *Exeunt severally; HAMLET dragging in POLONIUS.*

Similarly, Shakespeare employs a higher than usual number of stage directions immediately before and during Ophelia's funeral scene:

- [The Gravedigger] *Throws up a skull*
- [Hamlet] *Takes the skull*
- [Hamlet] *Leaps into the grave*
- [Laertes] *Leaps into the grave*
- [Hamlet] *Grappling with him* [Laertes].

Clearly these directions are important enough for Shakespeare to make them explicit to the actors. The Gravedigger's tossing up of the skull conveys his irreverence and casual indifference to death, how he has become so acclimatized to it that he has lost any sense of fear, pity or horror. In this way, this crude, comic character provides a model of fortitude for the habitually sensitive and philosophical Hamlet. Making Hamlet pick up the skull allows Shakespeare to generate a stage picture that has become one of the most iconic in all theatre. The theme of mortality that has haunted the whole play becomes tangible, emblematized in the image of the thinker staring into the empty eye sockets of a skull.

As a rule, Shakespeare does not try to describe action in vivid flourishes. Instead he uses short, basic, straightforward instructions. Hence action can appear rather flat on the page. The verb 'leaps' is striking in this context, suggesting wild abandon and a loss of control. Additionally, exactly the same stage direction is given to both Hamlet and Laertes, yoking them together. How exciting and serious the 'grappling' is will depend on the director and actors. Later, the rapier duel between the two avengers is introduced with the understated phrase, 'they play'. This can look rather flat on the page. On the stage, however, it can be electrifying. Unlike most directors of modern productions, Shakespeare would have hired highly trained, specialist duellists for this scene, so that it would take on for the Elizabethan audience the added frisson of watching an intensely dangerous sport take place dangerously close at hand.

Even without the spectacle of stage directions realised physically on a stage, the sudden and chaotic violence of the play's climax is evident:

- *LAERTES wounds HAMLET; then in scuffling, they change rapiers, and HAMLET wounds LAERTES*
- *QUEEN GERTRUDE falls*
- [Hamlet] *Stabs KING CLAUDIUS.*

Embedded stage directions

These are stage directions contained within the dialogue. For instance, when Hamlet tells the guards to 'hold off' their hands in Act I, Scene 5 this tells the actors playing the guards that they need to try to physically restrain the actor playing Hamlet before this line. If they or the director miss the cue, then Hamlet's line won't make sense. Sometimes embedded stage directions also indicate specific facial expressions to actors. At the end of Hamlet's lyrical speech about man's potential to be the 'paragon of animals' in Act II, Scene 2, he reprimands Rosencrantz for an inappropriate response. Hamlet's lines indicate to the actor playing Rosencrantz that he needs to smirk or laugh in the run-up to this line. Similarly the Ghost's comment in the closet scene that 'amazement' 'sits' on Gertrude's face is a clear instruction to the actor playing Gertrude and Hamlet's plea to his mother 'Why look you there, look how it steals away –' [III.4,135] indicates that both actors should look in the direction of the Ghost, with one character seeing him and the other not.

More subtly, sometimes the way verse passages are set out on the page indicates stage directions that control the rhythm of the dialogue. Usually an iambic pentameter shared between characters is a signal that the second speaker should come in immediately after the other speaker has finished whereas an incomplete line, indicated by blank space on the page, frequently signals that the speaker needs to pause, with the bigger the space the longer the pause. A good example of these type of embedded stage directions working in concert is in the play's opening scene.

This scene starts in prose, with short stichomythic snippets of lines. The lack of metre, an underpinning structure to the play's dialogue adds to the sense of uncertainty and unpredictability. The dialogue then moves swiftly at line five into a mixture of prose lines and verse ones. On the page, the typography looks odd and, superficially, rather random [we've emboldened some of the syllables to indicate where stresses probably fall]:

Francisco:	For **this** relief much **thanks**, 'tis **bitter cold**
	And **I** am **sick** at **heart.**
Barnardo:	Have you had quiet guard?
Francisco:	Not a mouse stirring.
Barnardo:	Well, good night.
	If **you** do **meet** Horatio and Marcellus,
	The **rivals of** my **watch**, bid **them** make **haste**

Why does the 'and' at the start of the second line quoted have a capital letter? Why is Francisco's second line indented? Why is there a big blank space after 'night'? By convention, capital letters at the starts of lines indicate that the dialogue is in verse [check the rest of the play and you'll find that it stays in verse until well into Act II and the conversation between Hamlet and Polonius.] Francisco's first and second lines above are in iambic verse. Barnardo's response appears, however, to be in prose. Nevertheless, Francisco completes this line as if it were verse and a rough pentameter is shared between the lines. That is why this line, 'not a mouse stirring' is indented. It tells the reader and the actor that we are in the process of transitioning from prose to verse. The blankness after Barnardo's response signals that this line is also in verse and therefore that the line is incomplete, which informs the actor to pause after 'night'.

Straight after this exchange several lines, now securely in verse, are shared between characters:

Horatio:	Friends to his ground.	
Marcellus:		And liegemen to the Dane
Francisco:	Give you good night.	
Marcellus:		O, farewell honest soldier
	Who hath relieved you?	
Francisco:		Barnardo has my place.

The typography emphasises that each speaker must come in promptly after the other, giving the dialogue a swift snappy quality. In passing, also note how Marcellus doesn't explicitly express loyalty to Claudius, but rather to the more ambiguous figure of 'the Dane', a word that Hamlet will claim for himself at Ophelia's funeral.

Entrances and exits

Obviously in a play that has twenty scenes there are a lot of entrances and exits and we've no intention of going through all of these. However, paying close attention to who is and who isn't present in a scene, who comes in and who goes out and when and how they do so, is always rewarding. Often the significance of a character's silent presence is more obvious on a stage than it might appear on the page and a character's absence from a scene may also be important. Think, for example, of what the actor playing Hamlet could do in Act 1, Scene 2 before he or she has a line of dialogue. The way Hamlet has entered the scene – dragging his heels, out of place at the back – already draws the audience's attention away from the apparent main focus of Claudius and Gertrude and implies his presence in this scene will be disorderly. Amplifying the effect, Hamlet's incongruous costume also picks him out visually among the throng of characters. To this an actor can then add appropriate body language to convey Hamlet's out-of-kilter gloominess. When we read the play, we have to imagine what Hamlet might be doing during the long lecture given to him by Claudius at the end of this scene, but on stage at least half the dramatic effect of this episode depends on how Hamlet reacts to Claudius' forceful power play.

Sometimes a character's entrance into a scene has an immediately transformative effect on the mood and atmosphere. We might immediately think of the Ghost, but other examples would be the entrance of an enraged Laertes into Act IV, Scene 5 and the equally transformative entrance into this scene of his sister, Ophelia. Other good examples are Hamlet's sudden entrance at Ophelia's funeral and Fortinbras' entrance at the end of the play. How the latter is interpreted – is this a violent coup and invasion of a foreign force, or something gentler? – will shape how we interpret the play as a whole.

The presence on stage of non-speaking characters is most obviously significant in the two spying scenes of Act III. As we will discover in our commentary on these scenes, interpreting the tone and meaning of the dialogue between Hamlet and Ophelia and Hamlet and his mother is complex. The presence of an apparently unseen audience on stage adds to greatly to this complexity, particularly in the earlier scene. The presence of Polonius and Claudius means we are not sure whether Ophelia's behaviour is governed by this factor or just influenced by it. Is she, for instance, stiff and formal in the way that she greats Hamlet because she dare not show him the affection she might if she wasn't being watched by her father and the King? Ophelia's intense discomfort in the scene is likely to come from awareness that she is being used, awareness that she is betraying Hamlet and acute awareness that she also being watched doing all of this. And what of Hamlet? We already have the added layer of whether he is or isn't putting on his 'antic disposition' when he sees Ophelia. Now, we have to decide to what extent Hamlet's behaviour in this scene is aimed at Polonius and Claudius as much as at Ophelia. When, if at all, do we think Hamlet discovers they are being spied upon? Deciding this must affect the way we read his lines.

After the pivotal events of Act III, Gertrude has to wrestle with an internal dilemma. She cannot be loyal to both her husband and her son at the same time. Or to put this another way, which comes first, wife or mother? If we assume that her husband being a murderer is a revelation to her and that Gertrude doesn't dismiss this claim as evidence of Hamlet's madness, she must, surely, look at Claudius with new eyes. Shakespeare hints at tension between the royal couple by repeatedly having Claudius command Gertrude to follow him at the ends of scenes. At the end of Act IV, Scene 1, for instance, in the space of one short speech he tells Gertrude to 'come away', 'Come Gertrude', 'O come away'. This seems overly insistent. A director and actor have a decision to make. Does Gertrude immediately follow her husband here? Does she hesitate a moment or two and then follow him off? Or most radically, does she ignore him and exit in another direction? Act IV, Scene 7 concludes similarly with Claudius twice instructing his wife to 'follow' him. If she hesitated a little last time, perhaps this time, in anticipation of her actions at the end of the play, Gertrude needs to hold her ground.

Props

In many of Shakespeare's plays props in the form of physical letters are intercepted and fall dangerously into the wrong hands, moving the plot forward. Such letters are important because they provide hard, physical, almost always undeniable evidence; the written word in black and white. In *Hamlet* several crucial letters are sent, intercepted or received by their attended addressee: Letters from the King of Norway to Claudius seeming to confirm that Fortinbras' threatening behaviour has been curtailed; Hamlet's love letters to Ophelia, appropriated by Polonius and providing evidence that Hamlet is mad for love; a secret letter from Claudius to the King of England instructing him to immediately execute Hamlet, a letter that Hamlet intercepts and reworks, sending Rosencrantz and Guildenstern to their deaths instead of him; Hamlet's letter to Horatio about his improbable escape from pirates. In the last of these Hamlet hints that he has not written a complete description of events, perhaps because he fears that his letter might be intercepted by Elsinore's web of surveillance.

Props can also be used as emblems of character - heroes in Shakespeare's plays invariably brandish swords, while fops carry nosegays. Machiavellian villains, such as Iago, Claudius and Goneril use poison, albeit the first of these poisons via what he says, while the other two use actual bottles of poison. Props associated with Hamlet, such as the book he carries about with him and Yorick's skull function as metonyms, indicating his scholarliness and his confrontation with mortality. Hamlet also carries a sword, of course, as does Laertes. The poisoning of Laertes' sword is emblematic of his corruption from noble avenger to treacherous villain.

Before you read the next section, list any props you can remember appearing in the play. Try to arrange them in chronological order. Then write next to each one how they are used by Shakespeare.

- The guards' partisans

Partisans are long, pike-like weapons, essentially poles with a number of blades at the business end. The guards' pointing of these weapons at each other, implied in the opening scene, quickly indicates their tense nervousness and suggests mortal danger may be lurking somewhere unseen, but perilously close by. Their attempts to stop the Ghost with these weapons also usefully confirms its supernaturality.

- Swords

Rather than similar weapons such as the dagger, as used by Macbeth to murder Duncan, invariably Shakespeare's plays the sword is the weapon of the noble hero.

Hamlet uses his sword at various points during the action, finally, of course, stabbing Claudius with it. As we've already noted, Laertes' sword, like the  duel in which it is used, becomes symbolic of his corruption, itself a reflection of the corruption endemic in Claudius' court. The almost sacred quality of the sword is established in Act I, Scene 5 when Hamlet insists the other witnesses to the ghost 'swear' on his sword, as if it is a cross, bible or some other holy relic. Both Laurence Olivier and Kenneth Branagh in their films of *Hamlet* emphasise this association by having Hamlet turn his sword upside down at this point so that its handle forms a cross-like shape. This association of the sword with truth, honour and, particularly, holiness makes Laertes' corruption of the weapon seem more profoundly villainous.

- Bottles of poison

The Ghost tells us that Claudius poured a phial of poison into his ear. The Machiavellian villain of the play-within-the-play also pours poison into his victim's ear. The murderer's choice of the ear is perhaps significant because poison in Shakespeare's plays often seeps through what characters hear to corrupt their thoughts, such as Iago's poisoning of Othello's mind. Both victims in *Hamlet* are also killed while helplessly sleeping. Clearly this is the most ignoble, cowardly way to kill an enemy, the polar opposite to honourable single-handed combat.

- Ophelia's book

Polonius gives his daughter a book to pretend to read in preparation for meeting Hamlet in the nunnery scene. The lack of reference to this book in the subsequent action – it's just an empty, disregarded prop - emphasises a general lack of interest in Ophelia's thoughts and feelings. In contrast Hamlet is asked what book he is reading, because this is assumed to be of some significance.

- Pipes and recorders

Although Hamlet has quickly discovered that Rosencrantz and Guildenstern have been sent to spy on him and keeps an eye on them in return, superficially he appears to tolerate their companionship. That is until after the court have witnessed *The Mousetrap* and Rosencrantz and Guildenstern are sent to reprimand Hamlet and order him to go and see his mother. Pinching one of the recorders from the troop of actors, Hamlet uses it as a devastating conceit for how Rosencrantz and Guildenstern have been abusing their friendship: 'you would sound me from my lowest note to/ the top of my compass'. The prop makes concrete and tangible the way Rosencrantz and Guildenstern have been trying to play Hamlet and here the Prince, for the first time, makes it crystal clear that he fully understands this, and will tolerate it no more.

Like embedded stage directions, sometimes Shakespeare writes lines that imply the presence of props. For example, when an impassioned Hamlet is trying to emphasise to his mother how superior his father was to his uncle he tells her to 'Look here, upon this picture, and on this'. Where these two pictures may be is up to the director to decide. They could be portraits hung upon the closest walls, for instance, or Hamlet could, perhaps, keep a picture of his father in a locket close to his heart.

- Ophelia's flowers

We will discuss the specific symbolism of the various flowers that Ophelia gives out during her mad scene in Act IV in our essay on her character. Clearly the flowers are a metonym for Ophelia's feminine character, just as the book, skull and sword are for Hamlet. Repeatedly Ophelia is compared to flowers, her identity defined by just this single prop. Hence one way of reading this scene is of her divesting herself of this prescribed feminine identity. Later, the flowers strewn on her coffin confirm the impression that even in death she is still being constructed as essentially flower-like.

- Spades and gravediggers' tools. Various skulls, including Yorick's

The casual, irreverent way in which the gravediggers handle the skulls suggests that their work has dulled their sensibilities and numbed the natural aversion people normally have to corpses. Perhaps this is part of the brutality of conditions in Claudius' Elsinore, but certainly it provides a poignant contrast with Hamlet and his sensitive meditations about mortality.

- Osric's hat

Hamlet and Horatio take some grim pleasure from tormenting Osric. In particular, they confuse him over the correct conventions of etiquette. This exposes the fact that Osric is exactly the sort of jumped-up, on-the-make, eager-to-please, ignoble lackey who is thriving in Claudius court.

- The poisoned chalice.

The crucial moment of decision for Claudius is whether he stops Gertrude from drinking from this prop and, in doing so, exposing his villainy. It's a dilemma he isn't quick or decisive enough to resolve, ending up with both Gertrude killed and his conspiracy revealed. Fittingly, when he is finally killed, it is with both a sword and with his own poisoned instrument.

Costumes

Naturally, some playwrights are very specific about costumes, while others are happy for directors, actors and designers to make their own choices. In some of Shakespeare's plays he specifies how particular characters should be dressed in particular scenes. In *King Lear,* Edgar as Mad Tom, for instance, is dressed in nothing but rags, while Lear enters at one point with a crown of flowers on his head and stage directions informs us that on her return to England, Lear's exiled daughter, Cordelia is wearing armour.

Old Hamlet also wears armour, of course. Not only in life, but even in purgatory and even when he returns as a ghost to the world of the living. Surely in that other realm armour cannot function as protection. Nor can it do him much good in the living world. The suit of armour is also rather ironic – it seems Old Hamlet was fully prepared for honourable, man-to-man armed combat – but he wasn't ready for a more intimate and sneaky form of attack. Clearly the main point communicated by this costume, however, is how essentially Old Hamlet was a martial king, one who not only would lead his troops into combat, but would fight individual duels to settle wars and save his men.

Shakespeare leaves directors to decide how Claudius should be dressed. An expensive-looking, sumptuously upholstered, richly coloured costume with gallant red, royal gold and purple, perhaps, ostentatiously showing off his military honours - an array of medals pinned proudly across his chest? Certainly in his first scene Claudius needs to sound and look convincingly like a king, to banish any doubts in the court. He is also in celebratory mode and his costume needs to be strikingly different from Hamlet's. For Shakespeare does, of course, specify how Hamlet should be dressed, in his 'inky cloak', one of his 'customary suits of solemn black'. At odds with those around him, still in mourning, gloomy-minded, gothic, scholarly.

A director would also have to make an important decision about how the actress playing Ophelia should dress in her mad scene. Compare how Jean Simmons as Ophelia is presented in Laurence Olivier's influential film of Hamlet [1948] with Kate Winslet's costume in Kenneth Branagh's 1996 film. In the former, as shown here, Ophelia is dressed like a delicate fairy elf, a little dishevelled in her pale, silky, gently pleated dress, her long, unbrushed, part braided hair embroidered with a garland of flowers. Winslet, in contrast, is restrained within a dull brown, sack-like straight-jacket.

How Ophelia is dressed is clearly an essential aspect of her character and also a means of controlling perceptions of her. Although we don't see her on stage, Ophelia's death costume is described in some detail by Gertrude. Ophelia's 'fantastic garlands' of various types of wildflowers are called a 'coronet weeds' and 'weedy trophies' as if she is a queen of flowers. Perhaps the wild, uncultivated weediness of these flowers is significant, contrasting with the rose of May that Laertes calls his sister. As she drowns, Ophelia's clothes spread around her and she appears to float a while, 'mermaid-like', adding to the fantastical effect.

Lighting

Lighting can be used starkly and boldly, such as in picking out a main character in a bright spotlight, or it can be used more subtly to convey mood and generate atmosphere. Intense white light makes everything look stark. Blue lights help create a sense of coolness, whereas yellows, oranges and reds generate a sense of warmth and even passion. Floor lights can light an actor from beneath, making them look powerful and threatening. Light coming down on them from above can cause an actor to look vulnerable and threatened or even angelic. Changes of lighting between scenes are common ways of changing the pervasive atmosphere.

However, for most of his theatrical career, Shakespeare was writing for the Globe theatre where performances took place only during daylight hours. Only when his plays were performed at the indoor theatre at Blackfriars, from around 1608, could Shakespeare employ lighting effects. This, however, doesn't mean that Shakespeare doesn't create lighting effects, rather that he does so through the language rather than through stage directions.

Obviously, for example, *Hamlet* starts at night, in darkness. At the end of the first scene, after seeing the Ghost, Horatio, with apparent relief, directs the guards' attention to the sky: 'But, look, the morn, in russet mantle clad/ walks o'er the dew of yon high eastward hill'. This evocation of changing light - the red colour of the sky - a distant hill and the coming brightness of the morning is brilliantly audacious. Of course, the Globe audience could see none of the things Horatio directs their attention towards. Hence Horatio's lines indicate how successfully Shakespeare has managed to conjure a palpable sense of a cold, night and, perhaps, also suggest Horatio's wistful hope for a curative brightness that will, in fact, be long delayed in this play.

Music & sound effects

Music is a highly effective device for developing mood and atmosphere. In Arthur Miller's play, *A View from the Bridge*, for instance, a romantic popular song, 'Paper-Doll' is played while two young lovers dance together in front of a man who absolutely detests and opposes their relationship, and a charged, threatening atmosphere is immediately generated. In another of Miller's plays, *Death of a Salesman* a flute is used as a leitmotiv for the dreaminess of the central character Willy Loman. Shakespeare weaves music into many of his comedies and in *Hamlet*, Ophelia's madness is signalled by her singing of subversive, sad and bawdy songs, the music increasing the emotional impact of this scene.

There is a number of overt stage directions and several embedded ones relating to music and sound effects in the play. Obviously Shakespeare did not have the rich range of resources a modern theatre or film director would have. As with lighting and other aspects of stagecraft, the comparative lack of music and sound effects means when they are deployed they are more noticeable and significant. The cock crowing, in Act I, Scene 1, for instance, obviously signals the start of day. How exactly Shakespeare would have recreated this sound effect is a mystery, but the sound effect plays an essential part of the illusion Shakespeare creates of a night-time setting, now giving way to morning.

An example of an embedded stage direction for sound is Claudius' command in the following scene for a large canon to be fired in celebration:

'The great cannon to the clouds shall tell/ And the king's rouse the heavens all bruit again/ Re-speaking earthly thunder'.

Like the various flourishes of trumpets and drums, here the sound is being used as part of the theatre of the state, part of its pomp and circumstance. The cannon blast, specifically, is a symbol of royal power and of military might. Moreover, the booming effect in the sky is presented by Claudius as God's confirmatory signal for his rule. As Claudius' instruction is not followed by a stage direction for cannon-fire, a director will have to decide whether this oversight is deliberate – a subtle sign of Claudius' lack of real command – or whether to add a canon sound effect. If the latter, a symbolically feeble pop will make one impression, while a powerful blast make another. [We do know that the Globe theatre was burnt down when a cannon shot set fire to its thatched roof, so Shakespeare did use a real cannon at times.]

Four times in the play cannons or guns are fired. In contrast to this first time, when Claudius again order the cannons to fire in Act V – 'Let all the battlements their ordinance fire' if Hamlet makes a successful hit - there is a delay followed by a 'shot'. A little later, seemingly unbidden and randomly there is another 'shot within'. The significance of these two shots only becomes clear once Fortinbras appears on the scene. Either the second of the two shots or perhaps both of them were not, in fact, merely symbolic, purely theatrical displays of power, as we and the characters on stage had assumed, but real, actual artillery shots fired with real intent to harm, signalling invasion. Fortinbras' last instruction for the soldiers to shoot is followed by a 'peal of audience'. Whether this ordinance is harmlessly fired into the air as a tribute, or aimed at the remaining members of the Danish court is up to the director to decide.

In addition to Ophelia's songs, a couple of stage directions signal music is to be played: The death march at the end and the hautboys during the dumb-show prelude to *The Mousetrap*. The precursor of the oboe, the hautboy was an instrument particularly 'associated with doom and gloom... it would have made a harsh and noisy sound in Shakespeare's times – especially if multiple oboes were played together.'[2] Often Shakespeare uses hautboys to create an ominous and sinister atmosphere. In *Titus Andronicus* [1594], for instance, hautboys play as Titus brings in a pie stuffed with the dismembered corpses of the sons of the woman who's about to tuck into dinner. Hautboys also feature in *Anthony and Cleopatra* [1606] and repeatedly, to suitably sinister effect, in *Macbeth* [1606]. Clearly in *Hamlet* they signal evil is being done.

---

[2] www.shakespeare.org.uk/explore-shakespeare/blogs/ominous-oboes/

The nature of the play

What is a tragedy?

The exact nature of the literary genre we call 'tragedy' is much debated. According to *The Complete A-Z English Literature Handbook* a tragedy is a 'drama which ends disastrously' and falls into two broad types:

- Greek tragedy, where fate brings about the downfall of the character[s].
- Shakespearean tragedy, where a character has free will and their fatal flaw causes the downfall.

As you shall discover when you read our essay on the tragic protagonist of *Hamlet*, the second half of that second point is much disputed by literary academics and Shakespeare scholars. And, in fact, it seems that the description above of a Greek tragedy fits *Hamlet* quite snugly.

According to Jennifer Wallace in *The Cambridge Introduction to Tragedy*, 'Tragedy is an art form created to confront the most difficult experiences we face; death, loss, injustice, thwarted passion, despair'. Wallace goes on to explain that 'questions about the causes of suffering, which are raised in each culture, are posed powerfully in tragedy'.[3] That's helpful, but couldn't we say

---

[3] Wallace, *The Cambridge Introduction to Tragedy*.

the same sorts of things about the academic subjects of philosophy and religious studies?

While, on the one hand, there are critics, such as Terry Eagleton, who argue the only thing that the plays we label as tragedies have in common is that they are 'very, very sad', on the other, many critics opine that all literary tragedies share distinctive common formal features which separate them from real-life stories of great unhappiness. And, if we shrink our perspective down from tragedies as a whole art form to Shakespeare's versions, we'll discover there's not much academic agreement either about what attributes these plays share:

'An eminent Shakespearian scholar famously remarked that there is no such thing as Shakespearian Tragedy; there are only Shakespearian tragedies'.

So begins Tom McAlindon's essay *What is a Shakespearian Tragedy?*[4] The author goes on to point out how attempts to define tragedy, such as those we've quoted above, tend to 'give a static impression of the genre and incline towards prescriptivism', ignoring the fact that genres are constantly changing and developing over time.

So, to sum up: The definition of 'tragedy' is hotly contested. So too is the definition of Shakespearian Tragedy. Indeed, more fundamentally, the idea of defining both these terms is itself contested within literary criticism. So where does that leave us with *Hamlet*? Perhaps a sensible way to try to find a route out of the academic fogginess is to start at the beginning and then navigate our way from that fixed point. In terms of defining tragedy as an art form, Aristotle's theories of tragedy serve well as a starting point.

Aristotle

Often it is assumed that Aristotle was setting down a prescriptivist rule book for writing tragedies, a kind of classical instruction manual for aspiring playwrights to follow slavishly. This assumption is mistaken. In fact, Aristotle,

---

[4] McEachern [ed.], *The Cambridge Companion to Tragedy*, p.1.

in his *Poetics*, was describing the features of classical tragedies as he saw them. Taken as prescriptivist or descriptivist, what is certain is that Aristotle's ideas about tragedies have been hugely influential. In particular, four key ideas have helped shape the ways tragedies have been written, performed and read for hundreds of years. These ideas concern:

i.   the nature of the protagonist
ii. the cause of tragic action
iii. the significance of plot
iv. the emotional effect of tragedy on an audience.

For our purposes, the first two of these concepts are particularly interesting. The protagonist in classical tragedy is always high-born, a prince or king or someone of equivalent status. This means their fall is as precipitous, destructive and dramatic as possible - right from the top to the very bottom of society [imagine an elephant falling off a skyscraper] in a way that the fall of someone from the bottom to the bottom of society [imagine a mouse falling off a kerb] would not be. As the tragic hero or heroine is high-born and they fall along way down, the impact causes immense damage to society, sending shockwaves out across the whole world of the play, creating cracks and fissures in the social fabric. Crucially, according to Aristotle, the primary cause of the fall is a fault in the tragic protagonist. Historically Shakespearian critics often conceived of this tragic flaw, or hamartia, in character-based or psychological terms. Pre-twentieth century critics often identified Hamlet's sensitive and imaginative nature as his hamartia, while early twentieth century critics, such as the hugely influential A. C. Bradley, diagnosed Hamlet's melancholia. But, according to Aristotle, the hamartia could equally be a terrible decision made by the tragic hero.

Read through an Aristotelian critical perspective, *Hamlet* is a play fundamentally about its titular hero, whose tragic fall is precipitated by his hamartia. Different critics have argued about what this hamartia might be but agreed that Hamlet is at fault for not delivering justice through revenge.

Modern criticism

However, most modern Shakespearian critics argue that an Aristotelian approach to tragedy over-emphasises the importance of the tragic hero and of characters in general. After the cataclysmic experience of World War II, literary critics became more interested in the role of society and of the power of history and of ideology to shape the experience of characters. Reading through this modern perspective, individual humans appeared to have less agency than earlier critics had assumed, and so too had characters in literary texts. Shifting critical attention away from individuals to societies, modern critics tend to view the tragedy as stemming from irresolvable, conflicting forces at work within the period in which Shakespeare was writing, a period that historians call the early modern. So, for instance, a modern critic might argue that *Hamlet* stages a conflict between traditional, essential feudal values – of loyalty, duty, honour, revenge and so forth – and a new Renaissance spirit of individualism, questioning and self-determination.

Hamlet and tragedy

Hamlet is far from an archetypal tragedy, and Hamlet himself far from an archetypal tragic hero; Shakespeare incorporates some conventions, but also subverts and rejects others.

In 1902, A.H. Thorndike coined the term 'Revenge Tragedy' to describe a sub-genre of tragedies in which the protagonist and plot are driven by the desire for revenge. These plays, initially inspired by the works of Seneca [4BC - 65AD], gained popularity in Elizabethan and Jacobean England and the first popular Revenge Tragedy was Thomas Kyd's *The Spanish Tragedy*, first performed in the late 1580s. Scholars suggest it is likely that Shakespeare  performed as an actor in Kyd's play. Certainly *Hamlet* [which is argued by many critics to be the greatest example of this genre] was heavily influenced by *The Spanish Tragedy* and arguably also by Kyd's lost play *Ur-Hamlet*. *Hamlet* does conform to many of the most common features of a Revenge

Tragedy: murder, a vengeful ghost, madness [either feigned or real], metatheatricality - drawing attention to performance and the aspects of unreality through soliloquies, references to acting, instructions to the players and the play-within-a-play – as well as the inevitable death of the protagonist. Following the tradition established by Kyd, but diverging from Greek and Roman Tragedies, there are also dramatic onstage deaths, intensifying the audience's emotional response to the action.

In many ways, the character of Hamlet is a classic tragic hero, a young man with a 'noble mind' who 'was likely, had he been put on,/ To have proved most royally' [Act V, Scene 2]. In other words, his potential is recognised by the other characters and the audience and he is, despite his flaws, widely admired. Following the tradition of Aristotle, a tragic hero often suffers more than he deserves, and we can see this with Hamlet, who is presented with an irreconcilable moral dilemma, believing that he is cursed by fate and was 'born to set it right' so responds accordingly. Arguably, this, rather than indecision, delay or even madness, is his hamartia - simply an error in judgement, believing that he [or anyone else] can 'set' Elsinore 'right'. Either way, Hamlet lacks the hubris and ambition of many tragic protagonists, with his indecision and inaction making him atypical, but relatable to a modern audience. We, surely, can empathise with his confusion and self-doubt, seeing his existential uncertainty as simply an awareness of the human condition rather than as a flaw. In many tragedies, it is obvious when the protagonist is making a decision that will lead to his downfall, and it's ironic that in *Hamlet,* rather than by a decision, his downfall is instead caused by the lack of one. His determination to send Claudius to hell rather than simply avenging his father when he has the chance might be labelled as hubristic, but is as likely to be interpreted as simply an excuse to delay rather than evidence of excessive pride. For wouldn't such hubris be incongruous in a character as full of self-doubt as Hamlet?

Arguably, Hamlet is the only protagonist in any Elizabethan Revenge Tragedy who is genuinely a hero. Specifically, only Hamlet is aware of the moral consequences of his actions. In Greek Tragedy, revenge was seen as justice, while in Elizabethan England, although there was still sympathy for an heir intent on vengeance, it was seen by many as a terrible sin. Leviticus 19, for instance, commands that 'You shall not take vengeance or bear a grudge against the sons of your own people, but you shall love your neighbour as yourself', whilst the sixth Commandment is the simple imperative 'Thou shalt not kill'. In addition, regicide was generally considered a

heinous crime, and especially so by Queen Elizabeth. Consequently, Hamlet's belief that he was 'born to set it right' is flawed: No such thing is possible, as his duty to his father and his personal desire to punish Claudius cannot be reconciled with his duty to God and thus there is no way to make things 'right'. His claim that 'conscience does make cowards of us all' is perceptive. Unlike the pagan avengers of Roman revenge tragedies, Hamlet's awareness of the moral obligations of Christianity prevent him from being the single-minded murderer that the genre demands. He may be the protagonist of a play that at first glance fulfils many of the features of Aristotelian or Senecan Tragedy, but unlike Horatio who claims to be 'more an Antique Roman than a Dane' Hamlet directly identifies himself as 'Hamlet the Dane'. He is a modern protagonist with a contemporary perspective, and Shakespeare modernised the genre so that the primary conflict is an internal, ethical one.

Hero and villain?

Initially, it appears certain that Claudius is evil: He has murdered Old Hamlet, and in the Ghost's statement that 'the serpent that did sting your father's life now wears his crown', the biblical allusions make his betrayal and evil clear. Claudius has betrayed his brother, committed regicide and fratricide and Hamlet is tasked with restoring the natural order. It appears that Shakespeare, like Kyd and his contemporaries, has presented an obvious villain, and a hero who must kill him. However, the situation is not that simple. The Ghost, without whose intervention Hamlet would not act, is central to the plot, but so is our perception of it: Ghosts at the time were seen variously as hallucinations created by the devil, warnings from God and spirits returned in order to resolve unfinished business. A. C. Bradley may claim that Hamlet is 'unable to carry out the sacred duty, imposed by divine authority, of punishing an evil man by death', but it is hard to see the Ghost as 'divine authority' or revenge as 'sacred duty'; Hamlet's fear of God is so evident and the Ghost and his commands directly oppose biblical teachings.

However, despite Hamlet's references to 'a divinity that shapes our ends' and 'th'everlasting', he is himself morally ambiguous and Shakespeare further subverts the revenge tragedy genre by highlighting parallels between Hamlet and Claudius, parallels which lead audiences and critics to question their relative morality. In Act V, Scene 2, Hamlet refers to Claudius as 'He that hath killed my king and whored my mother,/ Popped in between th' election and my hopes' with the first line revealing motivation for revenge and the second showing self-interest. Thus it appears to be impossible for Hamlet to avenge his father without committing regicide, like his uncle, to become King and thus himself benefiting from Claudius' death. Arguably, this reflects the paradox of the play: Hamlet's awareness of his moral dilemma is the very attribute that prevents him from being an uncomplicated hero and *Hamlet* from being an uncomplicated tragedy. Like many tragic protagonists before him, Hamlet is faced with a dilemma. But *Hamlet* is an unusual play in that rather than a simple choice of right and wrong, this is a major philosophical dilemma; he feels bound to 'set it right' when right and wrong are unclear both to him and the audience.

In a tragedy, we often see poetic justice: Virtue is rewarded and evil punished. But in many Shakespearean tragedies and in *Hamlet* in particular, this is not the case. Although Claudius' death is well deserved, and a similar argument can be made for Rosencrantz and Guildenstern, *Hamlet* shows an absence of poetic justice – the story ends badly for everyone. Hamlet dies along with Claudius and although he does rid Denmark of evil, he does so at the cost of his own life and those of Laertes, Ophelia, Polonius and Gertrude, all of whose deaths could have been avoided had he acted sooner. Additionally, depending a little on how it's performed, the play ends with a foreign invader, the avenging Fortinbras, claiming the Danish throne.

Transforming tragedy

Shakespeare transformed the genre with *Hamlet*. In revenge tragedies up to this point, the hero was bloodthirsty, determined and pursuing an uncomplicated villain, delayed by external forces and acting on his first opportunity. None of these are true in *Hamlet*. The Prince's obstacles to revenge are internal struggles with morality, duty and indecision. Claudius can be argued to simply be attempting to maintain order in Denmark, and Hamlet lets opportunities to kill Claudius pass as a result of his own internal conflict. This difference and increased psychological complexity is highlighted by the use of foils. In Laertes and Fortinbras, we see more traditional, uncomplicated avengers, acting with determination to resolve external conflict, highlighting through contrast the paralysis created by Hamlet's internal conflict.

In addition, Shakespeare adds comic relief including Hamlet's mockery of Polonius and of Osric and the gravedigger scene. Although criticised by contemporary critics, not only do these moments offer temporary relief, but by doing so intensify the impact of the following tragedy. For instance, the comedy of the grave digger scene is immediately juxtaposed with the tragedy of Ophelia's funeral, creating pathos as the audience reacts to this in the knowledge that they and Hamlet have laughed at her grave. Similarly, Hamlet's interactions with Osric show light-hearted wordplay and relieve tension, further accentuating the sense of tragedy in the final scenes.

Revenge tragedies often include the degeneration of their protagonist, and although Hamlet's madness can be seen to be exactly that, some would argue that he overcomes this to become the hero that we hope for: when he finally avenges, he speaks in hexameter: 'The point envenomed too! Then, venom, to thy work!'. This 'epic meter' is common in Greek and Latin poetry and thus associated with great heroes, suggesting that Hamlet, too, may overcome his flaws to be heroic. In many Revenge Tragedies, revenge against the antagonist is achieved largely as a result of the antagonist's own actions rather than those of the protagonist. Hamlet delays avenging his father [and may never have managed to do so], but when Gertrude is poisoned in front of him, Hamlet is compelled to act impulsively.

Unquestionably the end of the play is cathartic. The audience is purged of emotions, feeling pity and fear for Hamlet and satisfaction in Claudius' just punishment. Tension is released and order appears to be restored, for Hamlet, for whom 'the rest is silence' and for Denmark, as Fortinbras, named by Hamlet's 'dying voice' will become King. Fathers have been avenged and deaths forgiven. Hamlet becomes a hero and successfully purges Denmark of evil, and although this involves losing his own life, it appears that there is no longer 'Something…rotten in the state of Denmark'.

Appearances, however, in this play are always deceptive. At a time when there was an aging monarch and succession anxiety was rife in England, the idea of an outsider, an invader in fact, claiming the throne would have been deeply unsettling. The ending of the play shows a confident monarch stating in ringing rhyming couplets 'Such a sight as this/ Becomes the field but here shows much amiss', thereby identifying a clear sense of right and wrong and suggesting resolution. But the play itself ends not on this, but on the half-line 'Go, bid the soldiers shoot,' a line in one production of the play that is a signal for the Norwegian troops to shoot dead all the remaining Danes.

The big themes

Themes are the dominant ideas repeatedly explored in a text. Shakespeare's plays cover so much ground that they touch on many themes. This is especially true of *Hamlet*, a play which features Shakespeare's most philosophical protagonist. Concerns of different readers and critics foreground different themes. For political criticism, for example, themes of power, control and punishment are likely to come to the fore, whereas critics more interested in gender might explore the themes of masculine and feminine identity and any fluidity between these unfixed terms. Not having the time, nor the space to cover everything, we have chosen to write about what we believe are, indisputably, major themes and in less detail about other important ideas in the play.

Its origins in the old Norwegian legend of *Amleth* and probably in a lost contemporary play called by scholars the *Ur-Hamlet*, as well as being a play about dealing with death and the processing of grief, indisputably Shakespeare's tragedy, *Hamlet*, is also about the enduring power of memory and of the past. As Laurie Maguire writes, 'Hamlet is trapped in memory'[5] and suffers from its most 'disabling form, an inability to forget'. Emma Smith has also written in detail about how the play looks backwards as much as forwards. With its obsessive doublings, retrospection and reiterations the play expresses the theme of the past overshadowing the present, Smith argues, with the past forcefully replaying itself and preventing anything, or anybody, from properly moving on.[6]

As these interconnected themes – death, mourning and memory - have been covered extensively and with great expertise elsewhere, we have turned our focus instead to some of the play's other major preoccupations.

---

[5] Macguire, *Studying Shakespeare*, pp 190-6.

[6] www.bl.uk/shakespeare/articles/hamlet-looking-backwards.

Revenge and justice

In a pointed parallel to Claudius' murder of his brother, Old Hamlet, the play-within-the-play, known variously as *The Murder of Gonzago* and *The Mouse-trap*, which Hamlet has asked the actors to perform, features a Machiavellian murderer, Lucianus, poisoning a king. Specifically, as Claudius had in murdering of his brother, Lucianus 'pours the poison in his ears'. Hamlet himself makes doubly sure that the parallel strikes home by providing a choric commentary immediately after Lucianus' lines: 'A poisons him i' th' garden for his estate' [III.2,260]. Having watched such a close re-enactment of his own secret and perfidious poisoning, Claudius is alarmed and, calling for lights rushes away, giving Hamlet the proof of his uncle's guilt he needed to whet his appetite for revenge.

In Act I, the Ghost establishes vengeance as a form of ultimate justice. Thus we might expect a clear and sharp divide in the play between the noble avenging hero - entrusted to deliver this justice - and the Machiavellian villain who will be justly punished for their crime. Their different choice of weapon and the way they kill signposts their opposite characters: Whereas the noble avenger chooses the sword and fights in the open, the Machiavellian villain uses poison and kills in secret. Compare how the martial king, Old Hamlet, defeated the Norwegian King in single-handed combat to the cunning strategist Claudius who seizes power by an underhand and cowardly murder. Yet, repeatedly in *Hamlet* this opposition between hero and villain is undermined, collapses even, with the avenger taking on the language and tactics of the Machiavel. In the play-within-the-play, for instance, Lucianus may kill the king in a stealthy, Machiavellian way using poison, but, crucially, he is not the king's brother. He is his nephew. This means Lucianus is a parallel to Hamlet, not Claudius. Moreover, his act of poisoning is motivated by vengeance. As Hamlet emphasises just before Lucianus speaks, 'the croaking raven doth bellow for revenge'.

Ravens, of course, are associated with evil acts and they are deployed symbolically by Shakespeare frequently as harbingers of doom. Lady Macbeth, for instance, hears a raven croaking the 'fatal entrance' of King

 Duncan into her castle. Dark, hellish imagery is carried through in Lucianus' lines in which he describes his 'thoughts' as being 'black' and his poison as composed of 'midnight weeds', 'thrice blasted' by the goddess of witchcraft, Hecate. So we have an avenger acting very much like a Machiavellian villain, a double for both Claudius and Hamlet.

Another avenger introduced via the troop of actors is Pyrrhus, son of Achilles. In the excerpt from the story of Dido and Aeneas, in Act II, Scene 2, first Hamlet and then the first player describe how Pyrrhus sought to kill Priam, king of Troy, to avenge his father's death. Hamlet recalls the visually striking description of Pyrrhus: 'Black as his purpose' with a 'dread and black complexion'. Although Pyrrhus' blackness is clearly not a racial characteristic, from a modern perspective, Elizabethan culture's symbolic association of blackness and blackened faces with evil deeds is, it goes without saying, deeply offensive and inexcusably racist. The blackness here appears to be generated by the smoke of battle and, moreover, over his blackened body Pyrrhus has also 'smeared' himself horrifically 'head to foot' with 'blood of fathers, mothers, daughters, sons'. Covered all over in 'coagulate gore', with 'eyes like carbuncles', Pyrrhus' sets off to find Priam and murder him.

Pyrrhus' emphatic black colouring links this avenger to Lucianus. But it is not just an exterior blackness, like Hamlet's 'inky coat' of grief in Act I or the colour of someone's skin. Specifically it is Pyrrhus' act of revenge that is described as 'black'. His whole body covered with blood and gore, eyes bulging like a maniac and labelled 'hellish', Pyrrhus seems more like a demon, something out of a nightmare or modern horror film, than a noble hero delivering justice. The first player's description of him confirms this impression of brutality and bloodlust, describing Pyrrhus as a 'painted tyrant' and comparing his frenzied attack on Priam to the monstrous Cyclops battering Mars. Meanwhile, his victim Priam is presented as old, meek and helpless, as 'declining his milky head', and as 'reverend'.. If that were not enough already, the story then moves on to show the despair of Priam's wife, Hecuba as she witnesses Pyrrhus' savage and sadistic dismemberment of Priam's body: '...she saw Pyrrhus make malicious sport/ In mincing with his sword her husband's limbs'.

'Malicious sport' certainly sounds like cruel slaughter, like butchery, like the brutal satisfaction of a personal vendetta, and not at all like noble justice.

Over the years, many critics have identified various reasons why Hamlet doesn't do what he promises the Ghost in Act I, Scene 5 and 'sweep to his revenge'. A.C. Bradley, for instance, homed in on Hamlet's melancholia, while Ernest Jones famously uncovered Hamlet's apparent oedipal complex. Most of these critics assumed that Hamlet's delay in carrying out the revenge task was a fatal flaw, Hamlet's hamartia, to be explained or excused or deplored. Very few critics questioned whether a son's duty to his father is absolute and binding nor whether carrying out the revenge the Ghost demands is indisputably the right, moral thing for Hamlet to do. Modern readers and audiences may not agree that sons must always do what their fathers tell them. Moreover, from a more modern perspective, although we may understand its continuing emotive potency, we can see that revenge is essentially a crude, medieval, eye-for-an-eye conceptualization of justice, one that is more likely to lead to a cycle of further bloodletting than to reach a just resolution.

Shakespeare, it seems, had profound doubts about both the absolute authority of fathers and especially about the justice of personal revenge. Though the playwright doesn't use Hamlet to expound on the ethical debates about revenge, as he does, for instance, on the nature of man and on mortality in his soliloquies, the ethics of revenge are questioned instead by providing us with several contrasting models of avengers and of acts of vengeful murder. Moreover, as we have seen already, Shakespeare seems to deliberately blur the distinction between the avenger and the object of his revenge, his supposed binary opposite, the Machiavellian villain.

When Hamlet tries to talk himself back into sweeping to his revenge in his second soliloquy in Act II, Scene 2, he briefly moves into the idiom of the bloody avenger driven to act by violent passions. Having, characteristically, chastised himself for cowardice, Hamlet winds his rhetoric up to new ferocious heights, claiming he should have 'fatted all the regions kites/ with this slave's offal' [i.e. slit Claudius stomach and spilled out his guts]. The wave of violent revenge rhetoric carries him to the tumultuous, 'bloody, bawdy villain/

Remorseless, treacherous, lecherous, kindless villain!', and rushes to crescendo in the triumphant apostrophe 'O vengeance!'. But just as quickly this wave comes crashing back down to earth. An embedded stage direction indicates to the actor the moment of self-realisation before the self-excoriating, utterly deflated 'why, what an ass am I'. Hamlet is too clever and far too self-conscious to trick himself into revenge. The language is false and excessive, because it expresses displaced, frustrated energies - big talk covering lack of action. He is trying to force himself into taking on a part, but he knows the costume doesn't fit and the script is cliched. A little later, after the play within the play, in his fourth soliloquy in Act III, Scene 2, Hamlet again steps into the role of revenger and adopts a suitably gothic idiom.

''Tis now the very witching time of night,
When churchyards yawn and hell itself breathes out
Contagion to this world: now could I drink hot blood
And do such bitter business as the day
Would quake to look on.'

Once again, rather than being associated with heaven, light and restorative justice, revenge is instead intimately conjoined instead with darkness, night-time deeds, foulness, disease and hell. As we will explore in more detail in our essays on characters, like Hamlet, his foil, Laertes will also associate his own revenge task with hell and damnation. Thus Shakespeare does not give us a clear, unambiguous, unequivocal line on revenge. Instead, as with so much else in the play, Shakespeare fashions compelling drama out of the clash of contradictory currents and perspectives in Elizabethan culture. On the one hand, personal revenge in this period was prohibited by both the church and the state, with revenge classed as a sin and anyone committing revenge punished for eternity. On the other hand, in certain circumstances revenge might not only be considered justifiable but as a moral imperative. Ever adept at arguing *in utramque partem* – i.e. on both sides of an argument, in *Hamlet* Shakespeare distils urgent debates circulating in early modern culture about the ethics of revenge, over whether regicide could ever be justified, on the value of loyalty and duty, on what it is truly to be a man, and even, as we will see next, on the nature of reality itself.

Appearance and reality

Scholars of renaissance theatre agree that almost all of the drama of this period is preoccupied, one way or another, with the theme of appearances and reality, probably because this theme is interwoven into the fabric of theatre itself. Theatre is, essentially, the art of illusion and of pretence, as the word 'play' indicates. Though audiences can forget this for the duration of a play's action, what we witness on a stage is, of course, not the real world, nor are the actors really the people they are pretending to be. Indeed those 'people' are really only characters, works of fiction made up by a playwright. We know a play is all pretence, but as the poet Coleridge says, we willingly suspend our belief. At least for a short while, we conspire in making theatrical artifice seem to be real.

But what is real? *Hamlet* is haunted by questions that constantly probe at the gap between authenticity and illusion within its staged world. Is the Ghost real or a fantasy? If real, is it a messenger from God or a demon from Hell? Is it Old Hamlet or just his image? Is Claudius a good king or a bad one? Is Gertrude a wise queen or weak and lust-driven? Does Ophelia drown herself by accident or on purpose? Initially Hamlet appears to set himself up as our guide to what is genuine and what is not: 'Seems, madam?' he inquires in Act I, Scene 2, when Gertrude wonders why his grief over Old Hamlet's death 'seems so particular', '...I know not 'seems'' [I.2,76]. But, despite his claim that he is only and honestly himself and above appearing to be anything else, Hamlet offers no stable authentic self to help us navigate the play's smoke and mirrors. Among the questions you  may find yourself asking of him are: Is he mad or is he sane? Does he love Ophelia or is he just pretending? Does he ever really intend to revenge the Ghost or simply to remember him? You might even ask: is he a tragic hero or as much a villain as Claudius?

Taking a broader view on the topic of appearances versus reality, this section will explore three linked aspects that emerge in the play: the Elizabethan sumptuary [clothing] laws, subjectivity, and metatheatre.

The sumptuary laws

Hamlet and Gertrude's exchange quoted above pivots around a discussion of clothing. Hamlet continues to wear his 'suits of solemn black' in mourning for his father, which his mother and uncle consider inappropriate now that Old Hamlet is buried and a new king on the throne. The dispute reflects the ways in which clothing could be used to control and regulate early modern society. From the twelfth to the eighteenth century, England used sumptuary laws which dictated what people could and couldn't wear, and when. Generally, these laws controlled the types, colours, fabrics and embellishments that were considered suitable for different social classes. While there is a powerful element of classism to these rules, not all of them were as snobbery-driven as they may seem. Often these laws were used to protect local industry [e.g. the wool trade] from imports of foreign fabrics. An example is the 1571 act that demanded all men over the age of six wear a wool cap on Sundays to boost the wool industry and prevent it being overtaken by trade in silk and cotton. The laws were also used to help demarcate periods of time, such as Sunday attire for a day of rest and worship, and for weddings, birth celebrations and periods of mourning.

The sumptuary laws were fraught and complex. Often they were at odds with individual acts of self-identification, as Ann Rosalind Jones and Peter Stallybrass have noted. Clothing, they argue, was a form of cultural memory in literally material form, form through which people understood their place in society: 'clothes permeate the wearer, fashioning him or her from within… Clothes, like sorrow, inscribe themselves upon a person who comes into being through that act of inscription'[7]. Hamlet's attire is, in this sense, both an honest reflection of his emotional state and simultaneously a blatant act of rebellion.

There is no question that Hamlet is mourning his father's death. His 'inky cloak' and downcast air are externalisations of his state of mind. But according to Elizabethan mourning rituals, Hamlet should have shed his 'nighted colour' once his father's funeral rites were finished and returned to ordinary clothes.

---

[7] Jones and Stallybrass, *Renaissance Clothing*.

By not doing so, indeed by parading his ongoing sadness, he publicly rebels against Claudius' endeavours to restore the kingdom to normality – a 'peevish opposition' to the King's desires [I.2,100]. As a courtier, and Claudius' presumed heir, he is also acting against his social place, showing disproportionate, 'unmanly grief', disrupting the carefully curated image of unity and stability that Claudius is projecting and thereby undermining the royal family.

While Hamlet's personal reality and appearance are aligned, even exaggerated, in this episode, he also argues that clothes are not actually a reliable marker of a person's interior self. His sorrow goes far beyond 'the trappings and the suits of woe' – he could wear a clown's costume and still be grieving. He also notes that mourning rituals can be performed with sad looks, dark clothes, and crocodile tears when those who wear them do not grieve at all. Pointedly he implies that both Claudius and his mother were simply going through the motions of sorrow about his father's death while hiding their real feelings. He exposes his own performativity here too: while he seems to be doing his duty to the royal family by standing by his mother and uncle at the public celebration, and even promises to stay and support them instead of returning to university, his moody clothing is a visual reminder that he is there only to honour is father's death and not the new ruler of the kingdom. The essence of his point is that how one presents oneself on the outside may not be a true representation of their feelings or behaviour, and that too may not be in sync with the place they hold in the social spectrum.

We might also note that the character's self-consciousness about his costume threatens the fourth wall – the invisible boundary between the theatrical world and the real world in which the play is performed. Hamlet the character calls attention to his costume as a costume, his performance as a performance, within the world that he inhabits and so reminds the audience of the theatricality inherent in the world that they inhabit too: what are the sumptuary laws if not costume? The social codes of conduct if not performance? So the question arises, just how much of the real world is really real either?

Subjectivity

It is the lengthy, self-reflective investigation of the potential for divergence between appearance and reality, inner and outer selves, which makes *Hamlet* seem such a peculiarly modern play. This modernness is extended into its exploration of self-hood Among the other questions that that play brings up are those that concern individual identity. To die or not to die? To love or to hate? To tell the truth or lie? To act or not to act? Tortured by moral uncertainty to the point of mental fragmentation, as a character Hamlet exists in a state of permanent psychological crisis. Today, Hamlet might be scathingly referred to by older generations as a 'snowflake', paralysed in the face of his uncle's treason because he is so sensitive to the moral complexities of his situation. His experience does not deserve such scorn. Despite his Christian faith, he finds himself in a predicament where there aren't any simple, pre-set moral codes to follow. Instead he has to determine the morals for himself within a number of competing and irreconcilable frameworks. If

Hamlet struggles to present us with an authentic self, it is not just because he is as much a performer as the smiling, lying Claudius, it is also because the various aspects of himself are pulled in different directions by a range of social and moral obligations. For Hamlet, his course of action could be determined by the divinity of kings, a son's duty, an heir's political responsibility, a soldier's honour, a Christian's piety, a prince's authority, or a scholar's philosophy. Put another way; to murder the king is treason; to honour his father he must kill the king; as heir he must support the king; as a warrior he must be avenged by killing the king; as a Christian, murder is wrong; as a prince, it is his duty to act on Claudius' treason; as a scholar, he cannot conscience killing. Hamlet's identity comprises all of these facets of himself. To choose one to override all the others is a form of self-denial and self-destruction. No wonder he cannot decide what to do!

Hamlet's psychological crisis is epitomised by the collision of being and seeming that he articulates in his debate with his mother and uncle about his costume. But he is not alone in this. Most of the key characters battle with similarly conflicting aspects of their identity or are provoked into action by accusations that if they do not act then they are not who they appear to be. Hence a disjunction between being and seeming is at the core of the social crisis of the playworld.

As the section on Gertrude will investigate, the Queen is caught between how her son and his father both see her - a loyal and much-loved wife, seemingly turned traitor by her own lust - and how her second husband sees her as a respected partner and 'imperial jointress' to the state. She's caught too between how she presents herself as rational peacemaker for her realm and family and how she comes to see herself, i.e. as an unwitting betrayer of Old Hamlet, her son's fierce ally and traitor to her new husband. Claudius seems to be the perfect Machiavellian ruler, able to pretend virtue to his people no matter how much he manipulates the law – he can 'smile and smile and be a villain' [I.5,107-08] – but, ultimately, he is unable to maintain the charade before God and his seemingly straightforward villainy is complicated by his authentic genuine guilt over his act of treason. Ophelia wrestles with her contesting roles as Hamlet's prospective wife, her father's daughter, brother's sister, and lady of the court. Unable to determine who she is in the face of all she is supposed to be, like Hamlet, she breaks down mentally and seeks escape in terminal not-being. Rosencrantz and Guildenstern are supposed to be Hamlet's friends, yet sacrifice their own moral code as scholars and Christians to become his prospective executioners at the order of their King. Laertes is compelled to seek stealthy revenge on Hamlet by Claudius, but such deceitful dealings collide with his identity as a perfect courtier [IV.7,10]. While the historical circumstances that have provoked this state of social turmoil differ to the present day, we see in Shakespeare's Denmark a familiar and very contemporary sense of individual purposelessness and nihilism, provoked by too much choice, too much information, and too many colliding frameworks through which one is supposed to locate a place in the world.

Metatheatre

If Hamlet's world resonates with ours, it also deliberately echoes the world of Shakespeare's England. Playworlds became well-known for being microcosms of the social world, re-presenting it to itself. An extremely self-conscious play, *Hamlet* exemplifies theatre's capacity to shape the reality in which it takes place. Despite his constant railing against the divide between acting and authenticity, Hamlet turns to performance in search for the truth behind other characters' appearances. Having claimed to his mother to be exactly what he puts on show, he promptly makes a liar of himself by assuming an 'antic disposition' in order to minimise the threat he presents to Claudius' throne as heir apparent, while also giving him free rein to investigate the Ghost's accusations against his uncle. He further orchestrates a company of players to perform *The Mousetrap*, re-staging Claudius' presumed crime by way of a play 'to catch the conscience of the king' [II.2,601]. Despite his distrust of 'actions that a man might play', Hamlet uses acting to determine authenticity in others and to stimulate action in himself. His hatred of artifice in others is acute, yet he will use artifice when it serves his quest for authenticity. As Gillian Woods puts it, Hamlet is aware that 'theatrical performances may be mere pretence, but they produce a real impact on those who view them'. Contrary to the true anti-theatricalists of the early modern period, who viewed theatre as 'fundamentally fraudulent because they work by illusion'[8], Hamlet knows that performance is an essential part of reality.

Kingship

Before writing *Hamlet*, Shakespeare was most famous for his History plays, of which the two parts of *Henry IV* [1597-1599] were his most popular. Hence contemporary audiences were prepped to read his latest work through this

particular prism, as concerning kings, queens and princes. The issue of kingship would have been especially resonant for an Elizabethan audience as a woman was currently on the throne. And not just any woman, an elderly woman without children and therefore with no legitimate heir. Concerns about who might succeed Elizabeth I and a potential succession crisis had swirled around Elizabethan culture so dangerously that the monarch had felt impelled to issue the Treasons Act in 1571. Not only did

---

[8] www.bl.uk/shakespeare/articles/hamlet-the-play-within-the-playBritish.

this act make any attempt to usurp the English monarch an act of high treason, it also entirely outlawed any discussion of her succession.

It was audacious then for Shakespeare to produce a play where the issue of succession is so prominent, albeit hidden under the thin disguise of the Danish setting. The action of the play raises some fundamental questions, including how a monarch should be chosen. Hamlet, for instance, seems to think he has been usurped by his uncle and we might assume that, through the rights or primogeniture, he was the natural heir and should therefore have succeeded his father as King of Denmark. However, as the Shakespeare scholar Anjna Chouhan has pointed out the word 'election', in the sense of some form of democratic process, appears a couple of times in Hamlet, both times used by Hamlet himself. Though the Prince may feel usurped, he acknowledges that Claudius has 'popped between the election' and his hopes, implying his uncle may have been chosen as the new Danish King [though, of course, such a process could be open to manipulation]. Later, Hamlet again implies some sort of rudimentary democratic process operant in the choosing of a new monarch, when he prophesies that the 'election' will  'light' on Fortinbras. Hence the issues of succession in the play echoes the forbidden debate in Elizabethan England about whether a new monarch could be elected by the commonwealth rather than chosen, somehow, by God.

There are three other interrelated questions about kingship that the play raises:

- What are the key characteristics of an ideal king?
- What are the key characteristics of a king who is to rule medieval Denmark?
- In what circumstances might it be justifiable to overthrow a king?

Tot them up and there are six actual kings and two potential kings in the play – Old Hamlet, Old Fortinbras, the current King of Norway, the King of England, Claudius, Gonzago, plus Hamlet and the younger Fortinbras. As with the multiple avengers, and as the doubled names of fathers and sons implies, the play creates a hall of mirrors from within which, perhaps, an ideal king might be identified.

The off-stage characters of Old Fortinbras, Norway and the King of England are only dimly present in the play, shadowy backgrounds that make the on-stage characters more vivid. Ostensibly none of these provide a model for perfect kingship. Defeated in single-handed combat, Old Fortinbras failed in one of the prime responsibilities of a monarch – to defend his land from external threats. His successor is like Claudius - a brother, not a son - and appears to be old or ill, and ineffective. Described by Claudius as 'impotent and bedrid', he seems unaware of his nephew's martial preparations, suggesting he is poorly informed and that his grip on power is weak and shaky. Meanwhile, the King of England is also presented as being weak, operating like a vassal state, having to do Claudius' bidding in executing Hamlet without trial, under the threat of suffering more wounds under the Danish sword.

Arguably, the end of the play corrects the misconceptions of Norway we have received via Claudius. While it is possible that Norway was, in fact, even more impotent than we thought and young Fortinbras deceives him in his promise not to attack Denmark, another possibility is that Norway's assurances to Claudius were a ruse and that the king was complicit in his nephew's plans. Such a reading makes Norway a more Machiavellian figure, but one who still relies on the more martial Fortinbras to achieve his ends.

As his ever-present armour signals, Old Hamlet provides another example of a martial king in the chivalric-heroic mode. He seems also to have been a successful king, defeating Old Fortinbras and presumably having some hand in the cowering of England before the Danish sword. Certainly Hamlet idolises his father and the more independent Horatio also attests that he was a 'goodly king', in appearance at least. Old Hamlet seems a good fit for a medieval conception of an ideal king - the strongest warrior who defends his people in person through armed combat – but we develop little sense from the play of how he ruled Denmark. Was Old Hamlet a fair, just sovereign who ruled with shrewd intelligence for the benefit of his people? We cannot judge. What we can say with confidence is that in Elizabethan England this concept of kingship, though perhaps attractive in a nostalgic way, was already appearing to be old-fashioned, outmoded, not fit for purpose for the complexities of early modern culture.

At least superficially, Claudius seems, in fact, a better model for a new type of king. Clever, cunning, perceptive, diplomatically adroit, a good orator, he

seems to be able to run the state effectively. Whereas Old Hamlet represented the chivalric-heroic past, Claudius represents the future; a more political type of king with some kind of democratic mandate rather than God-given legitimacy. However, before we rush to celebrate Claudius as an ideal king for a newly emerging early modern Denmark, we need to remember he's a murderer, moreover a regicidal and fratricidal murderer, that the state he runs is a surveillance state, a state corrupt from head to foot, that he both corrupts Laertes and conspires to have Hamlet murdered and that he fails to protect Denmark from the external threat of Fortinbras. In short, Claudius is a Machiavellian and, even in Machiavelli's limited proscription for effective kingship of the ends justifying the means, a failure.

Claudius' rule also raises the issue of regicide, specifically whether it can ever be right to kill a king, however corrupt he may be and however noble the apparent justifications. While Claudius does not behave in the merciless tyrannical fashion of Macbeth or seek absolute power like Julius Caesar, the play does sail perilously close to opposing Queen Elizabeth's Treason Act by countenancing the idea that Hamlet is not only justified, but, in fact, has a moral obligation to kill Claudius.

And what of the two young pretenders to power, Hamlet and Fortinbras? If tested, would Hamlet have made a good king? The Hamlet other characters describe as existing before the events of the play - Ophelia refers to him as the ideal noble, scholar and soldier and calls him the 'expectancy and rose of the fair state' – may, perhaps, have made a great king. But though he may have the intellectual acuity, perspicacity and articulacy as well as, in the end, the courage, surely Hamlet's character is too prone to excess, too introspective and too unstable. Perhaps, we could concede that if he had survived, the Hamlet whose mettle had been tested by killing Claudius could have gone on to become a good king.

Surely the most successful of our candidates for the ideal king is Fortinbras. He combines the martial courage of Old Hamlet with the shrewd calculations of Claudius. Either he tricks his uncle or they both trick Claudius. He shows military prowess in taking Elsinore easily and an assured political touch in immediately shaping the narrative about Hamlet's death. His actions not only return land lost by the previous generation, but gain new, rich and powerful lands from Denmark. The only problem with Fortinbras, from a Danish perspective, at least, is that he's an invader. How he will rule his new territories will also, of course, never be known.

The nature of man

'What a piece of work is a man?' asks Hamlet. And whatever faults we might find in the Prince, and there are many from which to choose – including his cowardice, his procrastination, his self-centredness or his misogyny – Shakespeare gives him some of the most beautiful lines in English drama, lines that express both a profoundly inspiring, humanist conception of mankind's almost infinite capacities, as well as an equal and opposite annihilating sense of existential despair. And isn't this a poignant part of Hamlet's tragedy; that he is able to recognise the awesome beauty of the world and of humankind and of the potential to create a better world, and he is also able to articulate this, but he remains resolutely trapped in his own corrupted one?

What are, for Hamlet, the key attributes of a man? Ostensibly, for him at least, one figure best embodies what it really means to be a man, Hamlet's father. 'Here was a man,' he opines in Act I, Scene 2 with an invisible, but nevertheless implied adjective 'proper'. Describing his father to his mother, Hamlet adds that on his father's form, 'every god did seem to set his seal/ To give the world assurance of a man'. However, this identification of the chivalric martial hero with ultimate manliness is counterbalanced by Hamlet's faith in the scholarly Horatio as another proper man. Specifically, Hamlet pinpoints qualities in his friend that make him a man, his honesty and integrity as well as the fact that he is not 'passion's slave' but uses, instead, his reason to guide his behaviour.

The sense of what it is to be a man is also constructed through two binaries; women and animals. Superficially, these binaries may appear to be like men, but they are, for Hamlet, fundamentally different and, moreover, inherently inferior. Hamlet sees women as the binary opposite of men essentially because they do not demonstrate one of the three key qualities - honesty. His mother's speedy recovery from her deep mourning at her husband's funeral makes Hamlet wonder whether her grief was genuine or shallow. Ophelia's betrayal in the nunnery scene amplifies his sense that women are not trustworthy because they pretend to be what they are not: As he accuses Ophelia, 'God hath given you one face, and you make yourselves another'. Hamlet's most famous misogynistic comment, that 'frailty, thy name is woman', is prompted by the idea that his mother cannot resist temptation. Hence, in her son's eyes, she lacks another of the three essential masculine qualities - the ability to use reason to govern one's passions.

Similarly, Hamlet sets up an oppositional relationship between what he calls 'god-like', 'noble reason' and shameful 'beastial oblivion'. The key difference between man and beast is that the latter lacks the 'discourse of reason'. Furthermore a man without a moral purpose in the world, a man who is not prepared to sacrifice himself for a noble cause and only wishes 'to sleep and feed' is no more than a 'beast'. Both the Ghost and Hamlet call Claudius a beast: 'That incestuous, adulterous beast'; a 'lord of beasts' - in both cases associating beastliness with lustful corruption.

Hamlet also compares Claudius to an 'ape' and to a half-man, half-goat creature; a satyr. Other men who are not real men in Hamlet's estimation are compared to animals: Rosencrantz and Guildenstern are like adders, while the foppish Osric [a name that may imply ostrich] is described as a 'water-fly', a 'chough' and a 'lapwing' - all belittling and dehumanising comparisons, of course. So, a man is the opposite of a woman and a beast. In essence he is defined by the core qualities of honesty, capacity for heroic action and, rather than being driven by emotions, by a 'god-like' ability to reason.

However, Hamlet's use of the word 'man' is ambiguous. While at times, he is referring specifically to a male human being, at other times it seems that he uses the word in the more expansive sense of humanity. Certainly Hamlet rails against women, but he also rails against men, describing all men as 'errant knaves'. He accuses women of false pretences, but he also levels the same accusations at everyone, regardless of gender. Perhaps, sickened by the corruption of Elsinore, Hamlet is as much misanthropic as misogynistic. Nevertheless, unlike women, there are two men who escape the general gloom about human nature; Horatio and, of course, his father.

Unable or unwilling to carry out the task of revenge, pretending to be what he is not and fearing that he may not even be true to himself, for most of the play Hamlet is emotionally fragile and volatile, 'very much at the mercy of the emotions swirling around inside him'[9]. In other words, what Hamlet venerates most as manly qualities are the qualities he feels he most lacks. However, for a modern audience, in particular, what makes Hamlet a compelling, sympathetic character might very well be his uncertainty, his willingness to think things through, to reflect and feel deeply. Fundamentally, despite his self-excoriation for being like a 'whore' in unpacking his 'heart' with words, it is Hamlet's unrivalled capacity to express himself so compellingly that makes us invest so much in what happens to him.

Corruption and health

In Act II, Scene 2 Hamlet laments to Rosencrantz and Guildenstern that, since his father's death, the air around him seems 'a foul and pestilent congregation of vapours'. His sense of a world where every breath has been poisoned is a theme that runs throughout the play. From plague, apoplexy, leprosy, and pleurisy, to accusations of madness and images of poisoned wounds,

---

[9] Noble, *How to do Shakespeare*, p.16.

Shakespeare uses the language of disease as a metaphor for the corruption of the state caused by Claudius' fratricidal ascent to the throne.

There are three key things to be aware of when examining the language of [ill-]health in *Hamlet*. Firstly, the relationship between the monarch and the state was often represented in terms of physical and spiritual bodies. Arising through legal and theological tracts to explain the reigns of Mary I and Elizabeth I – women heading up a highly patriarchal society where men were seen as the dominant sex – the monarch was considered to have two bodies; a 'body natural', subject to the predations of age, disease, and sin, and a 'body politic', a pure representation of their divine right to the throne. The body politic transferred between monarchs with the succession and was separate from their own souls, which could go to heaven or to hell. The relationship between the royal, physical and spiritual bodies was complex. Though the body politic was theoretically untouched by any flaws in the body natural, sickness – particularly sinfulness – could spread from the monarch's body natural to infect and corrupt the political body of the state.

Essentially an ailing monarch, whether physically, mentally, or spiritually ailing, could spread their sickness into their politics. Claudius refers to this when he predicts a war with Norway to come: Its current ruler, he says is 'impotent and bed-rid', no longer able to uphold the agreement Old Fortinbras reached with Old Hamlet; Claudius implies that the state has been weakened by its leader's impotence and will be subject to takeover by the feisty Young Fortinbras, who plains to reclaim some Danish lands. Likewise, the restlessness of the Ghost – who may be Old Hamlet's soul, or even a figure for the body politic itself – suggests to Marcellus that 'something is rotten in the state of Denmark' [I.4, 90]. When graves spit up their corpses, especially the corpses of previous rulers, something is very wrong in the country, as Horatio tell us. It is not difficult to trace that rottenness back to Claudius, though Hamlet's accusations of bestiality, 'mildew' and infection in his uncle.

The second key association between bodily damage and political corruption emerges through wound-imagery, linked to revenge. Francisco speaking to Barnardo in the Act I, Scene 1, describes himself as 'sick at heart', representing a neglected populace and prefacing Marcellus' portrait of the body politic rotting at its core. The cause of the rot is connected to the murder of Old Hamlet when Claudius describes his brother's death as a 'memory…green', as if it were a fresh wound. Though Claudius [ironically] suggests everyone feels it, he and Gertrude tell Prince Hamlet that he is the only one still picking at the scab before it can heal. Claudius' use of the colour green echoes Francis Bacon's description of revenge as a wound that, if studied, remains 'green [meaning fresh] which would otherwise heal, and do well'. The guards, however, imply the wound has already gone septic.

This imagery is picked up again after *The Mousetrap*, when Guildenstern tells Hamlet that he has made the King 'distemper'd…with choler', or sick with anger at the insult; Hamlet counters that the King was already sick and is merely now self-medicating with alcohol. He adds that 'for me to put him to his purgation would perhaps plunge him into far  more choler' [III.2, 305-7]. In other words, the proper treatment would be worse than his current suffering. As most medical treatment in Shakespeare's time consisted of imbibing a concoction that included alcohol or releasing the sickness by inducing bleeding, vomiting, and other bodily fluids, Hamlet is suggesting that Claudius' intoxication will be preferable to him than Hamlet's preferred cure for his distemper [and by extension, the rotten state] – letting all of Claudius' blood out until he is dead.

The third key thing to note is the connection between love and madness. Hamlet's show of madness is explained by his mother and uncle as stemming from his great love for his father and grief at his death. Exploring early modern madness, Will Tosh notes that Robert Bruton's *Anatomy of Melancholy* [1621] – a treatise on mental illness – argues that the state of world affairs, such as 'rumours of war, plagues, fires, inundations, thefts, murders, massacres, meteors, comets, spectrums, prodigies, apparitions…towns taken [and] cities besieged'[10], could all drive someone to madness. Alongside death and grief, romantic love, or indeed sexual desire, was also perceived to be capable of driving someone to distraction. Hamlet suggests his mother is mad for marrying Claudius in a fit of 'the compulsive ardour' [III.4,85]. Hamlet himself is also misdiagnosed by Polonius, who suggests 'the madness wherein he now raves' is not because of his father's death but Ophelia's rejection of his affections [II.2,146-50]. It is, of course, Ophelia who ultimately succumbs to a kind of love sickness. However, we might well argue that being slighted in love is less of an issue than being manipulated by her father, King, Queen, and Prince to serve their differing agendas. Here familial love and patriotic love may be greater killers than romance, once again aligning political corruption with bodily friability.

For the influential critic, Caroline Spurgeon, the imagery of sickness, disease, blemishes, ulcers and tumours of the body is the predominant one in *Hamlet* But you might have noticed that these images do work in isolation. You might, for example, have seen that images of bodily ill-health and political corruption are often intertwined with other similes and metaphors, such as gardening, ghosts, and rotten corpses. Consider, for instance, Hamlet's vision of the court as an 'unweeded garden', Laertes' description of Hamlet as a garden pest [the canker worm], and the herb-based poison administered in the orchard that murdered Old Hamlet.

It is, then, not just living human bodies that exemplify the rot. Dead bodies too show the corruption of a kingdom: From the restless Ghost and Horatio's images of walking corpses in Rome to the disjointed heads and bodies that the gravediggers scatter, which foreshadows the severing of the political heads of Denmark [Claudius, Hamlet, and Gertrude] from the political body of the state. Wilting, dying, and decaying images of the natural world, such as Ophelia's dead flowers, rampant weeds, and holes in the earth also combine to create portrait of a world turned toxic, as if not only the human inhabitants of Denmark, but the very land itself is soured by its poisonous politics.

---

[10] www.bl.uk/shakespeare/articles/shakespeare-and-madness.

Religion and mortality

Unsurprisingly, Hamlet is the chief interrogator of the nature and meaning of death in the play and of its relationship to religion. Although he acknowledges God's strict prohibition against suicide, Hamlet considers self-murder, for example, and doesn't automatically assume that as a consequence he would  be sentenced to hell. Indeed Hamlet wonders about the nature of death and what may come after, imagining the afterlife as an 'undiscovered country', decoupling it from specifically Christian notions of heaven and hell. Hamlet also meditates on death as the great leveller, the one, ultimate, inescapable force that brings a king down to the same level as a beggar. And, of course, his father's death casts an enormous shadow over Hamlet, forcing him into the role of avenging bringer of death.

From Hamlet's lament that God has 'fix'd/ His canon 'gainst self-slaughter' to the Ghost's complaints about purgatory, Claudius' painful confession that halts Hamlet's vengeful dagger, and the debate over Ophelia's 'maimed [funeral] rites', representations of death in *Hamlet* are inextricably linked to faith. This is hardly surprising in a period during which faith formed the main framework for understanding of both life and death. It is even less surprising when we recall that the play was written in the wake of enormous religious upheaval. The rites and rituals that structured life and death in early modern England were rewritten almost constantly in the seventy years before the play's production, as the country oscillated between Catholicism and Protestantism. Consequently, the concept of death in this period was continuously being re-imagined.

Although how people mourned, memorialised, and even planned for death was often in flux, the need to die a 'good death' was one consistency that transcended denominational divides. In its simplest form, a good death was a natural one that the dying had time to prepare for, to say goodbyes, and to confess and be absolved of all human sins. There were variations, such as 'noble' deaths in combat which were generally viewed as good too – and sometimes better than a peaceful natural passing for those who had lived their lives as warriors. 'Bad' deaths, however, were much more wide-ranging, encompassing sudden deaths – natural or unnatural – for which the dead person had not been able to prepare or confess, to suicide, which tended to be viewed as a disgrace in the eyes of society and of God. A bad death was something to be feared in a time in which the dead were seen as having an active afterlife, their soul set to suffer in hell or purgatory, or seek solace in heaven, awaiting the Day of Judgement when their fate would be fixed forever. However, the many deaths in *Hamlet* show us that whether a death was good or bad depended on a variety of factors, including the type of person, the type of death, the context in which it happened, and how it is perceived or even appropriated by those around them. Not only could a death be good or bad, it could also be suitable or unsuitable for the individual and, particularly where the death was unnatural, it could also reflect the goodness or badness of those responsible.

At the start of the play, King Hamlet's death is portrayed by Claudius as a sad but natural passing that has been commemorated with appropriate Protestant brevity. Socially speaking, it seems to be a good death for a good man. To depict his passing as a normal event is politically convenient, of course, since it conceals Claudius' regicide. A 'good' death also allows the kingdom to move on and celebrate their new king. However, Old Hamlet was unable to prepare for death and thus went to his judgement with 'all [his] imperfections on [his] head [I.5,79]. Foreshadowed by the wandering of the Ghost, Old Hamlet's death is subsequently exposed as a brutal murder, a 'most horrible!' ending for a good man and one that has condemned him to purgatory. This bad death is decried by Hamlet and his father as grossly inappropriate for a good man and marks out Claudius, the murderer, as the primary villain in the play. Triggering Hamlet's campaign against his father's killer, it also sets him up as the avenging hero.

Claudius' imagined death in Act III, Scene 3 is almost the inverse scenario. To be surprised with a dagger and murdered would, it appears, be a fitting death for Claudius. Socially speaking, the brutality and abruptness looks like a bad ending, but the Prince stops short of acting upon it when he realises that it is not sufficient punishment 'to take him in the purging of his soul,/ When he is fit and season'd for his passage' in the eyes of God [III.3,85-86]. To allow

Claudius to die well, prepared for death, would be to insult Old Hamlet who died with no such luxuries. Hence Hamlet vows instead to wait for a moment when he can give Claudius a more suitable 'bad' death, 'when he is drunk asleep, or in his rage,/ Or in th'incestuous pleasure of his bed…about some act/ That has no relish of salvation in't'.

Relatively speaking, these are simple cases: A good man dies badly at the hands of a bad man; the bad man responsible should die at the hands of another good man and he should not die well. But many other deaths, and the responsibilities of the living for those deaths, are more complex. What of Polonius, who dies abruptly in an act of spying? A 'foolish prating knave' perhaps, but even Hamlet, preoccupied with revealing the truth of his father's murder to his mother, recognises that the death he has meted out to Polonius is 'bad', 'bloody' and undeserved. This killing warns us of the recklessness of revenge, which turns the revenger from one seeking justice into the doer of even greater wrongs.

What too, of Ophelia? In apparently taking her own life, in the eyes of the gravediggers and the church, she has committed a great sin against God and society; at best she deserves stunted mourning rites and at worst to be buried in unhallowed ground, condemned to hell. Yet, in the eyes of the Queen, King, her brother, and even Hamlet, she has been driven out of her mind by the Prince's mistreatments and the pressures placed on her by her family, so cannot be held accountable for her actions. It is another bad death, both socially and in the eyes of God for a good person, and one that again underscores the wildness of revenge, further tilting the balance for Hamlet from hero toward villain, while simultaneously reinforcing Claudius' villainy. The more deaths that mount up, the more the boundary between hero and villain seems to blur, and the more the concept of what is a good or a bad death in the eyes of God and the eyes of society seem to diverge. If Claudius, from the outset, seems destined for hell, then what about Hamlet? With at least Polonius', Laertes', Claudius', and potentially Ophelia's deaths on his hands, it seems unlikely that he can pass to heaven. Fortinbras promises to celebrate Hamlet's life and commemorate his death, as suits a noble prince, suggesting he will be remembered well in the kingdom. But surely the best he can hope for, dying with only a partial confession of his responsibility via an apology to Laertes, is to go to purgatory – if purgatory still exists in a kingdom that appears, under Claudius' rule, to be Protestant.

It is worth exploring some of the other deaths in this play to see if you can find your own answer to this question. You might want to consider the murders of Rosencrantz and Guildenstern: Do they die well or badly? Who is responsible and does it reflect well or poorly upon them? [We will consider this in our essay on them]. What about Gertrude? Did she commit suicide? If so, does it matter that she dies a noble death trying to save her son? Who is responsible for her death? And what about Horatio's desire to die that is stalled by Hamlet, who hastens his own death with the remaining poison? Think too about Laertes and Hamlet – to what extent do their dying confessions redeem these two very different avengers and spare them from suffering bad deaths?

Shakespeare's language

In the 1930s a literary academic, Caroline Spurgeon, wrote a hugely influential critical study of Shakespeare's language, called *Shakespeare's Imagery and What it Tells Us*. The central idea of Spurgeon's study was that Shakespeare's figurative imagery falls into groups or clusters and these clusters vary from play to play. Moreover, Spurgeon opined that these image clusters are the most important generators of the distinct mood and atmosphere of each play and also convey key thematic concerns. For instance, we might quickly think of the multiple images of animals in *Macbeth*. Like *King Lear*, the Scottish play houses a teeming menagerie of creatures, from poor 'wrens' and 'mewing' cats to 'hell-kites', a 'Russian bear' and even an 'armed rhinoceros'. *Hamlet* rivals these two tragedies in terms of the number and range of animals used in imagery, from Osric as a water-fly to the crocodile Hamlet claims he could eat. Spurgeon's approach is, as you can see, incisive, allowing us to fillet each play for the seemingly richest cuts of language.

However, since the 1930s her approach has been criticized and refined in various ways. There are three main criticisms, the first of which is less obvious, the other two probably a bit more predictable: As a pioneering female literary academic writing in the 1930s Spurgeon was constrained by decorum; hence she entirely ignored sexual imagery. Critics have also contested her choices of image clusters in each play, suggesting that alternative clusters are just as or even more significant. Other critics have gone a step further, disagreeing with the privileging of imagery above other features. Why, for instance, is imagery more significant than repeated single words [think of the importance of 'rank' in *Hamlet*] or other literary devices such as antithesis and doubling language ['To be, or not to be']? What about the use of verse, and prose, and Shakespeare's bending and meshing of iambic pentameter with syntax? Aren't characters also pretty important, especially in a text that is written to be performed by actors on a stage? Words, of course, matter, but there's an old cliché that actions speak louder. And so on. No doubt there's a literary academic out there

Image clusters in *Hamlet*:

As we've already explored the first two major patterns of imagery in terms of their thematic significance in our essays on major themes, we're going to keep this section as short and to the point as possible.

Appearance and reality

If there's one image cluster predominant in Shakespeare's work as a whole this one might well be it. And we might pause to wonder why Shakespeare seems so obsessed with ontological and metaphysical issues. Arguably, it's because of the nature of plays themselves. Pretending, acting and putting on masks are inherent features of drama texts in a fundamental way that is not true of poetry or novels. The Romantic poet, Samuel Taylor Coleridge, wrote about audiences' willing suspension of disbelief when we watch plays. Obviously, when watching *Hamlet* in a theatre, on one level we know that we are in a theatre and not really in Denmark. We know too that in front of us is a stage and not really the royal palace of Elsinore. Even with films, where directors can create a stronger sense of verisimilitude, we still know we are watching through a screen and that the characters depicted are not real people and are being played by actors. And, yet, for films and especially for plays to fully cast their spell on us, we have to let ourselves go with the spectacle, fill in the blanks with our imaginations, take what we see to be real, at least for the duration of the performance.

In other words, ontological or more broadly metaphysical issues, issues concerning what is real and what is pretence, what seems to be and what actually is, are the essence of theatre, and especially so for plays that are highly literary – written, for instance, in iambic pentameter – and yet want us to feel as we watch them as if the characters and actions are absolutely real. In the 2018 Globe Theatre production of *Hamlet* the director decided to cast a very tall man in a dress as Ophelia. While this decision might remind us that in Shakespeare's time Ophelia, and all female characters, would have been played by men, it made it hard for some audience members to suspend disbelief and invest fully in the character.

The word 'play' appears over thirty times in *Hamlet*, more times than it does in any other of Shakespeare's plays. There's an abundance of imagery taken from the theatre. The second scene, in the throne room of the royal court, is itself a piece of political theatre. Both Claudius and Hamlet seem acutely aware of this. The former knows he has to deliver an effective unifying speech to secure his authority as the new king and that the royal family itself must present themselves as unified. Hamlet knows this too, but is not going to play ball. Dressed for dramatic, theatrical effect in his incongruous 'inky cloak' costume, he takes the first opportunity to expose the nice little domestic display for the sham it really is. When his mother asks why he seems so gloomy, he pounces on the verb: '**Seems** madam? Nay it **is**'. And there we have the metaphysical issue in a pithy antithetical nutshell.

Hamlet then goes on to list the 'actions that a man might play' if pretending to feel as he feels. And the only way to tell the difference between this counterfeit of feeling and the real thing? Something you cannot see at all from the outside. So, it's almost impossible to distinguish between the real and the false, the truth and the lie. A little later in the same scene, Hamlet rages about how his mother has seemed so swiftly to recover from the extravagant grief she displayed at his father's funeral. Was this also just a performance?

Disguise, pretence and misreadings are everywhere you turn in Elsinore, perhaps because everyone is being watched and therefore everyone is always playing some sort of part for someone else's benefit. Frequently, we are not sure if Hamlet is playing a part, putting on his 'antic disposition' or not. More fundamentally, though he says he has something sincere within him that 'passes show', Hamlet worries that he is only ever like a bad actor unable to find the right part. Like Hamlet, we are really not sure for much of the play whether the Ghost is really the dead spirit of Old Hamlet or something malign, a 'goblin damned' perhaps, pretending to be the King. Meanwhile Polonius and Laertes advise Ophelia not to judge Hamlet's intentions towards her by appearances and Polonius misreads Hamlet's madness as stemming from

Ophelia's rejection of his love. At the start of the play Claudius is certainly playing the role of King, devoted husband and kindly uncle/father. Until their flush is busted, Rosencrantz and Guildenstern pretend to be Hamlet's friends. And then to further complicate things and bring theatre right to the centre of our attention, in the middle of the play, Shakespeare brings the 'players' to Elsinore. With their arrival, we have several layers of acting and being - real actors pretending to be actors pretending to be different characters in a pretend play within a real play. The actor playing Gonzago has to pretend to be an actor who then is playing a character. Good luck to anyone distinguishing reality from pretence in this hall of mirrors.

Sickness and health

From the opening scene, where Francisco feels mysteriously 'sick at heart' and the appearance of the Ghost, presaging some strange 'eruption' to the state, images of various types of disease, rankness and rottenness permeate and spread throughout the play like a plague. 'Something,' famously is very 'rotten in state of Denmark'. Almost the whole landscape of the play and the characters therein are or will be infected - 'blasted', 'blistered' or 'mildewed' - with this moral 'rottenness'. For Hamlet, of course, the source of this

'contagion' of 'pestilent vapours' is Claudius, the 'canker' at the core of the Danish court. Specifically his murder of Hamlet's father, when he poured poison – a 'leperous distilment' into the 'ear' both of the King and of Denmark, fatally infecting both it seems. Hamlet's mother too and particularly her overhasty marriage is another source of the poison, polluting even the air in Elsinore, causing the 'foul contagion' to spread like the breath of hell. Incest is a sort of sexual moral illness. Madness is another sort of illness, a mental one, and both Hamlet and later Ophelia cannot escape infection. Increasingly, Claudius imagines Hamlet as a disease that has to be cured. Or cut out, rather, like a cancer. He is like the 'hectic' at loose within the court and, more intimately, more viscerally, the disease which 'raves' maddeningly within the King's own 'blood'.

Nature and the unnatural

There are several different classes of nature imagery in the play:

- Flora - especially flowers
- Fauna
- Reference to a garden
- Water.

Shakespeare's use of flower imagery will be explored in discussions of Ophelia elsewhere in this guide as flowers are closely associated with her femininity in the play. However, Laertes also labels Hamlet's affection for his sister as 'a violet in the youth of primy nature' [I.3,490] associating the flower with sweet perfume and impermanence. This is surprising as generally violets symbolise faithfulness in love – hence Ophelia's reference to violets withering. Laertes also imagines 'violets' springing from Ophelia's dead body and, more specifically what he is keen to stress as her 'unpolluted flesh', i.e. her virginity. Either it seems that, like so much else in the play, the symbolism of violets is unstable or that the flower takes on different meanings when associated with a man rather than a woman.

Perhaps, Hamlet's 'violet' is only a temporary softness and gentleness he can put on and take off, whereas Ophelia's floweriness is integral to her character, or at least, essential to how other characters wish her to be. Ophelia also uses a flower to describe Hamlet, calling him the 'rose of the fair state' [III.1,1843]. Though this also problematises too rigid an association of women with flower imagery in the play, again the image is about how Hamlet is regarded by the people, not about who or what he is essentially.

A menagerie crawls, roams, flies, wriggles or slithers through Elsinore, it seems. There are worms and maggots and various types of birds [especially birds of prey] a water-fly, snakes, deer, Danish dogs, a couple of moles, some sheep, an ape and even a crocodile. Mostly, of course, the animals are used to describe and define characters. Some characters are like birds: Ophelia, for instance, is compared to a 'woodcock' while Osric is a 'chough' and a 'lapwing' and either Rosencrantz or Guildenstern is a 'hawk'. The latter are also 'adders' linking them to the biggest snake in this particular garden, the 'serpent' Claudius. Clearly comparisons to animals reduce and dehumanise their subjects, emphasising certain, usually unflattering, characteristics. The woodcock, for instance, is easily trapped and the serpent is associated with Satan. Hence this imagery cluster contributes to the sense of almost universal corruption in the Danish state. Driven merely by base instincts, human beings are corrupted and degraded into dumb beasts.

Indeed, Hamlet refers several times to generic 'beasts'. He uses the word as a foil or opposite from which he might be able to distinguish humanity's essential characteristics. 'God-like reason' is, for Hamlet, the quality that lifts humans above the animal world and gives us a touch of the divine. Even when animals are not used to describe humans, they contribute to the play's mood and atmosphere. The worms and maggots, for instance, feed on decay.

Denmark is compared a couple of times to a garden, clearly referencing the Garden of Eden. The analogy makes Claudius' murder of Old Hamlet seem even more heinous, coupling Hamlet's uncle to the serpent and the fall of humankind. Elsewhere Hamlet laments that Denmark has become like an 'unweeded garden', both poorly ungoverned, but worse, harbouring within it 'things rank and gross in nature', creatures feeding on corruption like maggots, that will possess it entirely.

As Charlotte Unsworth-Hughes[11] has pointed out images or water also run through the play. Starting off as a life-giver, even water is subject to the same process of degradation and corruption in Elsinore. So that, by the end of the play, it has even become a source of corruption itself, getting into graves and corrupting bodies. Beginning as a symbol of natural purity water becomes just another poisoned liquid, like that in the vials Claudius and Lucianus use and the poisoned wine in the cup from which Gertrude drinks.

More broadly 'natural' and 'nature' also commonly used as a synonym for

---

[11] Hughes, *'Too Much of Water'*.

good and/or true to one's self, whereas crimes and transgressions are labelled as 'unnatural'. Twice the Ghost, for instance, insists that Claudius' killing was most 'unnatural'.

Darkness and light

Darkness is, of course, associated with both secrecy and villainy, whereas light has the opposite connotations. We'd expect a similar binary to operate with the colours black and white. The play starts both literally and metaphorically in the dark and the Ghost arrives, according to Horatio, in the 'dead vast middle of the night'. This darkness, however, connotes uncertainty and mystery more than immorality. When fired up to kill Claudius after *The Mousetrap* Hamlet is presented as a dark avenger, choosing the suitably 'witching' hour of night to carry out his supposedly moral and noble task of revenge. The Ghost, a figure not clearly immoral, has to flee at the coming of the morning light and the darkest things in the play, the black things, are not universally associated with evil. Most obviously Hamlet's clothes in Act I, Scene 2 are black, signifying mourning, not immorality. More subtly, Pyrrhus is compared to night and blackness, yet he is an avenger, not a villain.

Olfactory imagery

Maybe it's all those animals, but Elsinore does seem to be an especially noisome place. While we've generally explored imagery in terms of topic, rather than by type, it is striking how many references there are to smells in *Hamlet*. On the fragrant side, there are a few perfumes sweetening the air of the play, perhaps wafting from the array of flowers. The Ghost smells the 'scent' of morning, while Laertes tells his sister that Hamlet's affection for her is like a violet's perfume, an impression enhanced by Ophelia herself when she observes that Hamlet's love letters, composed to her with 'sweet breath', seem to have lost their perfume. Sweetness is also connected to the air by Claudius, who in his soliloquy hopes that 'sweet heavens' might open and wash away the stench of his sins.

However these good, wholesome smells are outnumbered and overpowered by references to the rank odour of corruption. Why the rank odour of corruption rather than some other figuration? Perhaps because pungent smells can easily get into our noses and into our bodies unbidden in a way that horrible tastes, usually, cannot. Smells also illicit an immediate powerful response, with horrible smells making us feel nauseous and disgusted. Historically, miasma has also long been associated with disease. Rather than using synonyms for the disgusting smell of rot – rancid, putrid, fetid and so forth – Shakespeare hits on one word and uses it repeatedly, 'rank', for obvious punning reasons.

No doubt you'll be able to find other image clusters, so rich and integral is Shakespeare's use of figures of speech. There are, for examples, lots of references to parts of the body, especially ears, in the play, as well as imagery drawn from hunting or weaponry and the language of commercial exchange [Hamlet, for instance, doesn't murder Claudius when he thinks of it as 'hire and salary'.] Close attention to these patterns of imagery always pays handsome rewards.

Other literary devices

Allusions

Rediscovery of classical culture and its literature was, of course, at the heart of the Renaissance and, having originated in Ancient Greece, the genre of revenge tragedy was itself imported from Roman culture, particularly the plays of Seneca. Classical literature provided Shakespeare with a range of well-known characters and stories which he could use to add a frame of reference as well as a greater depth and resonance to his own. A quick flick through the dramatis personae of *Hamlet* underscores this influence, with the guards given classical names and Claudius, for instance named after a Roman Emperor and Laertes after the father of one of the greatest of all Greek heroes, Odysseus.

As a renaissance scholar himself, Hamlet often draws upon classical literature. As we will discuss elsewhere in this guide, Hamlet compares his father to great classical heroes and even the mightiest of Gods – Hercules, Mars, Jove, Mercury, Hyperion – while denigrating his uncle Claudius a classical goatish, lust-driven 'satyr'. In addition, Hamlet compares his tearful mother at his father's funeral pointedly to Niobe.

Julius Caesar pops up several times in the play. Struck by the strange eruption the Ghost may presage in Denmark, Horatio, for instance, recalls the unnaturally wild storm before the political assassination of the most famous of

the Roman emperors. Later in the play, we learn that as a student Polonius had acted in a play based on this story, a revelation that leads to some punning derision from Hamlet. Later still, holding foul-smelling skulls in his hand at the graveyard in Act V, Hamlet notes how even the greatest of emperors, such as Julius Caesar and the greatest of heroes, Alexander the Great, are as mortal as anyone else. Of course, the most extended use of classical literature as a foil for the action of the play is, however, the story of Pyrrhus , Priam and Hecuba.

As we discuss in our essay on revenge, Roman literature, in particular, provided a different set of values from which to consider the play's central issues of vengeance and regicide. Whereas significant forces within Elizabethan culture sought to prohibit both – Queen Elizabeth ordered homilies against regicide to be read aloud in church, while aristocrats fighting duels over their honour were for the first time becoming subject to the common law – Roman literature provided powerful counternarratives. Julius Caesar, of course, was assassinated by a gang of conspirators afraid of the absolute powers he was appropriating to himself, while, the Roman general Titus Andronicus, in Shakespeare's first tragedy, commits an act of horrendous brutality – murdering, butchering, dismembering and cooking his enemies and feeding them to their mother – without any moral qualms or sensitive hesitations at all.

Repetition

Many critics have noted the pervasiveness of duplication in *Hamlet*. Linguistic duplication occurs in many different forms, from the use of rhetorical devices that embody repetition, such as hendiadys and antithesis, to key words cropping up time and again or variations of them in synonyms, to language being used like a double-edged weapon, such as in Hamlet's compulsive use of puns.

Doubling language

In *Shakespeare's Language* [2000] the eminent Shakespearian scholar, Frank Kermode opines that the language of Hamlet is 'dominated to an extent without parallel in the canon by one particular rhetorical device: it is obsessed with doubles of all kinds, and notably by its use of the figure of speech known as hendiadys'. [Hendiadys is a figure of speech in which two words, usually adjectives, are used to qualify one noun.] 'Compulsive duplication' occurs throughout various aspects of *Hamlet*, from its language to its characters and its structure. Think, for example, in terms of characters of the pair of ambassadors, or of Rosencrantz and Guildenstern or the various doubles for Hamlet as revenger. In terms of action, consider the reappearances of the Ghost, the play-within-the-play that replays twice Claudius' murder of Old Hamlet or the repeated use of soliloquies. Kermode reads this obsession with doubling as an expression of the play's concerns with the nature of 'identity, sameness, and the union of separate selves'.

Kermode identifies Hamlet's 'O what a rogue and peasant slave am I' soliloquy as especially peppered with doubling. For example, hendiadys in 'rogue and peasant'; 'the motive and the cue'; 'dull and muddy-mettled' and antithesis in 'heaven and hell'. This compulsive doubling climaxes in 'bloody, bawdy villain!/ Remorseless, lecherous, kindless villain!'[12]

Simon Palfrey also argues that Hamlet is riddled with doubling language and hendiadys in particular. Palfrey focuses, however, on the semantic tensions generated by one term being defined by two others, a micro tension and instability on a linguistic level that resonates with wider thematic tensions in the play. For example, Palfrey examines Hamlet's well-known phrase 'slings and arrows of outrageous fortune' [III.1,58]. He points out that 'slings' is really a rather odd word in this context, one in which 'bows' would make more sense. However, 'if Hamlet had said 'bows and arrows' the power of the phrase would largely be lost... because the two substantives would indeed collapse into a single noun phrase'. In contrast, 'the collocation of 'slings' with

---

[12] Kermode, *Shakespeare's Language*, p.96-125.

'arrows' has a subtly dislocating effect... It evokes unexpectedness and unpredictability'.[13]

Antithesis

Antithesis is the setting up of paired opposites, like weights at either end of a pair of scales. It is habitually a device used by Shakespeare and by Hamlet, because it is an efficient tool for structuring thoughts in order to explore different perspectives and options. It also encodes within the play an endemic sense of conflict. Often finding the opposites within a speech quickly allows a reader to follow the underpinning logic of the thought expressed. Probably the most famous example in the play is 'to be, or not to be'. The antithesis set up here, between living and dying, perhaps dying by committing suicide, can be held in equal balance or tipped one way or another by the intonation of an actor. But what is clear, is that opposite, conflicting courses of action are being weighed. As the soliloquy progresses so the essential antithesis develops and unfolds; 'Whether 'tis nobler in the mind to suffer' or to 'take arms against a sea of troubles'.

Claudius' first speech is dominated by antitheses. After all the new King is trying to pull off a difficult balancing act, providing time and space to publicly lament the death of his brother [even if this is a sham] and, at the same time, celebrating his marriage and succession to the throne. Claudius navigates masterfully between the opposite poles so that he is able to express both 'delight' as well as 'dole'. Indeed his use of antithesis concentrates audaciously into oxymoronic phrases; 'mirth in funeral' and 'dirge in marriage'. Whereas Claudius presents himself and Gertrude ['the imperial jointress'] as embodiments of forces that can combine and resolve opposites into harmonious unity, Hamlet uses antitheses to emphasise difference, particularly how different and superior his father was to Claudius. Whereas one is superhuman, like 'Hyperion', the other is subhuman, like a 'satyr'. Claudius himself uses antithesis in a similar way at the end of his soliloquy. Here the device expresses an unbridgeable gap between the two poles of

---

[13] Palfrey, *Doing Shakespeare*, pp. 44-45.

heaven and earth:

'My words fly up, my thoughts remain below'.

In these instances the opposition in antithesis appears, ostensibly, to be one of clear binaries. But, on closer inspection, these binaries can blur or collapse into each other. We will see this phenomenon, for instance, in the presentation of the antithetical characters of the avenger and the Machiavellian villain. The reverse of this is also true, so that two things that superficially appear to be the same are revealed to have a more complicated, perhaps even antithetical relationship on a fundamental level. In Hamlet's 'To be or not to be' soliloquy, for example, the Prince compares death and sleep. On the surface the sleeping and dead body look the same, but sleep is followed by wakefulness in a way that death is not. On the other hand, as Hamlet suggests, we can be 'wakened' in the afterlife into a new life, undermining the difference between the two states.

Words, words, words

Certain key words crop up over and over again in *Hamlet*. These words also appear in groups, as synonyms with similar meanings. We don't mean commonly used function words such as 'I' or 'and', but rather meaning-carrying words, mainly nouns, verbs and adjectives. Tracking who uses these words and when and whether the meanings they ascribe to them, the semantics, are stable or change with speaker or time or place is an incisive way of mapping the major concerns of the play. As we might expect, 'madness', 'play' 'revenge' and 'noble', for instance, are repeated many times. 'Knave' and 'villain' appear often too, as do the many various synonyms for disease. Sometimes the concentration of otherwise innocuous seeming words can make them significant, such as Hamlet's use of 'to be' and Ophelia's obsessive, perhaps guilt-driven use of 'my lord' in almost every line in the nunnery scene. Repeatedly too words are used to describe and control characters, such as the feminising adjectives, such as 'sweet' and 'pretty', that stick like gaffer tape to Ophelia.

Puns

We might associate puns with comedy. The prime user of puns in *Hamlet* is the Prince himself and often there is indeed a kind of dark, sardonic humour to his barbed and double-edged use of words. Take the first few lines he  speaks in the play. After listening to his uncle establish at length the new political paradigm, Hamlet responds to finally being addressed by Claudius as his 'son' with a 'little more than kin and less than kind'. Whether or not this is an aside, the words are pointed, charged, witty and riddling in a way we will come to see is characteristic of Hamlet's utterances and especially those he makes to his elders. What exactly is this thing that is a little more than 'kin' but less than 'kind'? We don't know and Hamlet doesn't tell us. The pun, of course, uses the two meanings of 'kind' to suggest that either Hamlet or Claudius really feels hostility, not affection, towards the other. Or that the menace is mutual.

The pun punctures Claudius' performance of fatherly affection to the assembled nobles and lets us know that Hamlet sees straight through such pretences. Whether it is heard by those on stage or not, Hamlet also immediately contradicts what the King is saying and saying in public. The interactions between Hamlet, Claudius and his mother which follow are similarly barbed and as tense as a drawn bowstring. Responding to his uncle-father-sovereign's comment that he is still too gloomy, Hamlet again contradicts Claudius, this time openly, aloud, so that the on-stage audience can hear him: 'Not so, my lord; I am too much i' the sun'. The respectful 'my lord' only just keeps the words from being brazenly insolent. What, though, does Hamlet mean? Too much in the sun, as in the centre of attention? Or too sunny considering he is still in mourning? The pun signals, of course, that he is too much 'in the son', which could mean he is being placed too forcefully in the role of Claudius' son and/or that he is still too much Old Hamlet's son and therefore still loyal to his actual father. Once again, the punning compresses a teeming set of possible meanings into Hamlet's curt, double-edged responses. This kind of linguistic and semantic doubling makes language itself a deceptive, unstable medium, a tool, potentially for duplicity as much as communication.

Sensing that Hamlet's hostility is only just being held barely in check, Gertrude steps into the conversation, gently reminding Hamlet that it is normal for fathers to die. Hamlet's punning reply is, 'ay, madam, it is common'. While this comment may seem more polite than the Prince's responses to Claudius – after all, ostensibly he appears to be agreeing with her – the subtext is witheringly disdainful. Loosen the pronoun 'it' from referencing death of fathers and the second meaning of 'common' as low, vulgar, cheap, disreputable almost breaks to the surface. Later in his career, Shakespeare uses 'common' as a synonym for 'promiscuous' in *Coriolanus*, so perhaps, the word is loaded with even more personal hostility, directed at Gertrude.

Other notable puns used by Hamlet include his impudent reference to Polonius as a 'fishmonger' and, after the old councillor's death, to Polonius being 'most grave', as well as puns directed at Ophelia, such as his instruction to 'get thee to a nunnery' and his reference to 'country matters'. Three of these four carry disturbing sexual connotations, indicating the pun's edgy, transgressive side. Calling the high-status courtier and chief councillor to the King a fishmonger is insulting enough, but it is much more stinging when we take into account that in Elizabethan slang 'fishmonger' could refer to a pimp. Typically for Hamlet, it is also astute and apposite; as we will see a few scenes later when Polonius uses his daughter as a form of bait and as a stool pigeon. The famous imperative, 'get thee to a nunnery' neatly encapsulates the fundamental tricksy unreliability of words in the play. The surface meaning is clear; that Ophelia should save herself from the sexually corrupt world of Elsinore in the one place safe from sex, a nunnery. But the self-same words also carry entirely the opposite meaning, as nunnery was Elizabethan street slang for a brothel. In this reading, Hamlet is saying Ophelia is already corrupted so she'd be at home in a brothel. The last example needs no commentary, other than to say it shows how nearly out-of-control and perhaps cruel Hamlet is in this scene, as in this case the pun is hardly hidden at all.

The playwright

Had we but the space and time [as well as the skill, the scholarship and, indeed, the inclination] we could, perhaps, provide you, our avid reader, with an exhaustive account of the life and work of the world's most famous writer. After all, the Shakespeare scholar, James Shapiro managed to write a highly engaging account of just one year, albeit a monumentally creative year, in the bard's relatively short life.[14] On the other hand, notoriously, very little information actually exists about Shakespeare's life; famously one of the only extant official documents is his will and its curious instruction to leave his wife his second-best bed. Of course, that gaping biographical vacuum hasn't stopped scholars, biographers and novelists; in fact it's invited them to jump right in and fill it with all sorts of colourful speculations, such as the story that Shakespeare originally fled Stratford because he'd been illegally poaching deer and the preposterous idea that Shakespeare didn't really write his own plays, nor presumably all of his own poems, because he wasn't from the right class.

But, we haven't the space or time for such fanciful speculating [whether we have the other qualities we'll leave you to decide]. So, what can usefully be said about William Shakespeare [1564-1616] in a couple of pages or so? Firstly, that he was a middle-class boy, grammar school educated, and that he

---

[14] Shapiro, *1606, The Year of Lear.*

didn't attend either of the great universities of Oxford or Cambridge. This fact partly accounts for the claim that Shakespeare couldn't have written his plays as, so the argument goes, he had neither the life experiences nor the sophisticated education to do so, a claim unpleasantly whiffing of snobbery. How did a middle-class boy from the provinces write so brilliantly about kings, queens and princes and different times and cultures? Perhaps he read widely, observed keenly and used his prodigious imagination.

Secondly, at the tender age, even for Elizabethans, of just eighteen Shakespeare married an older woman, Anne Hathaway, who was twenty-six and already pregnant. This is a point to be borne in mind whenever Shakespeare is writing about disinherited and bitter children, those born out of wedlock and therefore labelled as 'bastards' in his world.

Thirdly, Shakespeare was an actor and many scholars think he probably took roles, albeit relatively minor ones, in his own plays. He was a member of an acting group, called the Lord Chamberlain's Men, who had a theatre built to house their performances – the Globe theatre.

Fourthly, Shakespeare was not only a highly successful playwright, but also a shrewd businessman. By middle-age he had become wealthy enough to buy the 'second largest' house in Stratford. By this time, his acting company had been promoted up the social ladder to 'The King's Men', with a royal charter and King James I as their patron, and they had purchased a second theatre.

Fifthly, Shakespeare was a highly accomplished poet as well as a playwright. Writing a decent sonnet was considered de rigueur for an Elizabethan courtier. Shakespeare did not write one decent sonnet, of course not, he wrote a sonnet sequence, a bigger and better and more sophisticated sonnet sequence than anyone has managed before or since, arguably. Comprising over a hundred and fifty sonnets, the sequence dramatizes the story of an intense love triangle, involving Shakespeare, a handsome young man and a dark lady.

Sixthly, Shakespeare is absolutely everywhere. He is the only writer whose work by law has to be studied in English schools. His poems and plays are read, studied and performed across the globe, from Australia to China, from India to Zambia, and have been translated into almost every major language, including Klingon[15]. Unsurprisingly, he's the best-selling writer ever. Estimates suggest that there have been over four hundred film versions of his plays. Phrases and words Shakespeare coined are used every day by thousands, perhaps millions, of people, sometimes consciously and sometimes because they have become an integral part of the fabric of our language. And that's still not the be-all and end-all: His head appears on bank notes, cups and tea-towels and he is a crucial part of the English tourism industry and our national identity. In this country alone, there are several theatre companies dedicated to his work, including a royal one, the RSC. In short, Shakespeare was, and is still, a phenomenon.

Some critics suggest that the boy from Stratford got lucky; his work spread the globe because first the Elizabethans and then the Victorians explored and conquered much of the globe and everywhere the English went they took Shakespeare along with them. But, even then, that doesn't explain why Shakespeare and rather than any other English writer became so ubiquitous.

---

[15] Apparently 'taH pagh taHbe' is Klingon for the very famous opening to a speech by Hamlet.

Shakespeare's world

Picture this: A happy, stable, highly ordered, hierarchical society in which each man and woman knows their place and, moreover, knows that this place has been rightfully assigned and fixed by God. All things on earth are held together in a great, universal chain of being. Furthermore, this fixed and eternal orderliness on earth reassuringly mirrors the fixed, eternal order of the heavens. As God rules the heavens so the monarch, God's representative, rules the earth. And the present monarch, Good Queen Bess, Gloriana, is a semi-divine virgin queen who has ruled peacefully for four decades. A bucolic, Edenic society in which an especially blessed race of men live harmoniously with each other and with nature. A demi-paradise, in fact. Recent religious conflicts between Catholics and Protestants have been resolved. The arts are blossoming as never before. Trade with the rest of the world is flourishing. Sending her ships out across the furthest seas, England is becoming a global super-power, bringing peace and prosperity for all. It is a veritable golden age. A merrie England.

The only problem with this enchanting picture is that it is, according to modern literary critics and historians, largely just that, a picture, a construct, an attractive illusion. Whether Queen Elizabeth I's reign was ever a golden age is a matter of historical debate, but what is not really disputed is that by around 1600, the time Shakespeare was writing *Hamlet*, England had become a very different, swiftly changing, more turbulent and troubled country. To borrow a term from Gothic studies, at the end of Elizabeth's reign England existed in a liminal space, uneasily stuck between its medieval, feudal past and a new, early modern world still in the process of coming into being. According to Lawrence Stone, there was an 'almost hysterical demand for order at all costs' in late Elizabethan culture, 'caused by a collapse of most of the props of the medieval world picture… in England there occurred a phase of unprecedented social and geographical mobility which at the higher levels transformed the composition and size of the gentry and professional classes, and at the lower levels tore hundreds of thousands of individuals loose from their traditional kinship and neighbourhood backgrounds'.[16]

While it is true that English society had inherited the feudal idea of the Great Chain of Being, and with this ideological construct the idea that a static social order was divinely ordained, it is the case that this sort of inherited thinking was also being challenged vigorously on many different fronts. In politics, the power of the monarchy and the lords was coming under more democratic pressure to reform. Laws were changing in the same direction; it was in this period that aristocrats settling a dispute via a duel became subject to the common law and ships leaving England for trade and adventure no longer had to carry an aristocrat as part of their crew. Increasing trade was creating a newly prosperous merchant class, especially in London - merchants were growing rich and powerful and upwardly mobile, threatening the established aristocratic class. Science was evolving too from its origins in magic and developing an empirical method that would not just accept inherited understanding of the word, but instead tested evidence objectively via experimentation. At the same time, a range of humanist intellectuals were questioning some of Elizabethan society's fundamental principles. Meanwhile, Puritans were busily decoupling faith in God from loyalty to the church and to the monarch. England may have been relatively peaceful, but faced the perpetual threat of invasion by Catholic Spain or France as well as potential insurrection from within, such as the Earl of Essex's revolt. On top of this plague had swept through the country in the 1590s and would do so again in 1603.

---

[16] Stone, quoted in Dollimore and Sinfied, *Political Shakespeare*, p.5.

It is within this liminal world of intellectual, religious and cultural turmoil that Hamlet struggles to find any fixed bearings. Famously, Hamlet is given an essentially medieval task, revenge, but questions it using the intellectual capacities of a sceptical early modern mind.

The vision of Elizabethan England as a peaceful golden age is particularly associated in Shakespeare studies with E.M.W. Tillyard and his hugely influential book *The Elizabethan World Picture* [1943] which was, for decades, the core 'background' text on Shakespeare for English Literature undergraduates. In particular, new historicist and cultural materialist criticism starts from the position of rejecting the sort of conservative and nostalgic version of the past Tillyard articulated. As these critics point out, some major historical events undermine Tillyard's rather rose-tinted take on the past. Look backwards a little way from Elizabeth's I reign and we see political turmoil of the reigns of Henry VIII and his short-lived immediate successors; look forward a couple of years and the Gunpowder Plot of 1605 comes into view, when Catholic conspirators tried to blow up parliament in 1605 and assassinate the king. In addition, cast our eyes a little further forward, only two decades after Shakespeare had written *Hamlet* barely suppressed tensions in English society erupted and the country broke into violent civil war. While there is no doubt there were many great achievements of the Elizabethan age, including Shakespeare's own work, historians' investigation of the treatment of women and ethnic minorities, closer examination of the appalling living conditions of the poor, inspection of Elizabethan society's penal system and spy network and its most popular forms of entertainment, has uncovered a more complex, nuanced picture. Their fine-grained analysis of many different aspects of Late Elizabethan society reveal it to be a much more unstable, dynamic, dangerous and fascinating place - a maelstrom of clashing ideas and beliefs, or, rather, a cultural furnace that fired Shakespeare's imagination and powered his plays.

Critical commentaries on key scenes

How many scenes are there in the play in total? How many scenes are there in each act of *Hamlet*? Which act is longest and which the shortest? Which scene is the longest and which the shortest? At what points does Shakespeare crosscut from the main plot to sub-plots? When and where are the soliloquies placed? Time spent mapping out these details is always time well spent.

Much of this information will be revealed in the following commentaries on each act. As well as providing a broad overview of the major content of each scene, the following commentaries also include close analysis of one or two key short passages from within each act. These sections exemplify the sort of close reading of the drama that is both enriching and often a part of assessment at A-level.

As you will notice, the longest or our commentaries is on Act III. This act includes two major scenes, the nunnery and closet scene, and so we've paid both of these scenes, or more precisely, select passages within them some extended close attention.

There are twenty scenes in *Hamlet* in total. Act I has **five** scenes; Act II has only **two**; Act III has **four**; Act IV has **seven** and Act V also only has **two**.

Act One

Opening on the battlements of the royal castle in Elsinore, the first act of *Hamlet* stages the key elements of the plot, characters, setting, and tone. *Hamlet* is a revenge tragedy, a genre that emerged from the runaway success of Thomas Kyd's *The Spanish Tragedy* [c. 1587]. Like others of its time, such as Thomas Middleton's *The Revenger's Tragedy* [1606] and John Webster's *The Duchess of Malfi* [1614], *Hamlet* is characterised by 'blood, poison, and melodrama...teeming with corpses and dismembered body parts, steeped in occasionally raucous black humour'[17]. It looks both backwards to the past – to the Latin plays of Seneca, themselves imitations of Greek plays – and forwards to the future, sharing tropes with the ghost story and detective fiction. But *Hamlet* is also a curiously modern play, recognised as one that explores the inner lives of its characters, and the potential for appearance and reality to become disjointed from one another.

The first of Act I's five scenes begins on the platform of the ramparts. The guards are changing shifts on a cold night's watch. Barnardo takes over from Francisco and is then joined by his partner, Marcellus, and Horatio. The watch has been quiet, but Barnardo and Marcellus are anticipating trouble and have summoned Horatio to bear witness to a 'dreaded sight twice seen'. Horatio is sceptical, mocking his fellow soldiers. His scepticism is quickly challenged when he is confronted by 'a figure like the King that's dead'. It is, the trio agree, a spirit of some sort that resembles Old Hamlet, who passed away a month or more before. Its true identity and purpose are oblique; the guards can only speculate as to what this figure is and why it walks among them. Omens of war come thick and fast as they look on in wonder. The Ghost wears a 'fair and warlike form', marching 'with [a] martial stalk' that prompts Horatio to recall the King's historic conquests in Norway and Poland. Horatio suspects it is a sign of bad news, forecasting 'some strange eruption to our state' and setting the scene for a battle to come. But will it be a war waged by Norway, where young Fortinbras seeks to reclaim the lands his father lost to Old

---

[17] Pollard, *Revenge Tragedy*, p.58.

Hamlet some thirty years before? Or will it stem from the primary vehicle of conflict in the genre, 'revenge of a personal injury'?[18] With its ominous sense of foreboding, this scene leaves the audience hanging, unsure what to make of the spectre and its motives. The scene closes with the spooked guards' vowing to seek out the counsel of the dead king's son: Hamlet. Perhaps he will be a source of enlightenment, they think.

We first meet Hamlet in scene 2. Where scene 1 is clearly a relative of the ghost story, foggy with darkness, old buildings, phantoms, and bone-chilling uncertainty, scene 2 is bright with revelry deep within the castle's heart. Far from the lonely battlements, the new King of Denmark, Claudius, brother to the deceased Hamlet Senior, attempts to bring together the 'whole kingdom' first in mourning for their former ruler and then in celebration of his own ascension and marriage to his brother's wife. Young Hamlet, black-clad and silent, sits or stands pointedly apart, undermining his uncle's show of unity. Hamlet is the last character we meet while the scene revolves within the council chamber. Laertes, a nobleman of similar age and good standing within the court, first makes a petition to return to France where he is at school. His request is granted. King Claudius then turns, belatedly, to Hamlet.

Audiences familiar with the tropes of the revenge tragedy would immediately recognise Prince Hamlet as the potential revenger. Churlish and critical, he is a malcontent, rebuffing the gentle-seeming enquiries of his uncle and mother as to why his grief for his father seems so much more extreme than it is for those around him. He is quick to anger and believes that he, personally, has been wounded more deeply by Old Hamlet's death than any other. There are three possible reasons for his belief. Firstly, in keeping with Denmark's elective monarchy, but rather more alien in early modern England where hereditary monarchy was more common, Hamlet has been passed over for the throne in favour of his uncle. Secondly, while Laertes is allowed to leave, his own desire to return to school is thwarted when he is asked not to return to Wittenberg. Finally, he suspects his mother and his uncle, in marrying so swiftly after the

---

[18] Pollard, [from] *The Cambridge Companion to English Renaissance Tragedy* p.58.

funeral, to be careless of his father's memory. Slighted, resentful, and full of suppressed rage, he is already ripe to seek revenge.

Hamlet, however, is a more complex character than the stereotype of the malcontent or the revenger. He is often recognised through his soliloquies by readers and critics as a very modern man, one capable of deep self-reflection and acutely aware that people's inner selves and the selves they present to the outside world may not be aligned. His first speech of any length draws our attention to this idea. 'Seems, madam?' he replies, when asked by his mother why his grief 'seems…so particular', 'I know not 'seems''. Commenting on his own 'inky cloak' and 'customary suits of solemn black', he claims his sorrow is real whereas everyone else has simply been going through the motions, performing rituals of mourning divorced from real feeling. '[A]ll forms, moods, shapes of grief' worn by those around him, he declares, may be 'actions that a man might play', whilst he has 'that within that passes show' – authentic heartache that aligns with his clothing, but that would endure regardless of whatever costume he might wear.

This exchange subtly sets Hamlet up as a potential detective figure, a young man with a deep sense of justice who has nonetheless set himself apart from  the institution, and someone who is wary and interrogative of other people's motives and behaviour. It also begins the play's steady dialogue with Baldassare Castiglione's *The book of the courtier* [1561] – a how-to guide for aspiring courtiers. The handbook outlines the qualities of the ideal courtier, whose reception and potential for success within the court revolves around how they dress, behave, and speak. The textbook courtier is someone who perfects these ways of presenting himself and then conceals that he has studied them at all so that his attire, behaviour, and rhetoric appear to come naturally to him. Hamlet, though he possesses many of the characteristics of the ideal courtier – as Ophelia tells us in Act III, Scene 1 – is uneasy about the gap between artfulness and authenticity within Elsinore's court. He suspects his mother, uncle, and many of the other courtiers of performing their ideal qualities outwardly while inwardly failing to live up to them, as the true courtier ought.

His first soliloquy reinforces this perception of a gap between inner and outer selves, whilst simultaneously calling into question Hamlet's own integrity. Having appeared to give a 'gentle an unforc'd accord' to staying in Elsinore to support his family, Hamlet's hidden emotional turmoil is vented in a desire for 'self-slaughter' as soon as he is alone on the stage. He calls attention particularly to his belief that his mother is two-faced, lamenting that her apparently insatiable love for Old Hamlet has dwindled 'ere those shoes were old/ With which she follow'd my poor father's body' and wondering if she did no more than play the role of sorrowing womanhood, 'like [but not as] Niobe'. He also offers a counter to Claudius's self-portrait as a benevolent, practical, and just king in the scene's opening speech, by decrying his uncle as the antithesis of Old Hamlet. As with the Ghost in Scene 1, we are invited to distrust everyone within the court; what they seem to be may not be what they are, and their motives are as obscure as the Ghost's.

Having set up the detective story aspects of the play, the metatheatrical focus on language and performance which prepares us for the play-within-a-play, we are abruptly returned to the ghost story. Horatio invites Hamlet to join him and the guards on the battlements in the 'middle of the night' to watch out for 'a figure like your father'. The two genres – ghost and detective story – are yoked loosely together by Hamlet for whom 'My father's spirit – in arms!' leads him to suspect 'All is not well' and that 'some foul play' is afoot in Elsinore.

Leaving us again in suspense, the play then crosscuts to an exchange between Laertes and Ophelia, who are discussing the latter's relationship with Hamlet. We are again invited to distrust Hamlet's character, with Laertes declaring his peer's favour for his sister as 'a fashion and a toy'. The violets that recur throughout Ophelia's story are first invoked here as a metaphor for something temporal; Hamlet's affection for her is, Laertes insists 'A violet in the youth of primy nature,/ Forward, not permanent…suppliance of a minute'. Even if it were real, he warns her, Hamlet is the next likely candidate for the throne and the choices of royalty are circumscrib'd' for 'the sanity and health of the whole state'. Laertes continues to lecture her on appropriate courtly conduct for a young woman, which she listens to apparently attentively, but counters with a telling reminder of the appropriate behaviour for a young man, before they are interrupted by their father, Polonius. Unlike the siblings, who speak thoughtfully, Polonius parrots platitudes. He does, however, echo Hamlet's reflection that inner and outer selves may not be aligned, reminding Laertes 'to thine own self be true' lest he 'be false to any man'. Once Laertes has departed, Polonius picks up where his son left off, lecturing Ophelia on the falsity of Hamlet's apparent affection for her. While Hamlet, later in the play, will claim to renounce his love for Ophelia, this may be nothing more than an act since her death has him declare it once again. Ironically, it is to Hamlet that Laertes will later prove false when he conspires with King Claudius at the end of the play.

Scenes 4 and 5 return us to the cold dark night on the castle battlements. Together with Marcellus, Barnardo, and Horatio, Hamlet encounters the Ghost. Scene 4 pivots around its appearance, with anxiety rising amongst the group as to what it is that they are seeing, whether 'a spirit of health or a goblin damn'd' with 'intents wicked or charitable', which we explore further in the section on Old Hamlet. Urged on by the others, Hamlet tries to get the spirit to speak, but it beckons him away. Despite the protestations of his friends, who fear it may be trying to trick him, Hamlet runs after it alone.

Scene 5 weaves the ghost and detective stories more tightly together, braiding them with the concept of revenge. Alone together on the stage, Hamlet and the Ghost discuss the latter's reasons to 'walk the night'. The Ghost, who claims to come from purgatory [a dubious, popish, concept in Protestant England], demands that the Prince 'revenge his foul and most unnatural murder' It was, it claims, poisoned 'with juice of cursed hebenon' poured 'in the porches of my ears'. The finger of blame, he points directly at

Claudius: 'the serpent that did sting thy father's life/ Now wears his crown'. Hamlet is horrified. As if it already knows his resentment against his mother for marrying Claudius so soon after Old Hamlet's death, the Ghost quickly warns him to 'taint not thy mind nor let thy soul contrive/ Against thy mother aught'. Heaven and her conscience, it tells him, will punish her enough. The Ghost then departs, but not before coupling its demand for revenge with the concept of remembrance. Already struggling with the loss of his father, for Hamlet recollection is now reliant upon seeking revenge.

At this point, Horatio and Marcellus catch up with Hamlet and beg him to tell them of his exchange with the Ghost. Hamlet is circumspect, telling them only that he believes the apparition was 'an honest ghost'. He then orders them to 'swear by my sword/ Never to speak of this' again – the sword here taking on the iconographic significance of a cross or holy relic - and warns them that he plans to put on an 'antic disposition' while he seeks out a 'villain dwelling in...Denmark'. The union of the ghost and the detective story is solidified in his plain to hunt down what Sir Francis Bacon calls 'wild justice' – the righting of a wrong that falls outside the usual remit of the law. It is not just individuals who can seem to be one thing and yet really be another; time too, Hamlet tells us, can be 'out of joint' and needs to be 'set...right'.

What do you make of Hamlet the detective? Are he and the Ghost the only honest individuals in Denmark on a noble quest to restore justice to a broken system? Or is Hamlet being led astray by some unholy creature? Worse, are his mother, uncle, and Laertes right – that he is so caught up in his mourning and whimsical by nature that he is imagining the whole thing? You might rightly wonder if he is already losing his mind. Horatio is alarmed by his 'wild and whirling words', which are mirrored by his actions as he circles frantically around the stage, following a ghostly voice that only he can hear, as he extracts the oath from his friends. You might note too that Hamlet alone claims to hear the Ghost speak. So, what do you think: is Hamlet a reliable detective leading us through a crime-scene investigation, or a young man going out of his mind with grief? Just how closely are his outward appearance and his inner reality aligned before he decides to feign insanity as part of his investigation?

Act Two

There are only two scenes in Act II. With the first, the action switches from the main plot of Hamlet and the Ghost to the subplot of Polonius and his family. This switch has a number of benefits for Shakespeare. From a practical perspective, it allows the actor playing the Prince to recover from his exertions and wild, whirling words. This time off stage is important, as playing Hamlet is an emotional and intellectual marathon. Secondly the switch helps Shakespeare generate suspense – the audience has to wait to see Hamlet interact again with Claudius and to discover how he might 'sweep' to his revenge. Thirdly, as in all his plays, the concerns of the subplot echo and amplify those of the main plot. Hence in Scene 1 we have a parallel father-son relationship as well as the thematic concerns of trust and surveillance.

Having employed Reynaldo as an agent provocateur, Polonius learns of Hamlet's apparent madness through Ophelia's testimony. At this stage of the play, there is a number of possible explanations: Hamlet's distraught state might have been genuine, a consequence of the traumatic experience of seeing and talking with a ghost, apparently the ghost of his recently dead father, and of being informed that his father was murdered and murdered by his own brother. Hamlet's paleness and his knees knocking together suggests genuine, not feigned, distress. On the other hand, Hamlet has just told Horatio and the guards that henceforth he is going to put on an antic disposition. Isn't there something of a mad-man's costume to Hamlet's wild appearance? Wouldn't it have been easy for him to button up his doublet? Certainly we never see him this dishevelled. Might he be playing the part, knowing that Ophelia will inform her father who in turn will inform the King and thus lend credibility to his antic disposition? A third option is that Hamlet and Ophelia have cooked this scene up between them. As events unfold, the latter becomes an increasingly unlikely interpretation, but at this stage the audience cannot be sure, unlike Polonius who immediately assumes Ophelia's rejection has driven Hamlet mad for love.

Full of action, featuring a rich range of characters and several shifts of dramatic foci, Scene 2 is much longer. It includes the introduction of Hamlet's supposed friends, apparently good news arriving from Norway, the reading aloud of Hamlet's private love letters and the arrival of a group of actors more accomplished in their arts than Hamlet's school friends. These players bring into the play another story of murder and revenge from classical literature, with Pyrrhus' savage slaughter of Priam.

False friends

In the dialogue between Hamlet and Rosencrantz and Guildenstern, the audience initially knows something that Hamlet does not - that his former schoolfellows have been sent to spy on him by the King and Queen. The tension caused by this dramatic irony increases through the scene, as the audience wonders if and when Hamlet will discover the deception. At the outset, the characters exchange affectionate words ['honour'd', 'most dear', 'my excellent good friends'] with, on Hamlet's part at least, apparent warm sincerity. [Compare, for instance, Hamlet's more measured response to Horatio in Act I Scene 2.] Their conversation is harmless, bantering back and forth playfully in a faux-philosophical discussion about Fortune and the nature of ambition, with the balanced line distribution signalling how they are on an equal footing. As the conversation progresses, specific lines ratchet up the tension. For instance, Hamlet's terse contradiction, 'your news is not true' and dramatic 'Denmark's a prison', or Rosencrantz and Guildenstern's over-eager 'we'll wait upon you' - a line often used in productions as the trigger for Hamlet's suspicion. The actors and director must determine the exact progression of discovery and the moments at which Hamlet realises that something's not right.

Under the guise of polite enquiry 'in the beaten way of friendship', Hamlet's question 'what make you at Elsinore?', seems to come out of the blue. The directness of the question wrong-foots Rosencrantz and Guildenstern. Hamlet does a very similar thing to Ophelia in the next act when he springs the question 'where's your father?' on her and forces her into making a crucial decision – whether to lie or tell him the truth. Rosencrantz and Guildenstern face the same dilemma. Though it is a lie, the first half of Rosencrantz's answer is convincing enough, 'To visit you my lord'. But then, as if he cannot help himself, he follows this with the unnecessary and therefore revealing 'no other occasion'. There's a good opportunity here for a director and his or her actors to emphasise the pressure of this question on Hamlet's friends. Perhaps Rosencrantz hesitates a moment before answering Hamlet's question. Perhaps he exchanges a quick, nervous glance with the strangely silent Guildenstern. Perhaps they both avoid eye contact with Hamlet. Whatever actions are added, Rosencrantz's words and Guildenstern's silence are enough to arouse Hamlet's suspicions.

After this, things go quickly downhill for them. Hamlet is not to be put off from this line of questioning. Insistently, he repeats his question, and with more edge: 'Were you not sent for? Is it your own inclining? Is it a free visitation?' Rosencrantz and Guildenstern's hesitation in answering is implied in Hamlet's

next words, where he impatiently has to prompt them to answer him: 'Come, come… Come, come – nay, speak'. Guildenstern's lame response - 'What should we say my lord?' - is as good as a confession. The philosophical discussion has moved on rapidly with four quick-fire questions from Hamlet, again mixed in with the ostensible pleasantries of 'thanks' and 'dear friends'. Repetition of 'come' and the commands 'deal justly', 'nay, speak', are frightening in their intensity. The tension increases as Hamlet's drops his friendly front, flatly accusing his 'friends': 'you were sent for… I know'.

The pair's lack of 'craft' and inept deceit are no match for Hamlet's sharp perceptions. Embedded stage directions suggest they are unable to control their guilty expressions ['there is a kind of confession in your looks'] and they give themselves away through cack-handed phrases. When Hamlet implores them to be 'direct' with him and confirm whether they 'were sent for or no', Rosencrantz is unable to answer, turning instead to Guildenstern and asking lamely 'what say you?'. If we haven't already worked it out, Shakespeare gives Hamlet an aside to confirm he has seen through his supposed friends' deceit.

The reversal in power dynamic is tangible. Though Rosencrantz and Guildenstern started with the upper hand, knowing more than Hamlet and physically on stage being 'two against one', Hamlet is the one who ends up being the interrogator, and they, by contrast, defer to his authority rather desperately: 'what should we do?' 'what should we say?'. In the end, it is the two friends, tasked by Claudius with wheedling information out of Hamlet, who are the ones forced to confess: 'My lord, we were sent for'.

Rosencrantz and Guildenstern's unwilling honesty diffuses the tension. The charged, hectic dialogue settles down into Hamlet's much quoted 'piece of work' monologue, where he reveals something of his true mental state. The speech is constructed so that breath-taking images of the world's beauty build up, only to be cut down with Hamlet's current unhappy outlook: This 'excellent canopy... brave o'erhanging firmament... majestical roof fretted with golden fire' is 'foul and pestilent'. The same technique is repeated in the descriptions of mankind, with the anaphora of 'how noble... how infinite...' reaching a crescendo in from 'angel' to 'god' only then to be robbed of this majesty by 'quintessence of dust', a phrase that linguistically embodies a fall, with the high-flown polysyllabic Latinate noun brought down to earth by the Anglo-Saxon monosyllable. Hence Shakespeare conveys how Hamlet's entire outlook on the world has become diseased and he is no longer able to appreciate its beauty. And yet he remains aware of the potential for beauty and retains the poetic ability to beautifully express his loss. Tellingly, Rosencrantz and Guildenstern are deaf to Hamlet's poetic sensibility and can only snigger like naughty schoolboys at the line 'Man delights not me'.

The scene as a whole touches upon issues central to Hamlet's character. His troubled mind, his undermining of hierarchy, and his disillusionment with the whole world are three themes we meet in this scene and which are developed further in the play. Endorsing the idea that Hamlet's chief problem is an excess of thought, Hamlet describes the power that his mind has over him ['there is nothing either good or bad but thinking makes it so'] and how his mind is troubled. The contrast of a 'nutshell' with 'infinite space' in the subsequent line, coupled with the apostrophe 'O God' and alliterative 'count myself a king', convey Hamlet's longing for mental peace – peace he cannot attain due to his feeling of confinement ['Denmark's a prison'] and his 'bad dreams'. This phrase 'but that I have bad dreams', in such simple language as a child might use, comes at the end of the sentence, puncturing the beautiful image of 'infinite space' in the same way the 'bad dreams' are disrupting Hamlet's peace of mind.

Elsewhere in the play, Hamlet appears to disrespect traditional hierarchies – most memorably when he describes how 'a king may go a progress through the guts of a beggar' – expressing how rank and status are flawed constructs, since death makes all people equal. That idea is found here too. Describing 'monarchs and outstretch'd heroes' as 'beggars' shadows', Hamlet reverses typical associations by saying kings are less substantial than beggars, and effectively undermines his own position; as he himself is a nobleman, a class alongside monarchs and heroes, he calls himself not just a shadow, but a 'beggars' shadow'. This belittling of status is characteristic of Hamlet, showing his pessimism and disillusionment as well as, perhaps, his humility.

Thematically, this scene with Rosencrantz and Guildenstern furthers the ideas of deception and betrayal within the play. Hamlet already feels himself to have been betrayed by his mother and uncle, he is shortly to be betrayed by his lover, and he now finds himself being spied on by his two old friends. Hamlet invokes all the things his 'friends' have betrayed in an anaphoric list ['by the rights… by the consonancy….'], driving home the long-standing 'fellowship' and 'love' that has been betrayed. Similarly, by trying to conceal their motives, Rosencrantz and Guildenstern join the laundry list of people in Elsinore who are pretending to be or do something that they are not – yet another example of deception within the play.

Act Three

Act III really is a powerhouse of an act in a powerhouse of a play. It is filled with important plot-driving events, hugely significant soliloquies [from both Hamlet and Claudius] and contains two of the most important scenes in the entire play: the nunnery scene with Ophelia and Hamlet; and the closet scene with Gertrude and Hamlet, neither of which doing much for Hamlet's standing with the audience due to his uncomfortable misogyny. Act III is also significant for being where the much-debated unreliability of the Ghost is put to rest: the ghoul was right - Claudius _is_ a regicidal villain!

Tonally, Act III is also wildly unstable in terms of Hamlet himself: He begins it full of focus and determination to 'catch the conscience of a king' through _The Mousetrap_, testing Claudius, yet delivers soliloquies of devastating sadness and isolation. His 'antic disposition' also veers wildly from clearly feigned nonsense that allows him to frustrate and humiliate other characters to frighteningly unhinged outbursts of rage that are all too genuine. This oscillation between the performance and the experience of madness points to a disturbing, deep-seated instability in Hamlet's character. Explosions of anger are contrasted memorably with the whispery scenes of intrigue that surround them. Similarly, personal success for Hamlet, _The Mousetrap_ scene, is followed immediately by personal failure, his inability to kill the praying Claudius, which is then followed by the 'success' of Hamlet's appalling moral education of his mother. For a play with a notably procrastinating protagonist, this act certainly goes against the grain in terms of its emotional and plot intensity. Hence we're going to spend a considerable amount of critical attention on it.

The act begins with Claudius still fully in control of events as he continues his surveillance campaign on two fronts: using old friends Rosencrantz and Guildenstern to fish for information from Hamlet; and using old girlfriend Ophelia as bait so he can personally become involved in the surveillance. Ironically, but typical of Elsinore's political intrigues, Claudius himself will be undergoing Hamlet's special imaginative surveillance later in the act in *The Mousetrap* scene. Claudius' pincer manoeuvre unfortunately ends up backfiring badly for all involved, especially the unwitting pawns in this game of greats: The old friends and the old girlfriend [and her old father]. Audience sympathy is pushed primarily towards Ophelia who, being no more than an obedient daughter to her father and subject to her king, endures terrible abuse. Why he feels the need to scapegoat her in such cruel fashion seems unclear as she has already reported in Act II that they have met before in his feigned madness mode. Their interaction in the nunnery scene is raw and brutal by contrast.

The nunnery scene

The scene itself does start with a peculiar dramatic conundrum. With Ophelia waiting for engagement and Claudius and Polonius concealed somewhere how can Hamlet credibly deliver his most famous of soliloquies? Are we really to believe that Ophelia cannot hear his words or, even more importantly, Claudius? If they can't hear them then their spying methods are not very effective! Surely, they must. But if they do, then would the content of his soliloquy, with its return to feelings of world weariness and existential doubt, not arouse some sort of pity for the Prince? From Hamlet's perspective, the resolute determination he came to at the end of his previous soliloquy, only a few minutes of stage time ago, about catching the King with the device of *The Mousetrap*, has already given way. Echoing the sentiments of his first soliloquy, he seems once again to be in a trance of exhaustion. When he finally catches sight of Ophelia, he is almost jolted back to reality: 'Soft you now, / The fair Ophelia!' Shakespeare here tests our suspension of disbelief a little but relies on the frenetic momentum of the spying plot to dislodge any doubts from our minds, which is all fine in the melting pot of performance, but less so in the cool of academic scrutiny. As Shakespeare often does with such inconsistences, he ploughs on regardless! From a stagecraft angle, creative use of lighting can be highly effective here, creating changing pockets of shadowy darkness and intense bursts of light, which can allow characters to hide and reveal themselves [to each other and to the audience]. Lighting can also suggest Hamlet's emotional instability, while also emphasising his personal isolation in Elsinore.

This exchange between Hamlet and Ophelia in Act III, Scene 1 is the first and last time the two lovers are shown on stage alone together, and it is not at all what might be expected. The conversation goes about as badly as it could do. At first stilted and formal, it quickly turns terrifying for both Ophelia and the audience as Hamlet rails at his lover, ordering her to leave before storming out himself. The audience know that the whole conversation has been set up by Polonius and Claudius to spy on Hamlet, and this dramatic irony creates an undercurrent of tension from the very outset of the scene. Will Hamlet discover Ophelia's deception? How will he react? How might she?

Hamlet has just finished his 'to be or not to be' soliloquy when his musings are interrupted. Ophelia's address to him is strikingly formal and distant, possibly because she knows her father and the King are watching the exchange. Hamlet replies in the same polite manner. There is none of the intimacy we might expect between lovers, and no trace of the passion we have heard in Hamlet's love letter. This opening section is in verse, giving the exchange a measured, formal quality. However, when Ophelia tries to return Hamlet's love letters, Hamlet's 'no, not I', reinforced by the double negative, completes her line of verse to show his immediate denial, while the incomplete next line throws brutal emphasis on 'aught'. Having only three feet, the line implies a silence at its end, indicating that Ophelia does not know how to respond. She tries again, 'My honour'd lord, you know right well you did', maintaining her composure in the face of his unpromising reaction – after all, she is holding the love letters that Hamlet is denying having written. Her five lines of verse, concluded with a full rhyming couplet 'mind/ unkind', sound almost as though she had planned in advance what she was going to say.

At this point, things really start to go wrong. Hamlet's unexpected question 'Are you honest?' ushers in the next section of the conversation, one which

Ophelia could not have foreseen. With the knowledge that this conversation

is a set-up by Polonius and Claudius, and the couple are being watched, this direct question from Hamlet heightens the tension for both Ophelia and the audience. Has Hamlet smelled a rat? The pace of the dialogue increases, with short questions alternating between the two characters. It is now in prose, and the lack of metre increases the informal feel of the conversation and with it the sense that it is getting out of control. Ophelia is clearly wrong-footed, responding to Hamlet's questions with confused, defensive ones of her own: 'My lord?', 'What means your lordship?'. Hamlet has derailed the conversation and changed the subject completely. 'Honest' at this time also meant 'chaste', and Hamlet launches into a quasi-philosophic and rather confusing discussion of the 'paradox' whereby 'beauty' will sooner make a chaste person corrupt than 'honesty' can make 'beauty' chaste. These sexual references, found again in 'nunnery' - an Elizabethan slang word for brothel - create the impression that Hamlet is making unkind insinuations about Ophelia's sexual conduct.

Contrasting the complexity of the argument about honesty with its monosyllabic simplicity, 'I did love you once' comes unexpectedly. But Hamlet immediately contradicts himself: 'I loved you not'. This out of hand rejection of Ophelia is astonishingly cruel and Ophelia's short answers, 'you made me believe so' and 'I was the more deceived' indicate that she feels herself to have been misled and wronged by Hamlet. Their restrained quality also underlines Ophelia's need to remain respectful, no matter what Hamlet says or does. Hamlet, as a prince and a man, has a superior status, and Ophelia's use of the 'you' form of address and the respectful 'my lord' which appears in every single line except 'I was the more deceived' [its omission possibly suggesting that she is truly hurt at this point] reminds the audience of this. This imbalance in status means that even if Ophelia wanted to, she could not really push her argument or defend herself against Hamlet.

The imperative 'Get thee to a nunnery' bursts out - a direct order using the informal pronoun 'thee' as opposed to the 'you' which has been used up to this point. This marks the third section of the exchange, where communication breaks down completely. Hamlet is suddenly enraged, and spirals off into three long tirades about the corruption and falseness of mankind in general, and women in particular, during which he orders Ophelia five times to go to a nunnery. The line distribution, as Hamlet speaks far more than Ophelia, shows how she has lost control of the conversation, and equally, how he has lost control of himself. Twice, he says 'farewell' before starting to speak again, as though he is so impassioned that he simply cannot stop himself. Although Ophelia has triggered Hamlet's diatribe, it barely seems to be addressed to her at all. He expresses his hatred of himself ['I am proud, revengeful, ambitious'] at humanity ['we are arrant knaves all'] and at women ['wise men know what monsters you make of them'], but these are general feelings of Hamlet's, not personal accusations towards Ophelia. Similarly, Ophelia stops trying to address Hamlet. Her pleas 'O help him, you sweet heavens' and 'Heavenly powers, restore him' show her desperation and fear, and also that she does not dare, or thinks there is no point, trying to reason further with him.

Why does Hamlet act like this? His behaviour towards Ophelia is not only cruel, but inconsistent. When he first sees her, his words are 'Nymph, in thy orisons be all my sins remembered' – the tone of this, when she takes him by surprise, is loving and intimate, using the familiar 'thy', and completely different from his vicious quick-fire questions only fifteen lines later. His fury at the end of the scene not only does not fit with what one would expect from lovers or with the attitude of the love-letter Polonius read out, but is even out of sync with the start of the scene. Surely, it must be that Hamlet has guessed the deception and is punishing Ophelia for her betrayal.

His question 'Where's your father?' had come out of the blue at the end of his first tirade. Ophelia only had an instant to decide what to say. She replied with her first actual lie, often delivered as if with some difficulty by the actor playing Ophelia, 'At home, my lord'. This can be interpreted as the moment Hamlet realises they are being spied on. Equally, her earlier formality could have been what tipped him off that something is wrong, if it is not how they usually talk to each other. After all, he has been primed to spot betrayals by his earlier conversation with his supposed friends, Rosencrantz and Guildenstern in Act II. Productions often interpret Hamlet's anger as being caused by her betrayal. But nowhere in the text is this made explicit; it is left to the actors and director to decide how to interpret the exchange, and there is much scope for different versions. It could even be that Hamlet's volatile behaviour is him performing his 'antic disposition' for the unseen on-stage audience. Or it could be that he is actually becoming unhinged. The order to go to a nunnery might even be Hamlet trying to protect Ophelia, sending her away from the corrupt 'arrant knaves' of the world, and out of the manipulative and dangerous environment of Elsinore. Whatever Hamlet's motivation, his ferocity contributes to Ophelia's breakdown.

The audience have witnessed a shocking scene, one tantamount to showing abuse by a raging jealous spouse, who, it seems, would rather destroy what he claims to love rather than allow it to flourish without him. Modern productions often show Hamlet manhandling Ophelia about the stage, with one memorable production incorporating a rape of Ophelia earlier in the play. Shakespeare must have known it was an extreme scene because he is careful to ensure that Ophelia only feels shock, not at his reprehensible behaviour but, at his apparent mental unravelling. Her asides that pray for his recovery ['O help him, you sweet heavens!'] and her timely reminder of all Hamlet used to be once he stalks off stage ['The courtier's, soldier's, scholar's eye, tongue, sword'] recover some sympathy for the 'blown youth/ blasted with ecstasy'. To compound matters for Ophelia, but also to distract the audience from her hurt, the reactions of father and King, are distinctly indifferent to the traumatic attack she has suffered: 'You need not tell us what Lord Hamlet said -/ We heard it all'. Unsurprisingly, the play is back to surveillance yet again: 'Madness in great ones must not unwatched go' and Ophelia's plight is quickly forgotten in the assumed concerns for Hamlet's safety.

The Romantic poet, John Keats, coined the term 'negative capability' to describe Shakespeare's unique dramatic genius. Keats meant by this term Shakespeare's capacity to present any situation entirely sympathetically and empathetically from opposing viewpoints, without biasing the argument in one way or the other. As we have seen, Hamlet's behaviour in this scene is wild, cruel and abusive. But if he thinks he has discovered yet another betrayal and this time from someone he appears to have loved, while we must surely condemn his behaviour, we may at least understand his hurt and rage. In his

eyes, Ophelia has been used and corrupted by her interfering father and the villainous King and, like his mother, she has chosen to betray him. But before we rush to switch allegiances and condemn Ophelia's cowardly betrayal, we have to consider the brutality of Hamlet's treatment of her and her own limited options at this point in the play. Entirely dependent on the powerful male figures in her life, Ophelia has little or no agency of her own. She cannot simply go away like her brother to Paris. As an Elizabethan daughter, her duty is to obey her father. To go against this duty would not only lead to opprobrium, but present impossible practical challenges. Potentially, she could transfer her duty to a husband, but the prime candidate for that position is otherwise occupied at present, a danger both to himself and those around him. And perhaps also mad. If she had disobeyed her father what could she have done and where could she have gone? Though we must condemn his behaviour, we can appreciate how Hamlet feels about Ophelia's betrayal. At the same time, we must also appreciate that Ophelia had little choice and she surely suffers horribly for the only one she could realistically make. Hence, characteristically, our sympathies in this scene may be torn agonisingly between the two characters.

As mentioned previously, the great one under scrutiny in Act III, Scene 2 is not just Hamlet but also Claudius himself. With its curious contrast of the Players' highly artificial verse and the more unrestrained prose conversations between the royal audience, *The Mousetrap* scene is another example of Hamlet's deep hostility towards women. His crude sexual innuendoes to Ophelia about 'country matters' and what lies 'between maids' legs may be publicly shaming and mortifying for her, but these are nothing as excruciating as Gertrude's experience at seeing her remarriage publicly ridiculed by her son in front of the royal court. While it is true that his main objective is to gauge Claudius' reaction to the theatrical regicide, Hamlet seems also hellbent on making Gertrude suffer for her sins too.

Both King and Queen are remarkably restrained in their reaction, especially Gertrude's 'The lady doth protest too much, methinks' response to Hamlet's pointed question: 'How like you this play?' He must know, of course, how she must hate it, but also how she must exercise public restraint. This restraint ends when Ophelia exclaims that 'the King rises' after Claudius sees the re-enactment of his poisoning of his own brother, which is the cue for a swift, guilt-ridden exeunt.

Despite Hamlet's excitable exclamations of success, it has been argued that because the play presents reality so relentlessly from Hamlet's perspective the audience often mistakenly assumes Claudius' premature exit to be guilt-ridden. Indeed, Horatio, a much more stable observer of affairs and the one supposed to be monitoring Claudius while Hamlet is harassing his mother and Ophelia is much less convinced it is a sign of Claudius' guilt. While Hamlet proclaims his theatrical wheedling skills as worth a 'whole share in a theatrical company', Horatio declares it only worthy of 'half a share'. Moreover, is it right to assume that it is guilt that motivates Claudius' hasty exit? As the murderer in *The Mousetrap*, Lucianus, is the king's nephew, the stage action could be read as a warning of what Hamlet will do to his uncle. Therefore, is it not guilt, but fear that may have driven Claudius from the scene?

On stage this scene can be played along the entire spectrum of culpability from Claudius fleeing, ashen-faced from the stage to a defiant, curtailing of Hamlet's insolence by shutting the entire farce down. Patrick Stewart's[19] recent performance saw Claudius bring a lantern ['Give me some light'] close to Hamlet's face before shaking his head in sinister warning. Given the quality of Claudius' own acting to date - concealing the duplicitous murderer behind the mask of caring stepfather - it does seem an uncharacteristic lapse. *The Mousetrap* seems to prick Claudius' conscience as the next scene sees a praying Claudius, at the mercy of a preying Hamlet, confess his sins: 'my

---

[19] RSC, *Hamlet* [2009] directed by Gregory Doran.

offence is rank: it smells go heaven'. Ultimately, another opportunity to 'drink hot blood' and carry out the delayed revenge is missed. But Hamlet does not fail to take another opportunity to re-direct his frustrated violence and hurt his dear mother: 'I will speak daggers to her but use none'.

The closet scene

Despite his intentions to be only 'cruel, not unnatural' there is something distinctly unnatural about Hamlet's behaviour in the closet scene. This unnaturalness is all tied up in Hamlet's unhealthy policing of his own mother's sex-life – not the most obvious topic for most normal mother-son conversations. While closet simply meant a private room in Elizabethan England, most modern productions choose to stage this scene in Gertrude's bedroom, where the potential sexual charge between the two can be ramped up for maximum audience discomfort. And that's not to mention the various costumes that can be used to amplify Gertrude's sexual attractiveness or the various ways she can be manhandled around her bedroom by her son. Even 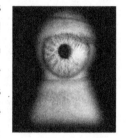 playing the scene as straight as the script allows makes it a challenging one for those sympathetic to the youngish Prince. However, there is the little matter of yet more state surveillance to deal with before diving into Freudian weirdness.

The closet scene begins with Polonius urging Gertrude to discipline her wayward son after his disgraceful behaviour in the previous Mousetrap scene. Parental discipline is one thing, but as has become characteristic of the world of the play it must be secretly observed. Polonius again, as he was in the nunnery scene, is the secret observer. He justifies his spying presence in the Queen's private quarters in terms of keeping tabs on Hamlet, naturally. But we may also wonder whether Polonius has other, more self-interested motives. Being party to this private scene could, for instance, furnish him with potentially highly useful and valuable information.

Whatever his motives, this time his spying will have fatal consequences for all, but most especially himself. Polonius ends up ignominiously skewered, mistaken for a rat, which in a way he is. However, what is of more importance dramatically, is why Polonius is mistakenly killed in the first place. Simply put, Hamlet's behaviour towards Gertrude has become so aggressive and threatening at this point that she actually fears for her life: 'Thou wilt not murder me -/ Help, ho!'. The fact that Gertrude genuinely fears for her life reveals a lot about how out of control things have become in this scene, and Hamlet hasn't even begun his moral dressing-down of his mother yet! So intense is his desire to berate her for her sexual misconduct that he is more than happy to allow Polonius' corpse to bleed out on the floor while he does so. As Graham Bradshaw[20] points out, the nausea about the incestuous nature of her remarriage, while theologically and legally inappropriate in Elizabethan England, is never mentioned by anyone else but Hamlet and the Ghost, who may or may not be a figment of his imagination. As this act has repeatedly shown, Hamlet's behaviour is becoming increasingly unpredictable and uncontrollable, by himself and others.

Ostensibly, Hamlet has been summoned to his mother's private quarter to receive a dressing-down for his wild conduct during the play-within-the-play. Such may have been Gertrude's intentions. But in no time at all the tables are turned and she finds herself the one being berated. Hamlet begins the closet scene full of linguistic insolence, a typical naughty child in defiance mode, taking his mother's words, twisting them and firing them back in her face. His intentions to be the berating force in the exchange is subtly signalled by Shakespeare through personal pronouns: Gertrude uses the more informal, and we would assume, more affectionate 'thou' whereas Hamlet uses 'you', which on one level is more appropriate when addressing his Queen, but also suggests the coldness, necessary for one assuming moral superiority:

Queen: Hamlet, thou hast thy father much offended.
Hamlet: Mother, you have my father much offended.

Hamlet's strategy of frustrating Gertrude, where he 'dar'st wag thy tongue/ in noise so rude against' her reaches boiling point straight away: 'You are the

---

[20] Bradshaw, *The Connell Guide to Hamlet*, p.82.

Queen, your husband's brother's wife/ and would it were not so, you are my mother'. Hamlet is careful here to emphasise the incestuous element of Gertrude's remarriage and doesn't hesitate to articulate his shame at her behaviour. Unsurprisingly, Gertrude feels that such a conversation is inappropriate and promises to 'set those to you that can speak'. While this decorum is unsurprising, the roughness of Hamlet's subsequent actions are. His imperative 'Come, come, and sit you down. You shall not budge' can be accompanied by all types of actions: a mere shaking before her mirror or a flinging to her bed as depicted rather crudely in the Mel Gibson film version of the play[21]. Of course, the latter action feeds the Freudian white heat that can sometimes be ignited in this scene.

The unfortunate killing of Polonius, an action that serves to accelerate the tragic plot, brings a potentially earth-shattering revelation for Gertrude: Hamlet suggests that she is not only an incestuous wanton, but also an accomplice to murder: 'Almost as bad, good mother,/ As kill a king and marry

with his brother'. Stagecraft considerations of lighting and sound can be highly effective here, with interrogating bright lighting to highlight guilty Gertrude and imaginative repetition of his words reverberating through the auditorium. While she seems to struggle to process the possibilities of such an accusation, Hamlet embarks upon his mission to chasten her or as he puts it, to 'wring' her heart. Gertrude's reasonable protests for Hamlet to calm down only aggravate the situation. Hamlet is driven to deliver a 36-line tirade, which builds in intensity until it overwhelms both mother and son. In fact, this tsunami of abuse only stops when the Ghost returns. Four times Gertrude asks for Hamlet to cease

---

[21] *Hamlet* [1990], directed by Franco Zeffirelli.

his invective. But he is unable to restrain himself; his venting cannot be contained: 'O, Hamlet, speak no more'; 'O speak to me no more'; 'No more, sweet Hamlet'; 'No more!' The increasing desperation of her protests, becoming shorter and more exclamatory, cannot stem the torrent of abuse. Hamlet at her third plea simply continues, as if he hasn't even heard her:

Hamlet: … A cutpurse of the empire and the rule
             That from a shelf the precious diadem stole
             And put it in his pocket, -
Queen: No more!
Hamlet: - a king of shreds and patches –

Enter GHOST

Unsurprisingly, Hamlet prefaces this tirade by describing Gertrude's decision to marry Claudius as a descent from idealised love to prostitution and a luxuriating in lust. Shakespeare cleverly uses props in the form of two portraits of the brother-husbands to explicitly compare like with like. While one is essentially Godlike, 'the front of Jove himself', the other is no more than 'a mildewed ear' [a neat reference to the method of regicide]. Increasingly, Hamlet's speech becomes more furious, reflected in the use of caesuras that suggest he is almost unable to articulate his mortification at his mother's choice. He assaults his mother with repeated pointed and barbed questions; five in all and all suggesting the utter incomprehensibility of her decision: 'Have you eyes?'; 'Ha, have you eyes?'; 'What judgement would step from this to this?'; 'What devil was't that thus cozened you at hoodman-blind?'; 'O shame, where is thy blush? His excoriation denies Gertrude the possibility of actually loving Claudius [that would surely drive this father-worshipping son into the abyss] or of making a reasonable political decision in remarrying. Instead he can only label her actions as licentious: 'You cannot call it love, for at you age/ The heyday in the blood in tame'.

Even Gertrude's admission that she can 'see such black and grieved spots' on her soul, is not enough. Hamlet insists on providing a graphically disturbing description of the royal marriage bed: The 'rank sweat' of the 'enseamed bed', a bed symbolically 'stewed in corruption', is sensually repugnant. 'Rank' certainly echoes Claudius' own description of his regicidal 'offence', but the language Hamlet uses is that of pigs, wallowing in their own stinking filth,  'over the nasty sty'. The adjective 'enseamed' suggests grease-saturated but also, even more disturbingly, semen-saturated sheets. A recent production memorably saw Hamlet wrap these soiled sheets over Gertrude's head in mocking fury. Additionally, to continue the accusations of prostitution that began this most untender exchange, 'stewed' also connects to brothels, which were known in Elizabethan England as 'the stews'. Is it any wonder Gertrude exclaims that 'these words like daggers enter in my ears'? These words are the very ones that direct all Freudian critics to suggest that part of Hamlet's madness at this point is his succumbing to Oedipal passions, his fragile, fragmented ego unable to control the wildly dangerous passions erupting in his id.

Thank God for ghosts then. If Hamlet won't listen to his mother, he certainly pays more attention to his father. And his father is much more considerate to Gertrude. The arrival of the Ghost jolts him from his relentless, self-righteous assault and Gertrude can successfully plead with her son to 'upon the heat and flame of thy distemper/ sprinkle cool patience'. While the arrival of the Ghost allows a much-needed dramatic pause in the heated action, it is not a cessation. Moments later Hamlet is making more demands, policing his mother's sexual practices again. Whilst more calm, he still insists on her considering 'the ulcerous place' in her soul that allows 'rank corruption mining all within' to infect 'unseen' and urges her not to 'let the bloat king tempt you again to bed'. The closet scene is not exactly a touching portrait of parent-child reconciliation, but at least they end slightly closer than how they began.

The scene ends with Hamlet issuing a double warning to his mother, the final one quite sinister in its wording: a) no more sleeping with her 'husband's brother' and b) keep the knowledge of his feigned madness a secret or 'like the famous ape' Gertrude will end up 'breaking her own neck. With that final warning ringing in her ears, Hamlet then prepares to try to atone for the unfortunate inconvenience of having to 'lug' away 'the guts' of the slain Polonius. The act ends with an acute sense of anticipation in the audience.

While Hamlet may have gotten away with mortifying the royal court to various degrees, Claudius will now have to respond. The intensification of Hamlet's threat will drive Claudius to much more overt, drastic strategies than the mere tolerance and surveillance that he has employed to date. How he probably now wishes he had let Hamlet go off to Wittenberg.

As we'll explore later in our essay on her, Gertrude's behaviour in this scene can be interpreted in several different ways. For example, was Hamlet's revelation that she has married a murderer necessarily news to Gertrude? It seems Gertrude cannot see or hear the Ghost, which suggests that Hamlet may be hallucinating and therefore actually going mad, albeit staging of the scene can strongly influence the audience's perceptions here. But, what if Gertrude can see the Ghost and is just pretending not to? What then? Whilst she seems to agree to follow Hamlet's instructions towards the end of the scene, to what extent does she tell him what he wants to hear, not least because Hamlet seems dangerously mad and might at any moment harm her physically?

Ostensibly, in this scene Gertrude shifts her loyalties from her husband, Claudius, to her son, Hamlet. Judging from her words, she moves decisively from being a wife to being a mother. In the following scene at the start of the next Act, she has to report the traumatic events of the closet scene to her husband. Exactly what she does and does not tell him will reveal more about where her loyalty now truly lies.

Act Four

While Act III represented a significant surge of dramatic energy, Act IV continues this upswing in narrative momentum. Like a sluggish beast waking up and flexing its muscles, the play now brings the audience face-to-face with more characters, offers more imaginative locations and finally unleashes Claudius' more overtly villainous side. Act IV also has seven scenes compared to Act III's four, the most scenes in any act, suggesting the act's more diffuse concerns as Shakespeare tries to balance events at home in Elsinore as well as abroad, on the seas to England. However, to begin with, Polonius' unfortunate manslaughter and its inevitable aftermath must be dealt with and this lamentable event brings great danger, not only for Hamlet, but also for Claudius.

In fact, the first scene with Gertrude after her straightening out by her son, sees clear cracks opening up in the royal marriage. For the only time in the play both husband and wife are alone together onstage, and it is notable that not only do they both lie to each other, but also that they hide their own emotional experiences from each other. Not only does Gertrude blatantly lie about her son's madness [rather than 'mad in craft' as Hamlet declares himself, she describes him as 'mad as the sea and wind when both contend/ which is the mightier']. She also declares that Hamlet 'weeps for what is done', at which the audience may only manage a grim, ironic smile as we remember Hamlet manhandling the bloody corpse of 'a most foolish prating knave' into the next room. A similar ironic smile may also decorate the audience's collective face once it hears Claudius' claim that 'so much was our love' for 'this mad young man', especially as we have already heard of the King's scheme to effectively exile his nephew to England.

More truthful, perhaps, is Claudius' naked self-interest, which sees him breathe a sigh of relief that 'it had been so with us had we been' behind the arras in Gertrude's closet. Despite his dramatic exhortation of 'O heavy deed!' he spends no time lamenting the passing of a completely loyal and rather inventive royal advisor. Indeed, he proceeds to count his own lucky stars and then worry about the political fall-out of such a calamity, hoping that the inevitable 'poisoned shot, may miss our name/ and hit the woundless air'. Further subtle evidence of a significant divergence in the marriage is seen in Gertrude's repeated ignoring of her husband's instructions to 'come away'. Three times he commands her to 'O come away'. Each time she apparently ignores him, leaving him exiting the stage with his 'soul full of discord and dismay'. Indeed, in some productions Gertrude leaves the stage in the opposite direction to her husband.

Claudius' soul is certainly not improved when he does finally apprehend his errant nephew/stepson and questions him about the whereabouts of

Polonius' body. Every time the two mighty opposites are on stage together the tension crackles like static electricity. Here is another episode in the feigned madness that sees Hamlet's riddling words needle the exasperated characters around him. When he declares that Polonius is at supper, he clarifies that it is supper 'not where he eats but where 'a is eaten'. Claudius regains control temporarily when Hamlet finally reveals the whereabouts of the body as well as accepting his mission to England.

Of course, this acceptance comes with a generous helping of customary insolence and yet another brazen rejection by his nephew/stepson:

Hamlet:	Farewell, dear mother
King:	Thy loving father, Hamlet.
Hamlet:	My mother. Father and mother is man and wife.
	Man and wife is one flesh. So – my mother.

It is little wonder that when Claudius finally has a moment to himself, he describes Hamlet like a fever that needs urgent medical attention: 'for like the hectic in my blood he rages'. And only a bloodletting will cure Claudius' diseased blood at this stage. The extent of his duplicitous villainy is revealed for the audience, which allows Shakespeare to restore some of the sympathy for Hamlet that he may have lost in the previous act. Claudius' explicit villainy can lend itself to all types of dramatic stagecraft, both subtle and not. An unsubtle lightning flash and crack of thunder has characterised many an amateur production, whereas professional productions have often played subtly with lighting colours and the use of over-lighting to cast striking shadows across the actor's face. The thin pretence that Rosencrantz and Guildenstern are Hamlet's friends and are acting out of concern for him is shredded in these scenes; quite clearly they are doing Claudius' bidding, taking on the role increasingly of Hamlet's guards rather than his companions.

Shakespeare surprisingly relocates outside the castle for the first time, to what must presumably be close to the port from where Hamlet will depart from England. Another frustrated revenging son, Fortinbras of Norway, embarks upon a similarly side-tracking mission. Whereas Hamlet journeys to England, Fortinbras marches to Poland to vent some of that warrior prestige that Hamlet so clearly lacks. The sight of 'the imminent death of twenty thousand men' for 'a fantasy and trick of fame' reduces Hamlet to shame and, not for the first time, another promise to swift and bloody action: 'O, from this time forth/ my thoughts be bloody or be nothing worth'. While this may seem rousing stuff, he is still referring to 'thoughts' and not 'actions'. In addition, the reality of his exile and potential murder in England, makes this another promise not to be taken too seriously given his track record of resolve being undermined by indecisiveness. Hamlet disappears from the play for the next few scenes, allowing Shakespeare to concentrate upon the terrible impact of Polonius' death on his own children: Ophelia and Laertes, last heard of in Act I, Scene 2.

Ophelia's madness

The focus on both children allows Shakespeare to explore both the deeply personal and deeply political ramifications of the old man's death. Ophelia's appearance in Act IV, Scene 5 must be one of the saddest in all of Shakespearean tragedy, up there with *King Lear* on the storm-tossed moor. The fact that Gertrude refuses to entertain her as the start of this scene is certainly revealing: 'I will not speak with her'. Why would she refuse this, especially when she has always held Ophelia in such high regard, in fact so high that she previously hoped Ophelia might ease Hamlet's madness? It is an odd reaction from another woman, but one that reveals a far tougher side to Gertrude. Regardless, Shakespeare cleverly employs a favourite strategy: detailed description of a character to the audience before unleashing them upon the stage. This works brilliantly here because the gentleman who brings news of Ophelia describes in detail her derangement - her preoccupation with

her father; her seemingly nonsensical speech and wildly unpredictable gestures and her general air of melancholy despair. It is a superbly charged dramatic moment when Ophelia enters the stage and one that can be played multiple ways. It usually depends upon how a production views her sexual relations with Hamlet, whether she deserved the sexual policing her father and brother were so keen to impose upon her or whether she was a sexual innocent. Modern productions, unshackled from old-fashioned prudery regarding female sexuality, have the option to present her in various degrees of undress. To maximise the pathos of her derangement, though, having her a sexual innocent is always a prudent choice.

Invariably, Ophelia enters the stage in a state of severe dishevelment; sometimes she wears a soiled wedding dress, highlighting her missed opportunity as future Queen of Denmark; sometimes she is dressed in some of her father's clothes, emphasising her status as a traumatised, grieving daughter; other times she wears very little at all, showing her rapidly loosening grip on reality. The First Quarto stage directions describe her with her hair down [shorthand for female madness] and playing a lute, badly and out of tune one would assume. Given the importance of flowers later in the scene, she has been shown wearing a badly-made crown of flowers. In fact, one production made her crown from broken twigs or branches, making it distinctly like a biblical crown of thorns, rendering her a suffering, Christ-like figure.

In this scene she sings fragments of songs, all with some sort of semantic importance, but none adding up to a coherent whole. Again, a significant array of options is available to the actress playing her: her singing can be sweet and moving, strong and melodious; however, sometimes, a weak-voiced, tuneless warble can be equally effective. Some actresses choose to alternate between these two modes, sometimes dolefully lamenting the loss of love and other times bellowing angrily about the sexual exploitation of women by men. The content of her song fragments loosely coalesce around the theme of loss: loss of certainty ['How should I your true love know/ from another one?']; loss of father or maybe even husband ['He is dead and gone lady']; loss of virginity and possibly innocence ['let in the maid that out a maid /never departed more']. There is more than a hint of male sexual trickery in her songs as Shakespeare points up her status as a victim of male heavy-handedness, firstly by her brother and father and, secondly, by her lover.

As we will explore in our essay on Ophelia, her madness has been interpreted very differently over time. Broadly speaking, traditional interpretations present Ophelia's madness as infantile, emotional and pitiful, whereas many modern interpretations highlight the subversive, rebellious and dangerous elements of her words and actions. Her pitiful exit off stage ushers in a change of focus from potential personal to potential political tragedy.

Laertes' return

Shakespeare uses offstage noise expertly to create spikes in narrative tension. He uses the stage direction 'A noise within' three times in this scene to suggest the movement of significant, unseen forces massing offstage. Two of these anticipate Laertes' dangerous arrival, whereas the final one is associated with Ophelia and works in a completely different way. It certainly doesn't take long for Claudius to switch from the 'poison of deep grief' to other 'sorrows' that 'come not single spies but in battalions'. The use of 'spies' is surely appropriate given that while Claudius may not be able to control the various sorrows he laments, he is fully aware of them, especially Laertes who 'is in secret come from France [...] and wants not buzzers to infect his ear'. Of course, when such turbulence is talked about it is always good to bring it to the stage. Laertes' entrance is as dramatic, just in a different way, as his sister's. Laertes brings not mental instability with him but political instability.

Claudius' fears of 'the people muddied, /thick and unwholesome in thoughts and whispers' are justified as the messenger brings the earth-shattering news that 'the rabble call him [Laertes] lord', implying a lawless regression to pre-civilised times. What the messenger is in fact describing is democracy in action! Again, Gertrude's reaction is both odd and telling: 'How cheerfully on the false trail they cry./ O, this is counter, you false Danish dogs'. Cue: outraged, Marxist howl of injustice! Despite the recent rift in her marriage and with Hamlet out of the way, she proves to be more than a loyal wife. Claudius' dramatic exclamation that 'the doors are broke' often presages an eruption of chaos onto the stage. This eruption doesn't last long, however, as Laertes almost immediately asks his followers to 'stand you all without'. Some productions merely have Claudius, Gertrude and Laertes retire to another room with the throng listening intently outside, thereby allowing all parties to remain onstage and a fragile peace to balance itself uneasily.

Two things are striking about this dramatic confrontation between an enraged, revenger son and the royal couple. Firstly, Gertrude's physical intervention between Laertes and her husband is surely the actions of a woman still in love, so much so that she must be ordered to release Laertes not once but twice ['Let him go, Gertrude']. Secondly, Claudius' absolute calm in the face of such political chaos is impressive. It is quickly revealed that Claudius believes himself divinely protected: 'do not fear our person./ There's such divinity doth hedge a king'. It has been remarked upon that having such a Machiavellian schemer voice such opinions makes an immediate mockery of them as mere wishful thinking. Divine protection certainly did nothing for Old Hamlet; Claudius of all people really ought to know this. Perhaps then, these words are aimed at cowing Laertes. Whether he believes his words or not, Claudius demonstrates a rather magnificent calmness and self-restraint, the absolute opposite of the enraged and armed man in front of him. So enraged is Laertes that he will 'dare damnation' so as to be 'revenged/ most thoroughly for my father'. This antithesis between dangerously, volatile subject and glacially calm king is absorbing drama, especially given the external pressure of the 'rabble' that lurks outside the room. The interaction between the two actors can be absorbing with the contrast in barely controlled emotion and supreme self-restraint shown through body language, gesture and stage movements. Claudius shows his formidable skills of diplomacy by sweet-talking Laertes into believing his side of the story before Shakespeare dramatically re-introduces Ophelia with 'A noise within' which changes the whole mood and atmosphere of the scene again.

While previously these two stage directions have suggested the sizeable explosive masses outside the castle walls, here they indicate more of the same only to deliver their opposite - a powerless, broken and vulnerable individual. Given Laertes' already heightened and fraught emotional state, the sight of his cherished sister [a relationship notably quasi-incestuous in Kenneth Branagh's 1996 film version] as deranged and dishevelled brings him to tears: 'tears seven times salt burn out the sense and virtue of mine eye'. Now whether Ophelia even recognises her brother is up to the individual production, but for drama's sake it would be better if she did not, or to limit it to a fleeting recognition in a storm of frantic detachment. Notably, Laertes calls her 'rose of May', associating her with flowery female innocence and this part of the scene sees her famous giving away of flowers to the various characters, with each flower carrying a very specific significance. Shakespeare does not specify the recipients, so, again, it is up to each production to decide this. The recipients can receive quite sincerely appropriate flowers or ironically inappropriate flowers. She hands out the following flowers:

- 'rosemary: that's for remembrance'
- 'pansies: that's for thoughts'
- 'fennel' for flattery
- 'columbines' for infidelity
- 'rue' for repentance
- a 'daisy' for unrequited love.

Ophelia claims that she would give 'some violets' [representing fidelity], but notably 'they withered all when my father died'. What exactly she means by this is unclear, but it suggests a marked loosening of morals once the policing figure of the father is removed. Again, whether this actually applied to her own behaviour or just some fantasy version remains open to interpretation. She exits the scene, and the play itself, never to be seen again, singing plaintively about the death of a father-type figure: 'He will never come again. / His beard was as white as snow'. Understandably, Laertes is devastated by this shadow of his sister and grieves now for a lost father and sister, essentially his entire family.

Ever the opportunist, Claudius is quick to exploit his grief. He gives Laertes an offer he can't refuse: prove me immoral and I'll make you king; if you can't I'll help you revenge your grievances: 'We shall jointly labour with your soul / to give it due content'. As several critics have commented, it is unclear what his ultra-loyal wife makes of his promise to ensure that 'where th'offence is let the great axe fall' as it is very clear that said axe should plummet down on her son's tender neck! Speaking of that particular neck, the scene ends to allow Horatio back on to the stage to read a letter from Hamlet informing him of a barely credible incident. Hamlet has become a prisoner of 'warlike' pirates, who have inadvertently become saviours, as they are depositing Hamlet back to Elsinore. Typically, Hamlet has yet to show any of the mettle required of a revenger - he is a passive player in his own rescue rather than an active instigator of it. With this unlikely news ringing in the audience's ears, they now know that Claudius's scheming has been foiled. But he doesn't, and it will be interesting to see his reaction when he finds out.

Of course, as everyone knows, Shakespeare is a masterful playwright and scene after scene in the play is complex, compelling and brilliantly crafted. But what about Act IV, scene 6? Surely it's the least dramatically convincing in the whole play, with a whole load of improbable backstory delivered through the clumsy device of a character reading out loud a letter. Fortunately it's a short scene, giving way quickly to a much more dramatically engaging one.

The 'seduction' or 'corruption' scene sees Claudius working his finest smiling villainy on Laertes, starting it with blatant lies and ending it with more. He begins by trying to justify Polonius' paltry funeral arrangements, which Laertes quite rightly sees as an insult to his long years of state service. Claudius also tries to explain his failure to punish Hamlet in two odd ways given his status as supreme ruler of the state:

a) he didn't want to upset Gertrude, who he cannot live without

b) he didn't want to upset the public, who also love Hamlet.

It's peculiar that he fails to mention Hamlet's madness and in general his explanation is sweet, but unconvincing nonsense, from Laertes' point of view, and every actor playing Laertes must decide how much to be swayed by what the audience knows to be blatant lies. However, before Claudius' explanations can be scrutinised too much he is interrupted by deeply unwelcome news: not only is Hamlet not dead, he is returning tomorrow. Faced with such a dilemma, Claudius arrives at an ingenious solution: let Laertes have his revenge and let Gertrude be damned. To do this, he carefully stokes up Laertes' fiery temper, which, to be fair, doesn't require much stoking. All he has to do is suggest that Hamlet is bizarrely envious of Laertes' swordsmanship and also that Laertes' love for his tainted family honour is already waning. Responding that he is ready 'to cut his throat i'th' church' [a claim that suggests both brutal recklessness and complete disregard for the supposed moral purpose of revenge and contrasts starkly with Hamlet's decision not to kill Claudius when he was praying] Laertes shows himself more than ready to take on Hamlet. Emphatically he is a very different type of revenging son. The complexity of the scheme and the complicity in its duplicitous villainy, casts Laertes in a distinctly unfavourable light. Defeating Hamlet in a show of swordsmanship is one thing, involving nobility and honour. However, scheming to poison him, is a corruption of his noble purpose and more like its opposite - cowardly, ignoble villainy. In other words, Laertes could have been an Old Hamlet, but he has chosen to be a Claudius and it surely damages his credibility with the audience, despite the validity of his claims.

Ophelia's death

The audience may be tempted to forgive Laertes, given the next sledgehammer blow he suffers: Ophelia has tragically drowned when she 'fell in the weeping brook'. Significantly, it is Gertrude who reports this to Laertes, and in such wealth of detail that it begs an immediate question: did she actually witness this death? If she did, why didn't she do anything about it?

Even if, which is more likely, this tragedy was reported back to her, why didn't the original witness do something to stop 'her garments, heavy with their drink' from pulling 'the poor wretch from her melodious lay/ to muddy death'? Given the high level of surveillance in Elsinore, it would be no surprise if some sort of potential help was near at hand. However, there are alternative conspiracy theories, such as Ophelia was found after clearly committing suicide and Gertrude conjures up this bizarrely beautiful death to spare Laertes' feelings. Or, perhaps, Claudius has had the mad, troublesome and uncontrollable Ophelia silenced and this oddly aesthetised account is part of an establishment cover-up.

If the royal court is trying to protect Laertes from the scandal of a suicide, this strategy clearly doesn't work, as even the Gravedigger in the next act is

convinced she was a genuine suicide. Understandably, Laertes leaves the stage a dervish of overwhelming, turbulent emotions. His sadness 'drowns' a 'fire' that would 'blaze', the imagery expressing acute inner conflict between rage and grief. Clearly, Laertes is in an unstable, emotionally-driven state, which is exactly as Claudius would have planned, despite his conniving protests to the contrary: 'How much I had to do to calm his rage!' Having already lied to his wife and hidden from her his plotting with Laertes to murder her son, once again Claudius has to order Gertrude twice to leave the stage.

What look does she give him when he tells her to 'follow'? Does she hesitate to leave? Or, more radically, not follow him off stage? How these small moments are depicted is crucial to our sense of the changing nature of the relationship between the King and Queen.

With Hamlet offstage for most of the second half of Act IV, Shakespeare has used the opportunity to build up Claudius' villainy in action and provide the audience with a reason to despise him. God knows they need it given Hamlet's antics at Ophelia's graveside in the next act!

Act Five

Rites, revenge, and remembering

The final act in *Hamlet* is all about endings. It is only two scenes long and, in fine revenge tragedy style, litters the stage with the bodies of all major characters. It draws together a number of key themes from the play, including: what revenge is and whether it is ever justified, the social rites and rituals of courtesy, and how to remember the dead in early modern society.

Act V Scene 1 continues the play's metatheatrical aspects, though with rather more subtlety than the play-within-a-play, and it primarily looks forward rather than back. *The Mousetrap* restages an episode from the past [the murder of King Hamlet] as part of young Hamlet's detective operation to establish his uncle's guilt and verify the story told by the ghost. Meanwhile Act V Scene 1 serves as a rehearsal for the play's climax. It harks back to previous episodes in the play, whilst providing a practice run of the confrontations between the major protagonists – including the duel between Hamlet and Laertes – that will take place in Act V Scene 2.

Death is already centre stage in Scene 1. Set in a churchyard, two clowns dig Ophelia's grave and discuss the influence of social class and religious beliefs on death rites. We are reminded that one of the few certainties in life is death: the gallows 'outlives a thousand tenants,' are 'built stronger than the church', and 'last until doomsday'. Hamlet and Horatio soon join the clowns and their musings. They reflect on the social levelling that death creates, discussing the demise of notable historic figures. Caesar appears again; the same Roman emperor whose assassination, Horatio recalls in Act I, was accompanied by the dead walking the earth. As he did in  Act I, Horatio breaks off when a king appears. The language in V.2 – 'But soft, but soft awhile. Here comes the King' – echoes that from I.1, 'But soft, behold. Lo, where it comes again'. This time, however, it is not the Ghost of Old Hamlet who arrives. Rather, in a moment that foreshadows his coming doom, King Claudius appears amongst the graves.

Claudius is accompanied by Queen Gertrude, courtiers, a priest, Laertes, and Ophelia's coffin, which is due to be buried as part of the 'maimed rites' afforded to her in the early modern era as someone suspected of taking her own life. There are allusions to earlier moments in the play through Gertrude's lament that 'thou shouldst have been my Hamlet's wife' and Laertes' cursing of the priest accompanied by his invocation of violets, which he hopes will bloom again on her grave. They had, Ophelia told us in her madness, 'withered all when my father died [IV.5,182-3]. Laertes' grief at losing a second member of his family then drives him to 'leap' into Ophelia's grave and embrace her coffin, seeking death alongside her. However, Hamlet leaves the gravediggers and Horatio to dramatically leap into the grave too. Claiming his love for Ophelia is worth that of 'forty thousand brothers', he fights with Laertes for the right to be buried with her. They are separated by Claudius and Gertrude. The former takes Laertes aside to restrain him, reminding him of the plan they have hatched to murder Hamlet. The latter is instructed by Claudius to 'set some watch over your son' - with the emphasis now significantly on 'your' rather than the 'our' he has been throughout the play - who is still presumed to be suffering from madness.

Gertrude's new alliance with Hamlet, secured during the Act IV closet scene, is affirmed at the start of Act V since Hamlet appears again with Horatio – clearly under no watch at all. They are met by Osric, an unknown courtier, who summons Hamlet to fight Laertes again – this time in a duel. The duel appears to Hamlet to be a formal dispute to settle the bad blood between the Prince and the courtier. In fact, it is another act of revenge, or wild justice, taking place with Laertes knowingly armed with a poisoned rapier. Hamlet's refreshment cup has also been poisoned by King Claudius in case the duel does not go to plan. As so often in the case of revenge, this is exactly what happens; instead of a single life being taken, all the major characters are propelled towards their early graves.

The duel scene

The legal or judicial duel in early modern England was imported from Italy, as a way to settle a matter of honour. According to William Thomas, who published *The historie of Italie* [1549], if one gentleman spoke ill or otherwise harmed the reputation of another, it was legally acceptable – under certain conditions – that he would 'die for it, if the party slandered may know it, and find time and place to do it'.[22] Indeed, it was part of the true gentleman's repertoire, noted Baldassare Castiglione's *The book of the courtier* [1561], that 'he should be skilful in the knowing of Honour and the causes of quarrel'. Duels were only acceptable in this period, however, if they were judicially approved; that is the injured party had sought permission from the Crown. Extra-judicial or personal duels – such as those fought by Tybalt and Mercutio, and Romeo and Paris, in Shakespeare's *Romeo and Juliet* – which took place

without permission - were a crime. Shakespeare's fellow playwright, Ben Jonson was branded on the thumb as a punishment for killing another actor, Gabriel Spenser, in an illegal duel in 1598. With Crown permission, however, a man could use arms to settle a dispute under strictly regulated and supervised terms that both parties agreed to at the outset.

At first, the duel between Hamlet and Laertes seems to be set up as a matter between gentlemen, with Hamlet as the injurer and Laertes the wounded party. The lengthy conversation that takes place between Osric and Hamlet over Laertes' gentlemanly qualities, and a reminder of Hamlet's own, is intended to make the duel appear to the Prince to be an approved legal challenge. In accordance with a legitimate duel, the terms are also laid out via the wager King Claudius is said to have made that Hamlet will win. These dictate the number of attacks acceptable [twelve], the type of weapons [rapier and dagger], and how the victory will be decided [the first person to land three strikes on the other wins]. More generally, duels could be won and lost in a variety of ways: by the sun setting, by the Crown calling a halt and declaring a victor, by one party spilling the other's blood, or by death. As another courtier refers to the duel as 'play' and Hamlet anticipates that if he loses, he

---

[22] Peltonen, *The Duel in Early Modern England*, pp.17-19.

will 'gain nothing but my shame and the odd hits', the Prince believes he is being invited into what is essentially an exhibition, a staged fight through which Laertes may try to regain his honour and that will culminate without blood being spilled. Naturally, Horatio is suspicious, however, and tries to discourage Hamlet from participating. His caution, along with Osric being sent to invite  Hamlet to combat [traditionally, the injured party, here Laertes, should cast down the gauntlet personally and in public] forewarns us again that the duel will be as corrupt as the court in which it takes place.

The extent to which 'something is rotten in the state of Denmark' is encapsulated in the contest, shows just how far the social poison has spread. John Webster's *The Duchess of Malfi* describes a similarly toxic court as being 'like a common fountain, whence should flow/ Pure silver drops in general, but if't chance/ Some curs'd example poison't near the head,/ Death and diseases through the whole land spread' [I.1, 13-16]. The reiteration of Laertes' noble qualities by Osric and Hamlet prior to the duel ironically underscores the extent of the contagion. The audience know that this once honourable man – held up as Hamlet's equal in exemplifying the ideal courtier – is now part of a secret and underhand plot to murder the Prince. The poison here is not just metaphorical, but also literal in its passage through the court: each of the main characters lives are lost to it during the duel.

Using cinematic precision, Shakespeare splices the duelling scene through the exchanges of words and blows between Hamlet and Laertes, and Claudius orchestrating the circulation of wine cups around the combatants. Tension is built steadily through the audience's knowledge that Laertes' rapier is tipped with venom and that Claudius has spiked Hamlet's drink. Whether at rest, or fighting, Hamlet's death hovers near him like the presence of the Ghost. Twice, Laertes lands a blow without drawing blood. Twice, Hamlet is offered the toxic chalice and declines a drink. Once, Laertes' commitment wavers – it is 'almost against [his] conscience' to go through with a such an ungentlemanly and deceitful attack. At least once, the duelling courtiers fight with no strikes to either side.

But the inevitable must happen. And it does so suddenly; the poison flows from person to person at unstoppable speed: Gertrude drinks from Hamlet's poisoned cup; the men engage again and Hamlet is wounded with the tipped rapier; in keeping with the rules of a duel, the ensuing scuffle – a product of rage and not discipline – is broken up, but it is too late: The rapiers have changed hands and Laertes too is stabbed with the poisoned weapon. First Gertrude, then Laertes, expose Claudius' treachery: 'The King – the King's to blame'. Finally, Claudius is killed with both the toxic weapons, stabbed first by Hamlet and then forced to drink the adulterated wine. Abruptly, the play comes full circle: from a king poisoned through the ear while sleeping in his orchard to his murderer's death from the same weapon. The Machiavellian and the heroic come together too in a fitting finale, as Claudius is both poisoned and run through with a sword.

The circular nature of history is also reinforced in the play's closing moments. Hamlet's 'dying voice' 'prophes[ies that] th'election lights/ On Fortinbras', once again suggesting some sort of nascent democratic principle at work. However, Fortinbras claims 'some rights of memory in this kingdom', reminding us of the single combat Old Hamlet fought to win some of the Danish lands from Old Fortinbras before the play began. But the contrast between the two acts of single-handed combat is stark. Where Old Hamlet's duel is remembered as an honourable one, Fortinbras grimly notes of the scene he has encountered that 'such a sight as this/ Becomes the field but here shows much amiss'. We might think again of Francis Bacon's statement that 'revenge is a kind of wild justice' that 'putteth the law out of office'[23] – Danish law here lies in ruins with its royal family.

But is it that simple? There are, you might have realised, distinctions between the kinds of revenge that are sought in the play, to which Fortinbras draws our attention. These distinctions echo those written down by Bacon. Hamlet's

---

[23] Bacon, 'Of Revenge.' Essays, civil and moral.

death, Fortinbras tells us, will be mourned ceremoniously: 'soldier's music and the rite of war/ Speak loudly for him'. Hamlet can be commemorated because he has not done wrong 'merely out of ill-nature' but has taken 'public revenge' 'for those wrongs which there is no law to remedy', namely here the murder of Old Hamlet by his brother [Bacon, *Of Revenge*]. All Hamlet's vacillating, and his reluctance to kill Claudius at prayer, lead us to this moment: a public act of revenge, such as the one committed against Caesar, that can be conscienced by the state. By contrast, the private revenge sought by Claudius – the attempted murder of Hamlet by Rosencrantz and Guildenstern, the deceitful duel, and the deadly drink [not to mention the murder of his brother] – is unpardonable and his end is ignominious.

Do you agree with this argument? You might want to think about what it means for the other characters who have died here, particularly Gertrude and Laertes. What sort of remembrance do they deserve for their parts in events? You might also want to reflect again on the distinctions between good and bad deaths in society and in the eyes of God. And what does the election of Fortinbras to the Danish throne mean for Denmark and the memory of Old Hamlet?

The soliloquies

What makes us who we are? What we say about ourselves? What we do? How we treat others? What we think and feel? Is the quintessence of identity external and revealed by our social interactions, or is it internal and revealed by what's really going on inside our heads, hearts and, if we believe in them, our souls?

What's the function of a soliloquy? This dramatic device is the equivalent of extended interior monologue used in novels; it takes us right into the thoughts of a character. Creating an empathetic link between audience and the character who soliloquises, the dramatic device also helps shape where our sympathies lie. Crucially, by convention, in Elizabethan theatre characters tell the truth in soliloquies. However untrustworthy and duplicitous the world around them, however much they need to put on masks and pretences in public, in their soliloquies characters drop these masks. Of course, Shakespeare is particularly adept at showing us how characters change and adapt themselves in different contexts. Often the public self is itself a kind of performance, a playing of a role, or, in Hamlet's case, multiple roles. Think, for instance, of how Claudius has to perform the role of king in front of the court at the start of the play or how Hamlet chafes under the pressure to play the dutiful son in the same scene. Or consider how Hamlet puts on an antic disposition and plays to the audience, such as in his public lampooning of Polonius or when he suspects he is being spied upon.

The public self is often a mask or façade and contrasts starkly with a hidden self that is only revealed during private interaction with a trusted partner, friend, lover or spouse. For Hamlet this confidante is, of course, tellingly, not his lover, Ophelia, but his friend Horatio. Together they conspire in secret – hiding the news about the Ghost's appearance, discussing the play within the play - while presenting an innocent appearance to the outside world. This private/ public duality of characters is another form of the doubling that so pervades this play.

Commenting on Shakespeare's 'transformation' of the inherited conventions of revenge tragedy and of sources for *Hamlet*, Emma Smith notes that 'the depiction of Hamlet's internal state, revealed, through soliloquy, is perhaps the most striking change of emphasis from his more plot-driven predecessors'. This play is not, she continues, structured around the 'crime and retaliation of the revenge tragedy genre', but instead, 'by rhetoric, punctuated by soliloquies that decisively displace action into reflection'.[24]

And, indeed, no Shakespearean tragic hero has more soliloquies than Hamlet. In no other of his plays does Shakespeare gives us such a rich and detailed insight into any of his characters' psyches. Examining these soliloquies in sequence reveals the contours and landscape of Hamlet's mind. Whether we judge Hamlet's character from what he says about himself or from how he treats other characters or from his actions, or from an amalgam of all of these, we'll leave you to decide.

---

[24] Smith, *The Cambridge Shakespeare Guide*, pp. 36-40.

Act I, Scene 2 - O that this too too solid flesh would melt

Hamlet's first soliloquy is pivotal in understanding his mental state after the death of his father, his resentment towards Claudius [even before the ghost reveals him to be responsible for Old Hamlet's murder] and the difficulties he has reconciling his desires with his duty to God. It begins with synecdoche, with his 'flesh' representing his whole existence and, depending on the edition, described as 'solid', 'sullied' or 'sallied'[25]. 'Solid' carries connotations of unwelcome permanence, linking to his wishes that it, and he, would 'melt, / Thaw and resolve... into a dew', while 'sallied' implies being attacked or besieged and 'sullied' suggests polluted - all plausible interpretations in the context of the rest of the soliloquy. Not only does Hamlet feel cursed by fate [as we will see again in his next soliloquy], but also as if Denmark and everything in it has been corrupted since the death of his father.

Hamlet seeks the impossible. He wishes for 'solid flesh' to both 'melt' and 'resolve itself'. These antithetical images of dissipation and creation reveal an essential truth; Hamlet's conflicting desires cannot be satisfied. In the aftermath of his father's death, Hamlet's confusion is evident. Initially he appears to reveal a nihilistic attitude in lines 134-135 - 'How weary, stale, flat and unprofitable/ Seem to me all the uses of this world!' [with 'seem' contradicting his earlier assertion that 'I know not 'seems']. However, this comment is an apostrophe, addressed directly to God, and, despite his wish for his life to end, his references to 'God' and 'the Everlasting' suggest a religious piety that will prevent him from both taking action and from fully believing that life is meaningless. Hamlet is conflicted as both his desires and his revenge role are opposed by religious teachings. At this point, he sorely wishes to escape worldly suffering, but the violently described 'self-slaughter', a sin against God, would lead to eternal suffering. When considering states of mind and being, the metaphor of physical states – 'solid', 'melt', 'thaw' 'resolve' and 'dew' - can be linked to the famous line that 'Something is rotten in the **state** of Denmark' from Act I, Scene 4. Hamlet, the seemingly rightful heir to Denmark, is thrown into in a condition or 'state' of confusion by the

---

[25] The first [or 'Bad']Quarto in 1603 had 'sallied' [which many editors choose to 'correct' to 'sullied' whilst the 1623 First Folio had 'solid'.

expectation that he should be a hero, and root out the 'rotten[ness]' embodied by Claudius. In addition, the use of the reflexive pronoun 'itself' reveals Hamlet's passivity and inner conflict: Ideally he would like the situation to 'resolve itself' without his intervention, even though he believes that it is his destiny to intervene. So, even at this early stage, Hamlet resists agency, anticipating his later reluctance to take revenge.

Further than that, does Hamlet really wish to commit suicide? If you were a psychologist, how at risk would you consider him to be? Not only is the way he conceptualises killing himself entirely passive – something he imagines happening to him rather than something he will make happen, but he also imagines death as an impossibly gentle transition from one state to another. The verbs 'thaw' and 'melts', for instance, mask and soften the violence inherent in 'self-slaughter', while the idea of being transformed into 'dew' suggests a refreshment, something associated with new beginnings, not death. Hamlet's choice of the verb 'resolve' is also significant. He wants his situation resolved without actually having to take action himself and it is, of course, his lack of resolve to carry out revenge that is the play's central concern.

Thoughts of suicide may float about in anyone's mind during times of suffering and depression. However, things only become really serious if and when people start to make plans for how they are going to die. Hamlet seems far removed from this 'at danger' stage, at present. Notice too how quickly his thoughts move on to other more animating matters.

Hamlet's awareness of corruption is also displayed in lines 135 and 136 when he claims that Denmark is an 'unweeded garden/ That grows to seed, things rank and gross in nature/ possess it merely'. Hamlet shows his disgust for his uncle/father, Claudius, who as king, now 'possess[es]' Denmark, with the metaphor of an unweeded garden reflecting social disorder and disruption of the Great Chain of Being. 'Unweeded' foreshadows Hamlet's later sense of responsibility, as it will be up to him to restore the natural order by uprooting Claudius and clearing Denmark of corruption. The crucial metaphor of the 'unweeded garden' can also be linked to the ghost's later words: 'The serpent that did sting thy father's life/ Now wears his crown' [I.5] through the concept 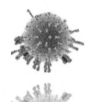 of Denmark as a ruined Eden, a paradise corrupted and destabilised by Claudius and his noxious sins. As well as evoking thoughts of Claudius' ill-gained status and linking to multiple images of disease throughout the play, the olfactory adjective 'rank' reveals foul corruption and expresses Hamlet's visceral disgust at Claudius and Gertrude's incestuous relationship. Meanwhile 'things' in this line both dehumanises the monarchs by referring to them as objects rather than people, and insults them, with 'thing' notorious Elizabethan slang for a phallus.

Hamlet idealises his dead father and establishes the stark contrast with Claudius. Describing his father as 'so excellent a king, that was to this/ Hyperion to a satyr', Hamlet refers to Claudius as 'this', rather than 'he', before establishing that he barely sees him as a man, let alone a worthy king. The Classical allusions to 'Hyperion' [the Greek God of the sun] when referring to his father and a 'satyr', a grotesque mythological half-man, half goat, associated with Dionysian excess, drunkenness and sexual debauchery, in reference to Claudius, highlight both the perceived difference between the two kings – one superhuman, the other subhuman, as well as Hamlet's fixation on Claudius' sexual relationship with Gertrude. The second classical allusion used to compare the two kings - 'My father's brother, but no more like my father/ than I to Hercules' - once more highlights Hamlet's view of Claudius' shortcomings, whilst self-deprecatingly comparing himself to Hercules, a hero and demi-god famous for physical strength and overcoming apparently impossible obstacles. This ironic allusion foreshadows Hamlet's later dilemma: As he acknowledges, he is not a natural action hero. In the face of a seemingly unsolvable predicament, unlike Hercules who is famed for the action he takes, Hamlet is paralysed by the moral quandary he faces and acts only on impulse and only when it is unavoidable. Notice too that these comparisons suggest that while Hamlet is unlike his father, he may be more like his uncle.

A third classical allusion is used to describe Gertrude at Old Hamlet's funeral as 'like Niobe, all tears'. The simile compares the Queen to a figure from Greek myth, referenced in Homer's *Iliad* and Ovid's *Metamorphoses*, whose grief was so extreme that Zeus took pity on her and turned her into a rock to relieve her of her suffering. But the rock continued to cry, creating a river. This image of ceaseless mourning reveals Gertrude's apparent devastation at the death of her husband, but is then juxtaposed with the wicked speed' with which she moves on. This raises three critical questions about Gertrude:

1. Was her grief genuine or was it an act?
2. If her grief was genuine, is she incredibly emotionally shallow?
3. If her grief was genuine, could she now be acting under duress of some sort?

For Hamlet his mother's behaviour highlights her apparent inconstancy. He believes that 'a beast that wants discourse of reason/ Would have mourned longer', focusing on the belief that Gertrude's hasty remarriage is unnatural. This 'little month' is shortened through further imagery, claiming that she remarried both 'ere those shoes were old/ With which she followed my poor

father's body' and 'Ere yet the salt of most unrighteous tears/ Had left the flushing in her galled eyes'. These hyperbolic comparisons reveal Hamlet's grief and outrage. The first refers to cloth or fine leather shoes worn by nobility that would wear out quickly, but implies that her grief is more short-lived even than these, while the second image implies that even as her eyes were still irritated by false tears for her dead husband,

she remarried. However, whilst criticising his mother for his actions, reflecting the attitudes of the period, Hamlet also appears to believe that Gertrude is not to blame. The famous apostrophe 'frailty, thy name is woman' reflects the misogynistic attitudes of the era, and appears to imply that all women are equally and innately inconstant, an attitude that is evident in his later abusive treatment of Ophelia.

Whilst a speedy remarriage like Gertrude's may seem shocking to a modern audience, it is worth noting that although it is not unreasonable for Hamlet to condemn his mother's remarriage as 'o'erhasty', it was common in this period for widows to remarry within a year as women were socially and financially dependent on men. For Gertrude it would have been the only way to maintain her status as queen. However, Hamlet also draws attention to his mother's sexual desires, describing with tactile intimacy how 'she would hang on [Old Hamlet]/ As if increase of appetite had grown/ By what it fed on', before, in the closing lines of the soliloquy, drawing attention to the 'incestuous sheets' of her new marriage bed. Although not forbidden by law, marrying a husband's brother [or brother's wife] is incestuous in the Judeo-Christian tradition and forbidden explicitly in both The Book of Common Prayer and Leviticus 18.16 and 21.21. In addition, Henry VIII, Queen Elizabeth's father, had to gain Papal Permission to marry Catherine of Aragon [his brother's widow] before later divorcing her on the grounds that to do so had been sinful. A contemporary audience would have been aware of this, which may have led to discomfort, mirroring the attitudes expressed by Hamlet. However, with awareness of Freud's reading of Hamlet, it is difficult not to attribute at least some of Hamlet's revulsion to jealousy as well as religious piety. Afterall, Hamlet feels revulsion, his disgust expressed in the spitting sibilance and plosives of 'O most wicked speed to post/ with such dexterity to incestuous sheets'. Notice too how the word 'dexterity' resonates in this context, forcing Hamlet to imagine his mother's physical agility in bed.

The soliloquy comes to a close with meiosis, with the claim that 'It is not [nor it cannot come to] good'. Watching a tragedy, the audience would have been aware of the heavy dramatic understatement of these words. Hamlet's grief and sense of abandonment are evident throughout his first soliloquy, as are themes that run throughout the play - betrayal, incest, misogyny, melancholy, mortality and the meaning of life. In this soliloquy, Shakespeare encourages us to feel sympathy for Hamlet - a confused young man whose heart is about to 'break', alone in his grief in a world that seems meaningless, cruel and corrupt after the unexpected death of his father.

Act II, Scene 2 - O what a rogue and peasant slave am I

Surely the dramatic crux of this, Hamlet's tonally disjointed second soliloquy comes about two thirds of the way through. Prompted by the first player's performance, Hamlet has been berating himself for the lack of progress he has made in striving for his revenge and analysing himself to try to find the single flaw within that might explain his inaction. The thought that he might be a coward prompts the Prince into working and winding himself up, talking himself into revenge, pumping himself up, like a boxer before a fight, with more and more violent, more inflated revenge rhetoric. This overheated, overblown rhetoric carries Hamlet away with its compelling momentum, swelling with intensity until a climactic crescendo in the apostrophe 'O vengeance!' The rest of this line is a blank – an embedded stage direction signalling a pause. It is a pause that implies Hamlet has inflated himself up as far as he can possibly go and only one thing can how happen. The following line is the prick that bursts the rhetoric balloon into shreds and sends a deflated Hamlet tumbling back to earth: 'O what an ass am I'. The tonal shift between these two lines could not be greater. In a nutshell they express Hamlet's condition. Fate has demanded that he has to try to talk himself into taking revenge, not agonizing about it, and while he can convince himself to do so, for moments at least, he is far too self-aware, too aware of acting and pretending, far too self-conscious to trick himself into the revenge role for long, and so he finds himself again self-reflecting, stuck with thoughts and words, not actions.

The soliloquy can be usefully broken down into nine mini sections, charting the build-up to the 'O vengeance' climax and back down again. The first section expresses Hamlet's response to the first player's tears and his consequent self-accusations. How can the actor emote so deeply for a mere fiction? Then, in the second section, Hamlet wonders what this actor would do if he had as much cause as the Prince has. In the third Hamlet contrasts the actor with his own inability to say or do anything. Is it because he's a coward he wonders in the fourth part? The fifth section overheats with the language of revenge, cooled immediately in the sixth and, typically of Hamlet's closed circuit pattern of thought, Hamlet is back berating himself – during the course of this soliloquy he calls himself a 'rogue', a 'peasant', a 'slave', a 'rascal', a 'villain', a 'coward' an 'ass' and a 'whore'. In the seventh section he accuses himself of prostituting his emotions with words. In the penultimate part of the soliloquy Hamlet forces himself to think rationally and then plans to use the play-within-the-play. This is only reasonable, he reflects in the final section as the Ghost is unreliable and Hamlet needs indisputable proof of Claudius' guilt before he can take his revenge. The couplet at the end lends the close of the soliloquy a sense of certainty and of definite resolution.

Linguistically, the most interesting sections are in the middle. After Hamlet has wondered whether cowardice prevented him from already having killed Claudius, his thinking and the pace of the soliloquy suddenly accelerate with a volley of short, emphatic rhetorical questions. Whereas in earlier sections of the soliloquy Hamlet had mulled over things one thought at a time, now his thinking takes on a rapid-fire, percussive urgency: 'Am I a coward?/ Who calls me villain? breaks my pate across?' Violent action verbs – 'breaks', 'plucks', 'blows', 'tweaks', – come in a rush, with the latter two given a little more emphasis by being placed at the starts of lines. The violence is also goading, intimate, personal, in and around Hamlet's face – 'pate', 'beard', 'nose', 'throat'. The volley of six unanswered questions culminates with the baffled 'who does me this'. Short, punchy monosyllables. Hamlet reacts as if flinching from actual blows with two quick angry exclamations, 'Ha!' and 'Swounds', the latter a shocking swearword in Elizabethan culture.

A brief pause, a lull in intensity, a moment of quieter reflection on his potential cowardice before the language of bitterness and poison ratchets up into the

most violent image so far. Typically for Hamlet, the viciousness depicted is of what he has not done: 'fatted all the regions kites/ with this slave's offal'. A grotesque image of Hamlet having slaughtered and eviscerated Claudius then violating the King's corpse by feeding his viscera to birds of prey; gross insult added to gross injury. The violence of this image might recall Macbeth's 'unseaming' of Macdonwald from the 'nave to the chaps' or the savagery of Titus Andronicus.

It certainly doesn't suit Hamlet. From him it sounds, false, inflated, hyperbolic.

Now Hamlet's imagination is really overheating, the revenge rhetoric sweeping him away on the wave of its own violent energies. Again a short percussive exclamation, '**Bloo**dy, **baw**dy **vill**ain', with the plosive alliteration and emphatic trochaic stresses leading into a run of three successive adjectives, each one sonically as much as semantically suggesting the next, each one upping the rhetorical ante a notch: '**Re**morseless, **treach**erous, **lech**erous'. Trochees accelerate into a three-beat scheme. But then there's another adjective 'kindless' before that word 'villain' again. The almost cartoonish excessiveness of these adjectives is enhanced by the metrical overload of the line. Composed of thirteen rather than ten syllables, this line also appears to have seven rather than five stresses. Unless that is the adjectives 'treacherous' and 'lecherous' are reduced to single syllables. That way would force an increase to the speed of the line, but would lose a little of the sibilant disgust. All these words form the runway to the final climactic fury of the apostrophe 'O vengeance!' which surely must be shouted and shouted with great brio by the actor playing Hamlet. Perhaps too accompanied by facial rictus, violent shaking of fists and some actual violence inflicted on the stage set.

How then to play the next line? It's such a huge tonal shift. Compare, for instance, the 'o' with the 'why'. The first is a long gathering of breath, building in intensity - ₒₒₒₒOO - like an excited crowd anticipating the entrance of a star turn. Here the star of the show is the huge, explosive release of the word 'VENGEANCE'. In contrast 'why' expresses deflation, disbelief and almost existential despair. In their versions, Kenneth Branagh and David Tennant both physically collapse at this line, falling down into a heap, the wind suddenly ripped from their rhetorical sails.

Even language it seems can also betray Hamlet. Even, indeed, and most troublingly his own language. Only after he descends into self-accusatory nonsense, the non-words - 'fie' and 'foh' – and his lines break into incoherent broken bits, reflecting the state of his thoughts, can he begin to put things back together again and arrive at a proper plan. Tellingly for a character so aware of acting and performance, who has just realised the ridiculousness of his own revenge performance, he settles on the idea of using theatre.

Before we move on from this soliloquy, a couple of other thoughts occur. Throughout the play Hamlet is very keen to distinguish himself from Claudius. Desperately, Hamlet wants to think of himself as being like his father and, like his father, the opposite to his uncle. But again and again Hamlet's words and actions link him to his uncle, not his father. In this soliloquy, for instance, Hamlet uses the insult 'slave' to describe both himself and his uncle, yoking them semantically together. That last adjective in the run of four in a row is also striking in this regard. While the other adjectives fit together the last one, which should surely be the strongest, seems less potent and less charged. Kindless? Maybe there's a small dip in intensity to allow 'villain' to hit home harder; a stronger adjective might take attention away from the cumulative noun. Perhaps. In any case, Hamlet may mean 'unkind', which would seem rather a low-level villainous quality [compare it with 'murderous' or perhaps 'sadistic'], but 'kindless' also echoes his first words in the play,' A little more than kin, and less than kind'. Even in his most inflated revenge rhetoric, Hamlet, it seems, has to insist on Claudius being different from him.

Act III, Scene 1 - To be or not to be

Hamlet's first two soliloquies are clearly immediate reactions to on-stage events. In the first Hamlet seeks escape from all the falsehoods of his uncle's court; in the second witnessing the actors prompts him to reflect on his own lack of passion. In contrast, his third soliloquy has no obvious external prompt, suggesting that Hamlet is becoming more lost in his own inner mental turmoil. This soliloquy also follows hard on the heels of his previous one. There is only one short scene and a few minutes of stage time between them. This adds to the impression that Hamlet's thoughts are overwhelming his powers to act, especially since his previous soliloquy had ended with apparent robust determination and a ringing final couplet. Clearly, this firm resolution has already become 'sicklied o'er with the pale cast of thought'.

Shakespeare's most famous soliloquy is one of existential doubt, confusion and a lack of resolution. We often think of Hamlet's dilemma being that of whether or not he should avenge his father, but in the aftermath of his encounter with the ghost, Hamlet feels cursed by fate, so the focus is also on his own existence and whether the act of taking his own life could end his suffering. The first line of the soliloquy reveals Hamlet's reasoned thinking. Unlike the previous two soliloquies, it reflects reason rather than passion and his whole dilemma is encapsulated by the dichotomy presented in the opening chiasmus 'To be, or not to be'. More ambiguous than often believed, 'the question' is both whether or not he should be alive and whether or not he should avenge his father. Either way, it involves balanced thinking and a final, irrevocable decision.

The next four lines echo this balance with lines 57 and 58 considering 'being' and continuing to 'suffer/ The slings and arrows of outrageous fortune' while lines 59 and 60 consider the possibility of 'not being' and the idea that he can end his torment. Shakespeare personifies 'fortune' or fate as an enemy. In Hamlet's mind, life is a battle and he feels attacked by his current existence and perceived fate, something impossible to resist. The only way for him to take action to defeat this immortal enemy appears to be death, as the only way to end his troubles is to end his life. Arguably, however, these lines show the futility of Hamlet's situation: the mixed metaphor of 'tak[ing] arms against a sea of troubles' may simply imply that his troubles are innumerable and an apparently overwhelming natural force which he must battle. Or, more cynically, since no human weapons can overcome a 'sea', the image suggests a flaw in Hamlet's belief that death would end his suffering.

Hamlet questions whether it is better to passively continue to live and suffer or to make the active decision to end his life. The comparative 'nobler' reflects Hamlet's dilemma, as he is questioning what best befits a man of his royal birth and attempting to find a preferable solution. But the fact that Shakespeare selects 'nobler' rather than the superlative highlights an issue that is central to the play. Hamlet is not an uncomplicated tragedy and Hamlet is not an uncomplicated hero: No clear right answer to his dilemma is presented to either the protagonist or the audience. Hamlet cannot do what is best or right as he is ensnared, here, as elsewhere in the play, between two conflicting ideologies. In this case, he is trapped between religion and revenge. Unable to resolve the contradictory impulses, instead he must aim for whichever is 'nobler' or closest to noble, identifying the lesser of the two evils he faces, deciding whether to live or 'take arms' and end his suffering, by ending either his own life or Claudius'.

As the soliloquy unfolds his thoughts, its focus moves unequivocally to suicide. It becomes clear that Hamlet really is considering ending his own life, not just briefly toying with it as he did in his first soliloquy. He dismisses death as 'no more' than sleep, and it becomes clear that if death could be guaranteed to be final and to give him closure then it would be highly desirable or, in fact [and perhaps sacrilegiously] 'devoutly to be wished'. He describes it as a 'consummation' - a perfect completion. The extended metaphor of sleep is then used to explore the implications of the afterlife as death. However, the anadiplosis in lines 63-64 marks the turning point. 'To die, to sleep, to sleep,

 perchance to dream...'. Increasingly Hamlet becomes aware that death may not be the escape, the oblivion he desires, and that this is what prevents him from taking his life. The 'rub' [a bowls metaphor for an obstacle that diverts the path that is being followed], or the obstacle which diverts Hamlet's plan to end his troubles, is the idea that death might not be the end. He identifies the fear of 'what dreams may come' and it is this that 'must give **us** pause' or delay action.

Throughout these lines, Hamlet's rhetorical questions persuade the audience that this speech is reasoned rather than emotional, even if we do not agree with his argument. He exemplifies the 'thousand natural shocks that flesh is heir to'. The synecdoche of 'flesh' links to 'must give **us** pause' in the previous line as it implies that the dilemma presented in this soliloquy is not just personal to Hamlet, but applicable to the whole of mankind, normalising 'natural shocks' that all 'flesh is heir to' - that all must suffer. Shakespeare uses a long, but diminishing list, beginning with the personified 'whips and scorns of time', which mixes physical with mental suffering, and encompassing the apparently trivial 'law's delay' and 'insolence of office' - minor inconveniences to those not already beset with grief. Hamlet refers to 'he' who 'might his quietus make' and uses plural pronouns to imply that this is the dilemma facing all those who are melancholic and suffer. The scale of human suffering and hyperbolic 'thousand natural shocks' is juxtaposed with the image of the bare bodkin'. A small dagger is all that is needed to end life, and it is implied that few would 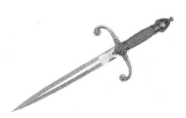 continue to suffer if they could find peace this way. 'Quietus' is primarily a release from life that allows someone to achieve peace, but also a legal term for settling a debt: Unless he avenges his father, although death is possible, 'quietus' in either sense is impossible for Hamlet.

Hamlet questions whether anyone would suffer the burdens of life unless they were scared of the afterlife, referring to 'the dread of something after death'. Hamlet fears a lack of certainty and the mysterious 'something' that 'puzzles the will' prevents him from acting - an idea that is prevalent throughout the play as Hamlet seeks a moral certainty that is absent from Elsinore. Death is poetically described as 'the undiscovered country, from whose bourn/ No traveller returns', but ironically, he has seen the ghost of his father, trapped in purgatory until he is avenged, a 'traveller' who, through necessity, has returned. This creates certainty that there is something after death and the 'ills we have' may not only not end with life, but in fact be much worse.

Hamlet again presents his experience in universal terms: 'conscience does make cowards of **us all**', a sentiment that applies equally to suicide and revenge. He equates conscience or morality with a lack of bravery, again showing the hopelessness of his situation. It is impossible to stick to his moral principles and to fulfil his desire to avenge or to die. Critics have suggested that 'conscience' here is not merely a sense of guilt, but also introspection and overthinking, qualities often attributed to Hamlet. Noticeably lacking from Hamlet's thinking about death is any sense of God and an afterlife in heaven. Here, as elsewhere in the play, he is expressing a new, modern religious scepticism befitting an Elizabethan intellectual. However, on the other hand, isn't there a religious aspect to 'conscience'? Despite his humanist doubts, a moral awareness of God's commandments may still prevent Hamlet from acting both to end his own life and Claudius'.

Hamlet suggests he is powerless to maintain 'resolution' when defined both as a solution to his problems and a sense of determination. The image 'thus the native hue of resolution/ Is sicklied o'er with the pale cast of thought', constructs thought as yet another disease blighting Elsinore and its inhabitants.

The passive construction also hides agency and adds to the sense that this is an occurrence over which Hamlet has no control. This is supported by the metaphor 'enterprises of great pitch and moment/ With this regard their currents turn awry/ And lose the name of action'. By making 'currents' the agent of the sentence, Shakespeare conveys Hamlet's sense of powerlessness. Rather than perceiving a loss of resolution as the result of outside influences, or of his own actions, he presents it as natural and universal that dramatic and significant plans and ideas, including revenge and suicide, will lose impetus through no fault of his own. Interrupted by Ophelia's entry, the soliloquy itself ends on a half line, reflecting the lack of resolution expressed, as the natural forces described, like Hamlet, 'lose the name of action' and fail to resolve.

To some, this soliloquy exemplifies Hamlet's core weaknesses: overthinking, making excuses for failure to act, believing himself to be helpless when he was not. However, this is one of the most famous pieces of Literature in English and this is not because audiences judge Hamlet, but because they empathise with him. Shakespeare's language allows us to understand a man who is attempting to deal with a situation that is not of his own making and who is fundamentally ill-suited to the task. He is also suffering and casting around for a solution to a situation for which one may not exist. Hamlet is relatable because this soliloquy reveals him to be an ordinary, intelligent man dealing with an extraordinary situation. It is easy to condemn Hamlet's indecision. But, remember his father has been murdered, his mother has married the murderer and nothing in his life makes sense. In this situation, would your response really be any different? And, lest we forget, there is also the overarching issue of whether revenge is ever just.

Act III, Scene 2 – Now could I drink hot blood

The mood, tone and style of this short soliloquy is very different from the philosophical musings of Hamlet's previous one. As we've noted already and will continue to note, no doubt, there's a circular pattern to the play, or perhaps a two steps forwards one step backwards motion and especially so for Hamlet himself. His language here, for instance, is closer to his 'bloody, bawdy villain – O vengeance' idiom than it is to the reflective 'to be or not to be'. Like the earlier 'peasant rogue and slave' soliloquy, this one falls roughly into two halves with the language of the first half completely at odds with that in the second.

The night-time setting is appropriate, of course, for a speech about the doing of the darkest of deeds. We might recall Macbeth heading across his castle to  murder the innocent Duncan in his sleep. Hamlet uses similarly gothic language to Macbeth here, as he contemplates exacting his terrible revenge. 'Now', he says 'is the very witching hour of night' almost conjuring up the atmosphere himself of midnight nefariousness, 'when churchyards yawn and hell itself breathes out/ Contagion to this world'. Spooky stuff indeed. The churchyards are asleep, like all good things of day, drooping and drowsing; this is the time for witches and witchcraft to do their wicked worst. This foggy, benighted world has been poisoned by the breath of a hell that has come eerily to life while goodness slumbers. Dialling the gothic rhetoric up to full gothic horror, Hamlet even imagines himself in vampiric mode, 'Now could I drink hot blood'. Hot in the sense, presumably, of fresh from a newly killed corpse.

Hamlet seems an unlikely drinker of hot blood. Clearly, he can only keep up this sort of exaggerated dark revenger rhetoric for a few lines before casting it off with a swirl of his dark gothic cape. To put it mildly, Hamlet calling revenge 'bitter business' and associating it with night, darkness, hell, witches and monsters suggests he might be harbouring doubts about its virtues. The gothic language he uses here echoes the descriptions of Pyrrhus and Lucianus and anticipates the imagery Laertes will use later in Act IV.

There's another huge tonal shift starting with 'soft' and continued with the plaintive 'o heart'. This change is so abrupt that some critics have wondered whether this soliloquy has been cobbled together from two separate speeches, with the first half sounding like something from an earlier, cruder revenge tragedy. The second half does little more than tell us what is going to happen, although it does include another reference to classical culture and feature the memorable injunction to 'speak daggers' but use none, which it turns out is rather ironic.

Act III, Scene 3 – Now could I do it pat

This soliloquy comes hard on the heels of the last one. The proximity means we are brought closest to Hamlet's thoughts during these crucial central episodes in the play. It's also immediately preceded by Claudius' soliloquy. There's dramatic irony here, as the audience knows what Hamlet does not, specifically that Claudius is not actually praying, as Hamlet supposes, because he's unable to do so honestly.

'To make anything very terrible,' Edmund Burke wrote in his famous essay on the sublime, 'obscurity seems in general to be necessary. When we know the full extent of a danger, when we can accustom out eyes to it, a great deal of the apprehension vanishes'. Burke opined that the 'heightening' of 'terrible things' is best achieved by 'the force of a judicious obscurity'. A hundred and fifty years earlier, Shakespeare, it seems, was well aware of the benefits of such obscurity. When Macbeth is considering murdering Duncan, for instance, he says, 'If it were done when 'tis done, then 'twere well/ It were done quickly'. Shakespeare understood when a device worked well and recycled many of this best ones many times over. The use of the vague, innocuous euphemism 'it' and the deceptively easy and straightforward verb 'done', in place of more precise words, such as 'murder' and 'kill' in *Macbeth* [1606] is anticipated by its earlier use in a similar scenario here in *Hamlet*.

For a character with a sophisticated, philosophical vocabulary and poetic turn of phrase, Hamlet's language at the start of this speech is strikingly simple and starkly straightforward:

'Now might I do it pat, now he is praying;
And now I'll do't. And so he goes to heaven;
And so am I revenged. That would be scann'd'

The first nine words are monosyllables. About 90% of the words in the three lines are monosyllables. These simple, basic words are also repeated close together – 'now', 'do', 'I', 'and'. Adding to the effect, Hamlet's thoughts are pieced together by the simplest possible conjunction. As with Macbeth the simple and euphemistic 'do' and 'it' stand in for the more troubling specifics. The 'it' Hamlet is contemplating 'doing' is murdering a man in cold blood by stabbing him in the back with a sword while he is praying. 'It' and 'do' mask and obscure the real, terrible nature of the act.

These opening lines crackle with tension. Not only is Hamlet tense, on the verge it seems of murder, but so too is the audience anticipating this. The tension is reflected in Hamlet's words, both in the semantic torsion between the words themselves and particularly between their meanings and their form. The adverb, 'now', for instance is repeated obsessively as if it is an imperative, and it means, insistently, at this very moment in time. But Hamlet's verbs describing the murder are doubtfully conditional ['might'] and imagine action taken in the future ['will']. While the overall meaning of these lines might be glossed as something like 'right, now I'm going to kill him' their form undermines the sense of definite and resolute action. The metre of the first two lines, for example, skips over the active agent, the 'I' doing the action, while landing more heavily on thoughts that Hamlet doesn't really want to examine, such as '**pray**ing' and '**heav**en'. In fact, these lines are markedly hesitant: Five words, pause - four words, pause – four words, pause - six words, pause – five words, pause – four words, pause. The uncertain, start-stop movement of the lines is a micro diagram in syntax of Hamlet's actions in the play as a whole.

Having apparently decided to act, by the end of the third line the only definite thing is that Hamlet is having doubts already. The verb 'scanned' introduces us to Hamlet's rational mind at work on the inner logic of his problem. It's like an equation he can't quite solve in the way he wants: A father murdered by a murderer goes to the son murdering the murderer + murdering the murderer at prayer ≠ equal revenge.

Tellingly, Hamlet's depiction of his father here is at odds with the idealised picture he creates elsewhere in the play. Rather than a god-like paragon, Old Hamlet is described as dying 'with all his crimes broad blown'. Perhaps this explains why Old Hamlet appears to be in purgatory and not in heaven. Quite how Hamlet killing Claudius will help him to reach heaven is not clear. Anyhow, Hamlet is appalled by the thought that he might end up inadvertently sending his uncle to heaven. The empty spaces in the speech after both 'to heaven' and the bluntly emphatic 'no' signal long pauses, suggestive silences into which we are to imagine Hamlet staring deeply. The imperative 'up sword' marks thought turning into action or, in fact, in action. It's an embedded stage direction that retrospectively tells the actor that Hamlet's sword has been drawn either before or at some earlier point in the scene.

Finally, Hamlet decides that he must kill Claudius at a more appropriate time, such as when the King is stewed in his sins. Unsurprisingly, Hamlet's mind turns to his uncle's corruption, and, firstly, to corruption through alcohol and incest. As it will time and again in the play, the way in which revenge is conceptualised here raises more troubling questions than it resolves: Hamlet's description of desiring his uncle's 'heels' to 'kick at heaven' before he plunges down to hell suggests sadistic cruelty. How much suffering does the criminal need to experience, we may wonder, for justice to be served?

Two familiar image clusters close the soliloquy. Both amplify the sense that while Hamlet might sound certain and definite, doubts, worries and complexities circle just below the conscious surface of his words. Hamlet imagines hell as 'black' and while this colour is obviously linked to villainy and foul deeds, such as the black 'spots' on Gertrude's soul, references to it in this play are often rather ambiguous. Think, for instance, of Pyrrhus' black 'purpose' and Lucianus' 'thoughts black'. We need to remember Pyrrhus is an avenger and Lucianus is a nephew. Moreover, Hamlet himself is dressed all in black, at least in Act I, Scene 2, where the colour symbolises grief, not villainy.

Similarly there's ambiguity in Hamlet's closing reference to disease: 'This physic but prolongs thy sickly days'. Overtly, this means that delaying the administration of the medicine of revenge will prolong Claudius unhealthy life. But, it also seems to mean the opposite, i.e. 'this medicine only prolongs your sickly days'. No wonder then that when he tries his hardest to be definite Hamlet tends to use the simplest words, though even these often betray him.

Act IV, Scene 4 – My thoughts be bloody

A director will have to decide where each of Hamlet's soliloquies takes place. Following the display of state craft in Act I, Scene 2, it seems natural for Hamlet to deliver his first soliloquy in the same state room where Claudius has so recently been addressing the gathered members of his court. Using the same stage space will help emphasise the completely different type of drama taking place. The 'To be, or not to be' soliloquy requires space for Hamlet's most expansive and deepest thoughts and takes place in the same space where Hamlet meets Ophelia, whereas 'O what a rogue and peasant slave' is preceded with the line 'now I am alone' which suggests a more private space, such as an anteroom or Hamlet's own study.

In the Kenneth Branagh film version of *Hamlet* this soliloquy takes place on a vast snowy plain with a chain of mountains behind. As the soliloquy nears its end the camera pulls back, zooming out to depict the small, dark-coated figure of Hamlet almost shouting his speech so that it reverberates within the epic landscape. Declaiming the soliloquy as if to an audience, like a rousing call-to-arms, reminiscent of Henry V before Agincourt, Hamlet's words are accompanied by the film's suitably stirring theme music which builds to a dramatic crescendo as the soliloquy finishes. In stark contrast to the intense nervous energy of previous soliloquies, where Hamlet is depicted as always restlessly on the move, forwards and backwards, Branagh stays entirely still while he delivers this soliloquy. What is it about this soliloquy that suggested such a different treatment?

Its content reprising many of the thoughts and feelings that Hamlet has often expressed in his other soliloquies, this soliloquy feels summative. Typically,

Hamlet is going back once again over old, familiar ground. The subjects he puzzles over here are:

1. The sense that fate is conspiring against him
2. The nature of man
3. Why he hasn't already carried out his revenge
4. Whether cowardice is the true cause of this delay
5. How the example of other people - here soldiers, earlier on actors - shame and prompt him to revenge
6. Arriving at a determination to take action.

As in his other soliloquies, Hamlet interrogates himself and asks questions – in this soliloquy there are four questions. So what's different this time? This final soliloquy seems more settled and measured, more rational, less emotionally driven, less frenetic and fragmentary. Rather than coming in fits and starts, with a restless stop-start motion, the subjects and lines lead naturally from each other and unfold in a coherent, logical sequence. Gone are the violent shifts in tone and topic common in his earlier thoughts. Nor is there any of the hyperbolic gothic imagery. This seems a calmer and more rational Hamlet.

A greater poise is evident too in the forward driving syntax and in complete line after complete line not fragmented by caesuras. Count the number of syllables in each line and you'll also discover nearly every single line has the regular ten present and correct. Mostly too, the metre runs smoothly with a regular iambic pentameter.

This soliloquy also feels more rhetorical. A sense of an audience being addressed is signalled with the invitation to 'witness this army of such mass and charge' and the predominantly interrogative mode of Hamlet's previous soliloquies is supplanted here, with the regular metre reinforcing a newly assured and decisively declarative tone:

' ...Rightly to be great

Is **not** to **stir** with**out** great **argum**ent,
But **greatly to** find **quarrel in** a **straw**
When **honour**'s **at** the **stake**.'

Hamlet may sound more resolute and determined here, but we have had smaller patches of similar language within other soliloquies, particularly at their conclusions. Often this more resolute language has, however, been undermined the next time we see or hear Hamlet. What's different here is the sustained resolute quality in this soliloquy and the fact that, as it's his last, he makes good on his promise; we will actually see him taking action the next time he appears in Act V. However, this more confident tone doesn't mean Hamlet is coming to the right conclusions necessarily. His description of the martial Fortinbras, for instance, as 'delicate and tender' seems like a projection, wide of the mark: Future events will suggest an entirely different Fortinbras.

From a modern, particularly post WWI perspective, it's also impossible to agree with Hamlet that it is honourable and admirable for 20,000 men to be led to the slaughter over a little patch of worthless land. Memorably the

Victorian poet Tennyson wrote of a doomed cavalry charge that 'theirs [was] not to reason why/ their's but to do and die', but few of us now would agree with the idea of such unquestioning obedience and self-sacrifice. For modern readers, the futile deaths of thousands of men cannot help recall the attritional warfare of the WWI trenches and the many thousands of men killed moving backwards and forwards across land reduced to rubble and mud.

Even though this is Hamlet's most rousing soliloquy, it functions more like a speech and a call-to-arms at that. Although the closing couplet gives it a decisive ring, there's still some typical Hamlet ambiguity. Crucially, even at his most decisive, it's still his 'thoughts' that are going to be 'bloody' and not necessarily his 'actions'.

Claudius's soliloquy

Images of illness, blight, corruption and malady infect the whole play. Think of all the references to things rotten, rank and foul. Sometimes these images concentrate within the human body or the body politic, within the country or even the time, presenting each of these as being fundamentally ill or 'out of joint'. Think, for instance, of Ophelia's madness or her description of Hamlet's disordered mind as being 'out of tune'. In this soliloquy we learn that even the head of the body politic, the King, is fundamentally dislocated, his mind knotted in irresolvable conflict with itself, arguably implying that here can be found the prime source of all Elsinore's corruption and out-of-jointness.

As we shall discuss in our essay on Claudius, this soliloquy humanises him. Giving him a rich interiority only hinted at previously and, crucially revealing a conscience, it fleshes him out from a two-dimensional villain. Like Hamlet, in his own way Claudius is caught in a bind. While he admits his crime was 'rank'

 and says it 'smells to heaven', connecting it to a wider pattern of olfactory imagery of corruption in the play and punning ironically on 'rank', despite his dire need for it, he finds himself unable to pray for forgiveness. To his credit, Claudius does not shy away from acknowledging the heinous nature of his crime. Tempting as it might be, he doesn't seek to hide its horror in euphemism. Instead, he uses franker, more honest, more moral language. As well as recognising its moral stench, Claudius alludes to Cane and Abel in his reference to the 'prime eldest curse' and bluntly uses the word 'murder'. At least, we might think, he is speaking the truth to himself and indirectly to us.

Several images powerfully convey Claudius' self-conflict: He says his, 'stronger guilt defeats his strong intent' and that he is a man in 'double business bound'. He feels trapped, incapacitated by conflicting currents of thought, and so, like Hamlet, uncertain how he can proceed, he pauses, hesitates, tries to think his way out.

His desperate desire for absolution is communicated through an image Shakespeare recycles and develop in *Macbeth* – the washing of bloody hands. Claudius is not quite as despairing as Lady Macbeth. His 'is there not rain enough in heaven' to 'wash' his hand 'white as snow' is couched as a rational question. Indeed, like Hamlet, Claudius's dominant mode in this soliloquy is interrogative. As Hamlet questions some fundamental Christian principles, such as the idea of salvation in the afterlife, here Claudius ruminates on the nature of prayer and of mercy.

Claudius reasons that the function of prayer must be 'twofold'; to prevent us from committing sins or to absolve us if we have committed sin and feel remorse. This line of thought leads him to the hopeful conclusion that he should therefore be able to 'look up' to heaven. Almost immediately, however, he sees the knotty flaw therein. How can he pray sincerely for forgiveness unless he feels remorse and is prepared to give up his ill-gotten gains? While on earth, he might be able to get away with this because 'offense's gilded hand may shove by justice', heaven's laws are fixed and just. A final reckoning will have to be made and reward and punishment dished out accordingly. Claudius' imagination makes this reckoning acutely real and present; to heaven we will be forced to give evidence 'even to the teeth and forehead of our faults', i.e. face-to-face with God.

The impasse, the dead-end line of these thoughts, arrives at a series of short, stunted and anguished questions: 'What then?'; 'What rests'; 'what can it not?' Despite his clear and logical thinking, Claudius is unable to answer these urgently pressing questions and instead plunges into a series of self-pitying lamentations, beginning with 'O wretched state'. Again, another image of conflict is located within the King's body. While he describes his bosom as 'black as death' [obviously the opposite colour symbolism to the white snow mentioned earlier] his soul is trapped within it, 'limed', like a bird within a cage. Moreover, the more it struggles to free itself the more trapped it becomes. The mind too seems to at odds with the body. Claudius has to command his 'stubborn' knees to bend in supplication and his heart to 'soften'. His final words express hope more than expectation, and are dramatically ironic: Just as he says this hope, Hamlet enters the scene.

Critical essays on characters

There are dangers in providing exemplar essays. Inadvertently, such exemplars can close down the space for your own thinking and encourage uncritical regurgitation of an essay's content in examinations. Our essays were not written in timed, examination conditions and they are not examples of what an examination board would expect from any student in those conditions. Hence, primarily, our essays are not designed as model answers. Moreover, fundamentally we don't believe there can be one model answer to literary questions. Instead, we contend that the best essays express pupils' own critical thinking and opinions, aided by their teachers and informed by engagement with other readers. Hence our aim in the following essays is to provoke, stimulate and inform your own thinking about the play's major characters and make you reflect more critically on their roles and functions.

Hopefully, our essays will make you think again, perhaps even make you think differently. Sometimes you may also encounter readings with which you disagree. Good; so long as you can explain and justify why you have come to different conclusions. You may also find our writers offer slightly different shades of interpretations in these essays. Again, good, particularly if you can evaluate these differences and decide where you own opinions lie. Whether you mostly agree with the interpretations or not, these essays should, however, provide plenty of information you can digest, ponder, alter, reformulate and contest in your own words.

Remember when you are writing about characters to try to lift your perspective above the character-level action of who said what and who did what to the author-level perspective of why these words and actions are significant.

Hamlet & me

I've sat down to write this essay several times, but somehow keep putting it off. That may be a rather weak joke, but it's also true. Because what can anyone say about Hamlet that hasn't already been said and said better by many major critics of the play? *Hamlet* is one of the most written about plays in the whole of the literary canon and, as we've already established, for many critics Hamlet himself is its most compelling feature. An overview or survey of critical opinions about the Prince, charting how these have changed over time, from contemporary responses to the Romantics' over-identification with Hamlet [William Hazlitt claimed sweepingly that 'we' are all Hamlets] up to the present day and modern criticism of his less winning characteristics, such as his misogyny, might be helpful. But this material has been covered here and there throughout this guide and similar information can also be found elsewhere. So, instead of a formal essay, we're going to offer a more personal perspective on the literary world's greatest gloomy, poetic procrastinator.

A personal response isn't a mere indulgence, by the way, nor is it unacademic or irrelevant. Reflecting on how we, individually, respond to the play and interpret aspects such as the character of Hamlet is vital part of the assessment at A-level, a part sometimes overlooked by students. Currently, it is assessed through AO3: Students should 'demonstrate understanding of the significance and influence of the contexts in which literary texts are written and *received*' [our italics]. In our own times and places - schools, classrooms, theatres and at home - with our unique individual life experiences, we ourselves are vital contexts of interpretation. And our contexts are just as important in the process of meaning making from the text as the Elizabethan world or theories of tragedy.

Before developing this personal response further, however, we need to establish a few key points about Hamlet: Firstly, as the range of critical responses to him suggest, and as he himself seems to understand, there are many different Hamlets. Not only does the character have many shadow selves within the play, most obviously Laertes and Fortinbras, but he also plays so many different roles and parts – son, heir, prince, malcontent, lover, satirist, friend, revenger, madman and so forth - that Hamlet struggles continually to distinguish a separate sense of self behind or under all his acting. As Simon Palfrey has written, 'Hamlet can be understood as an actor never at one with his part'.[26] But that suggests a more stable, integrated identity than Hamlet really possesses. For it is not just the fact that he is like an actor, nor only the roles he plays, that define his identity. How different characters perceive him, what Hamlet says, what he does, how different audiences and readers respond, how different actors portray him and how Hamlet thinks and how he thinks about himself generates a hall of dizzying mirrors, multiple reflections from which it is impossible to distinguish a true, singular, authentic Hamlet. Moreover, the play's action divides Hamlet fundamentally against himself; some roles are mutually exclusive, most notably those of pious Christian and bloody avenger. It is not possible for Hamlet to integrate these irreconcilable roles into one coherent sense of self. In fact, the figure we call Hamlet is composed of so many fragments from so many different perspectives that he is like the most radical of cubist paintings.

I first came across Hamlet studying A-level English Literature at school in the sixth form. This was in the late 1980s, at the height of Thatcherism and during

---

[26] Palfrey, *Doing Shakespeare*, p.280.

a decade and more of Conservative government. My school was an all-boys comprehensive with a general, unstated bias towards maths and the sciences and deep distrust of non-conformity. The area I lived in was an attractive, prosperous, conventional small town in the South East of England, though to my teenage self it seemed to be a cultural abyss and the perfect definition of absolutely nowhere.

Against this dull and mundane backdrop, Hamlet seemed dazzlingly brilliant, able to express in majestic and moving poetry a complexity of feeling and thought beyond anything else I had read, seen or heard. Like a teenager, Hamlet was also acutely uncertain and self-conscious, questioning every idea he had inherited, trying to think his way to a new and different understanding of himself and the world. Angry at the cruel injustices of the world and the waste of human potential, he was also raging, albeit rather ineffectively, against the machine of the Danish state. Although there was, of course, an unbridgeable, comical gulf between Hamlet's huge tragic world of court intrigue, murder and revenge and my own petty provincial teenage problems, he seemed a cleverer, sharper, deeper-thinking, more eloquent, braver, more charismatic version of the sort person I thought I wanted to become. I felt I understood and shared his existential despair. Hamlet, it seemed, was the ultimate version of a familiar character type we often venerate in our culture;

 the tortured artistic genius, teetering on the edge of brilliant madness. And my teenage self thought, yep, that's how I'd like to be. Thinking of a fictional character as a real person is considered a naïve sort of category error in literary studies, but Hamlet seemed larger-than-life to me and glamorous, albeit in a gloomy, gothicky kind of way. It helped too that Hamlet looked pretty cool. Or, rather, the dashingly handsome Laurence Olivier looked pretty cool as Hamlet in the moody film version we watched in class. Despite being in black and white, Hamlet shone brightly.

Politically, socially and economically, England in the 1980s was a deeply divided country. While some sections of society were prospering though the economic liberalisation of Thatcherism like never before, getting rich and getting rich quickly, other parts of society were struggling to cope with the breakdown of the post WWII social contract. To a tentatively bohemian, literary-minded student from a comfortably middle-class background, a student who had never had to earn a penny in his life, capitalism, or at least the free market kind espoused with a fervour of religious converts by the most ardent Thatcherites, seemed merciless, destructive and fundamentally unjust – something worth fighting against, if only via the medium of angry guitar songs. Additionally, Thatcher's Britain, or at least what I saw of it, seemed angry and ill-at-ease with itself, an often ugly, often philistine place, where the only language anyone really listened to was the language of money. Everything in life, it seemed, was being commercialised. Greed was not only considered good, gluttony was often admired. Self-interest, or actual selfishness, trumped selflessness. Compassion was often disdained as sentimentality or soft-heartedness. English nationalism too often reared its ugly head, shaming the nation through hooliganism at events such as England football games. Members of the British government were even sympathetic to the apartheid regime in South Africa and decried Nelson Mandela as a terrorist. In short, this was the sort of brutal, unjust and heartless society that made many young people like me feel depressed and alienated, angry and fundamentally at odds with the world.

But, other than forming a band and writing some angry, self-righteous lyrics and listening to equally angry or gloomy music, what could teenagers do to change society for the better? Very little, it seemed. And so Hamlet's righteous indignation at the sordid iniquities of Elsinore and the 'insolence of office' echoed my own anger and alienation, while his inability to carry out the task of cleansing his country of its corruption mirrored my sense of helplessness and futility. He was the underdog, the individual fighting an oppressive state. Naturally I was on his side. Probably too, like Hamlet, I rather enjoyed languishing in my self-righteous misery. Probably too I tended to be rather blinkered and partial, simplifying and caricaturing everything I opposed – mainstream, conformist society, the Tory government and the Prime Minister - as brutish and villainous. There was also something rather theatrical and posed about my rather small-scale rebellion against society. Mainly I dressed almost always in black.

The young are also, often, winningly idealistic. When Hamlet spoke of the great wonders of the world and of the awesome potential of human beings to be like gods he struck a chord in my impressionistic teenage heart. I believed in the potential of human beings to be good and kind and decent and generous-hearted. I believed in the potential of society to become better and fairer. I believed in the obligation to try to leave the world a better place than you found it. England in the late 1980s may have appeared to me to be an unweeded garden where things rank and gross in nature were doing very well indeed, thank you very much, but underneath the concrete and the shopping malls it was still a garden, with the potential to become again a healthy, nurturing place. The heavens, fretted with golden fire, may have been obscured by foul and pestilent vapours, but the heavens were still there, only temporarily obscured. Political winds could change. The world was charged with potential. But where in life could meaning, purpose and beauty be found? Where could something to believe in more than just making a quick buck be located? In the natural world, in music, in friends and the opposite sex, of course, and in books. Literature and, in particular, poetry and Shakespeare's poetic drama had power and beauty. And the most powerful, most magnetic, awesome figure in the little literature I had read was Hamlet, Prince of Denmark.

Remarkable as it may seem now, I don't remember at school, in my all male class with my male teachers ever noticing, let alone discussing, let alone  condemning Hamlet's unhealthy, probably misogynistic, attitude towards women. Rather sharing Hamlet's disdain for old men keen to impose their tired and self-interested worldviews on the young, I don't remember either having much ethical trouble with Hamlet's dispatching of Polonius, nor with the lack of remorse he shows for this killing. Polonius, it seemed to me, was an apparatchik of a despotic regime and so didn't deserve much pity. Things can also be more black-and-white when we are young. And our close friends at this age are incredibly important. Hence Rosencrantz and Guildenstern's betrayal and their obsequious lackeydom to a corrupt court meant that, for me, they got what they asked for. Hamlet doesn't always behave well, of course, that I would have acknowledged. His treatment of Ophelia, in particular, seemed horribly cruel and humiliating. However, the fact that as well as having intoxicating qualities Hamlet also had flaws only humanised him. Among these flaws I didn't, however, count his delay in murdering Claudius. To me, Hamlet thinking hard and seeking conclusive proof before killing someone was entirely to his credit. Compare this to Laertes.

Coming back to *Hamlet* decades later, now older than the Prince, teaching the play to classes of boys and girls, it is obvious that my teenage reading of his character was too partial and sentimental, too wowed by his stellar qualities and too blind to his myriad faults. That put in me in some good company, however, with many male critics historically overidentifying with Hamlet and losing their critical distance. Though he is alienated and rages against the state, I'm no longer sure, either, that Hamlet had a very radical social agenda or can really be seen as a champion of the poor.

At least one influential critic has, however, suggested that Hamlet is a kind of proto-Marxist, a mouthpiece for Shakespeare's radical sympathy with the

dispossessed. What evidence could be cited to support this claim? Hamlet certainly expresses hostility towards the Danish state and its officials, whereas he mixes comfortably with various commoners, such as the guards, the actors and the gravediggers. The fact that he also

compares himself to a 'peasant slave' has also been presented as evidence. However, unlike that other great tragic protagonist, King Lear during his transformational storm scenes, Hamlet doesn't express any pity for, or sympathy with, the poor. Nor does he offer any cutting criticisms of the institutions of the state, such as the law, or imply that he is likely to reform them. Does Hamlet want to dismantle the monarchy and develop a more democratic, let alone a more Marxist, Denmark? Seems highly unlikely. Shakespeare emphasises time and again how Hamlet admires his father, worships him in fact as a paragon of Kingship. Hamlet also admires Fortinbras and is impressed by the idea that thousands of innocent men will be slaughtered when there is a question of honour at stake. While he does mix easily with the commoners, that could be interpreted as an aristocratic virtue and he is as likely to express elitist as egalitarian sentiments, such as when he

 refers to great plays as 'caviar' for the general. When Hamlet returns to Denmark from his rather improbable pirate escapade, he announces himself at Ophelia's funeral as 'Hamlet, the Dane' [V.1,260], asserting that he is the rightful king; an odd move for a Marxist. He may, indeed, compare himself to a 'peasant slave', but he is scorning himself as such, and couples this phrase with the derogatory word 'rogue'. Elsewhere Hamlet compares himself to many other things, such as a 'stallion' and a 'whore',

but only in visceral self-disgust. It seems improbable that in these instances he is expressing any radical sympathy with prostitutes. Surely Hamlet feels such hostility towards the Danish state not because the way in which it is constructed is iniquitous, unfair to the poor and destitute, but because it is being led by Claudius and his cronies. Put his father or himself on the throne and Hamlet's passion for social form would surely disappear.

As Simon Palfrey notes, the word 'Hamlet' is repeated more than eighty times in the play, far more than any other character in any of Shakespeare's plays[27]. So Shakespeare too seems to have been rather obsessed with his protagonist. Of course, many critics have been preoccupied by Hamlet's procrastination. As Kiernan Ryan puts it, 'it's hard to resist the conclusion most critics have drawn, which is that the main cause of the whole tragic train of events is Hamlet's compulsion to postpone. And for those who assume that to be the case, all that remains is to crack the conundrum with which the play confronts them: why does Hamlet delay?'[28] But, for me, despite the changes to how I have perceived Hamlet over the decades from when first encountering him to

---

[27] Palfrey, *Doing Shakespeare*, p.66.

[28] www.bl.uk/shakespeare/articles/hamlet-and-revenge.

now, despite the fact that his faults are more starkly apparent and profound, and despite the idea of being a tortured genius teetering on the edge madness now seeming a rather less attractive and unrealistic career option, there is still something glamorous and entrancing about this embattled, emotionally volatile character, wrestling with himself and the world, raging against hypocrisy and shallowness, skewering others with the sharpness of his wit. Moreover, Hamlet is given by Shakespeare the capacity to express himself and his situation in lines of extraordinary, heart-aching, unforgettable beauty.

Shakespeare is, as Ben Jonson puts it, 'not for an age but for all time'. His works survive because they are infinitely adaptable, their characters, dilemmas, and political challenges malleable to multiple contexts. Shakespeare's plays have lengthy afterlives in adaptations and they seem to speak to moments in time other than their own. Thinking of your own responses to *Hamlet* and, especially, Hamlet, how might he be relevant to your present moment? What political and individual issues does the play speak to now?

Claudius

At first glance, Claudius appears to be the archetypal 'bad guy' – the villain to Hamlet's hero. Having murdered Hamlet's father out of ambition and lust, he spends most of the play seeking to murder Hamlet himself. 'Something's rotten in the state of Denmark,' complains the guard, Marcellus, in Act I – surely, it must be Claudius. Surely, he is the evil at the heart of a corrupt system, and once Hamlet has killed him, all will be well once more in Elsinore.

Despite being outlawed in England in Shakespeare's time, the writings of Niccolò Machiavelli [1469-1527] were widely circulated, and Claudius is a textbook Machiavellian prince; an ambitious and ruthless man who uses underhand and unheroic means to achieve selfish ends. As Claudius says in his soliloquy, 'I am still possess'd/ Of those effects for which I did the murder / – My crown, mine own ambition, and my queen' [III.3,54-55]. Repeatedly he uses poison, the weapon of the Machiavellian villain: To murder Old Hamlet; to taint Laertes' sword – a sword which should be a symbol of traditional values of honourable revenge – as well as in the cup of wine he intends Hamlet

to drink in Act V. Contaminating other characters with his corruption – Gertrude, Rosencrantz and Guildenstern, and Laertes – Claudius runs a surveillance state and secretly orders the cold-blooded execution of Hamlet. As Old Hamlet told his son, 'A serpent stung me, so the whole ear of Denmark/ is, by a forged process of my death/ rankly abused'. In light of all this, it is hard to disagree with Hamlet, that Claudius is a 'smiling damned villain' – murderous, treacherous, guilty, and, like the serpent in the Garden of Eden, evil.

On the other hand, as much as Hamlet might like to think of himself and Claudius as 'mighty opposites', they are not so much opposites as mirror images. In many ways, Claudius and Hamlet are very alike: Both are highly perceptive and are quick with words; both are more thinkers than fighters – Hamlet spends the vast proportion of the play vacillating on his course of action and uses the ruse of the play-within-a-play to confirm Claudius' guilt, while Claudius deals with the threat from a returning and enraged Laertes not with weapons, but with nothing other than some well-chosen words. Both Hamlet and Claudius apparently love Gertrude, both are overshadowed by Old Hamlet and both have either killed a king, or seek to do so. Indeed, an Oedipal reading of the play suggests that Hamlet hesitates from killing Claudius exactly because of their too-close similarities and desires. In this sense, Shakespeare's depiction of Hamlet and Claudius is another example of the mirroring which is so characteristic of his play: multiple revenging sons, two mad lovers and even two Hamlets.

In terms of his character development, Claudius' soliloquy in Act III, Scene 3, is key. Up until this point in the play, there has been no overt indication that Claudius feels any moral qualms about his actions, other than one brief aside. The only character other than Hamlet to be given an opportunity to bare their soul to the audience, in his soliloquy, Claudius debates with himself in strikingly similar ways to how Hamlet expresses his inner conflicts about revenge and suicide. Inevitably, his soliloquy humanises Claudius for the audience and he graduates from a cardboard villain to a nuanced, complex character in his own right. By giving a soliloquy to the 'bad guy', Shakespeare complicates the traditional form of the 'revenge tragedy'. The Claudius we see in the soliloquy is not a heartless murderer nor a serpentine embodiment of evil. What we see and hear is a man tortured by what he has done and who cannot see a way out of his predicament.

The soliloquy puts paid to a black and white perception of Hamlet as morally superior to Claudius, particularly to a predominantly more religious audience such as the Elizabethans. Hamlet is full of doubts about death and the afterlife, and at no point does he seem to have an orthodox faith in a Christian heaven, either Protestant or Catholic, to be reached through faith and confession of sins. Claudius, by contrast, seeks forgiveness, calling on angels for help. Arguing back and forth about the nature of divine forgiveness, his soliloquy is theological in content. In contrast, Hamlet considers revenge with little reference to a religious standpoint. The soliloquy also reveals Claudius' active conscience; arguably far more active, in fact, than Hamlet's. Hamlet, when asked about engineering the deaths of his two old school-friends, Rosencrantz and Guildenstern, says only that 'they are not near my conscience'. Moreover, straight after Claudius gives this contrite soliloquy, Hamlet enters and expresses a merciless and sadistic desire to kill his uncle in such a way that 'his heels may kick at heaven/ And that his soul may be as damn'd and black /As hell whereto it goes'. The negative contrast with Claudius' remorse is unavoidable, and Claudius ends Act III, scene 3 as, arguably, a more sympathetic character for the audience than Hamlet.

In fact, it is possible to interpret Claudius as barely a villain at all. Isn't he, for instance, loving to Gertrude, saying that 'she is so conjunctive to my life and soul… I could not but by her'? Though he admits to having killed Old Hamlet, he is not only deeply remorseful about it, but probably also becomes a more effective king than his brother ever was. Using diplomacy, he swiftly resolves the threat from Norway, whereas Old Hamlet wagered his kingdom on a courageous but irresponsible single combat. If Claudius' use of poison makes him a Machiavellian villain, it must be remembered that, to a follower of Machiavelli, the ends justify the means: Claudius does seem to deliver stable rule in Denmark. Of course Claudius committed regicide [a scene we are never made to witness] but from that point onwards, Shakespeare shows him to be loving, politically effective, repentant and courageous.

In an interview about his 2001 RSC production of **Hamlet**, the director Steven Pimlott claimed 'the real villain is Hamlet'. The literary critic, G. Wilson Knight, in *The Wheel of Fire*[29] argued Hamlet has a 'diseased consciousness' and that he poisons the world of the play. If Marcellus is not sure what the corrupt 'something' is in Denmark, then Pimlott and Knight provide a clear answer. And there is a textual basis for this judgement. While Claudius is an effective king, Hamlet is the mad, bad vigilante, moping around Elsinore, sulking, cruelly abusing Ophelia and his mother and killing people by turns. In fact, it is only after the murder of Polonius, when Hamlet has demonstrated that he is an imminent danger to the court, that Claudius explicitly expresses the desire to have his nephew killed. Before this, the attempts to spy on Hamlet through Rosencrantz and Guildenstern and later Ophelia could be interpreted as Claudius' genuine concern for his flamboyantly troubled nephew. Throughout, Claudius is embracing the 'realpolitik' of the modern political sphere, while Hamlet is seeking to exact an old-fashioned revenge – spurred on by instructions from a ghost that only he hears and of whose provenance he cannot be sure.

Hamlet's seven soliloquies may make the audience automatically side with him. But, viewed more objectively, Hamlet's is a terribly flawed, tendentious perspective. Though he calls Claudius 'a murderer and a villain', he is seeking to do exactly the same thing he is vilifying; murder a king. He is young, grieving, and morbidly suicidal – can his judgement really be trusted? In Elizabethan England at this time, the Queen was ageing and succession was unclear. Perhaps therefore, to an Elizabethan audience, the diplomatic, effective Claudius would have been a preferable king to Hamlet, who, viewed rationally, is not only borderline mad and definitely murderous, but also chronically indecisive.

Not totally convinced by our argument? What counterarguments could you cite? Perhaps you could argue that we have underplayed the significance of the murder of the rightful king, Old Hamlet, and the crime of regicide. Or that in allowing Gertrude to drink from the poisoned cup at the end of the play Claudius reveals his true colours, putting his own self-preservation first. You

---

[29] First published in 1930.

might also add that, actually, Claudius' court is corrupt to its core, as exemplified by the rise of a character such as Osric and the surveillance network of Polonius. In addition, Claudius' spying on Hamlet is not really motivated by concern for the Prince's wellbeing, but from the King's fears for his own safety. Moreover, Claudius cunningly exploits Laertes for his own ends, he may have had a hand in Ophelia's death and his lauded diplomatic strategies are not, in the end, successful. After all, though it appears for most of the play that he had dealt effectively with the threat of Fortinbras, the ending makes it clear that he had been deceived.

Whatever line of interpretation you take on Claudius, one thing is clear: Claudius is a more complex, nuanced and sympathetic character than the 'remorseless, treacherous, lecherous' villain Hamlet imagines him to be.

Gertrude

If Old Hamlet and Prince Hamlet are to be believed, Denmark's Queen is nothing more than the early modern stereotype of the wanton widow. Her first husband and son seem obsessed with her sexuality and her relationship with Claudius. Prince Hamlet spends an unhealthy amount of time fretting about her 'incestuous sheets' and 'enseamed bed,/ Stewed in corruption [I.2, 159; III.4, 93]. Old Hamlet, meanwhile, speaks of her in the pained clichés of the betrayed husband, as a 'radiant angel' who has succumbed to the lure of lust in marrying Claudius. Gertrude's decision to unite with Claudius' all but overshadows his crime of regicide: by 'marry[ing] with his brother' she commits an act her dead husband and son deem 'as bad…as kill[ing] a king' [III.4,27-28]. Although critics have long recognised her importance in the play as 'the mother of the hero, the widow of the Ghost, and the wife of the current King of Denmark,'[30] until the late 1950s literary criticism sided with her first husband and her son. Her character was oftenest interpreted through their offended male eyes. But, while the play denies her a full soliloquy, Gertrude's own speeches and actions suggest a clear-sighted, strong-minded and politically savvy figure, a character whose so-called passivity does not reflect her character but rather the limitations of women's social roles in Elizabethan England and beyond.

The first clue that Gertrude is more than the Hamlets claim lies in her name. While the second element of her name means 'beloved, dear,' the first derives

---

[30] Helibrun, *Hamlet's Mother*, p.201.

from the words for 'spear' and 'strength'. Combined, her name suggests a precious source of strength or a trusted weapon, harking back to Genesis and God's creation of woman as man's 'helpmeet' – someone who is able to make man better than he could be alone. Claudius echoes this idea of Gertrude as a powerful partner in his opening speech of Act I, Scene 2, calling her 'Th'imperial jointress to this warlike state'. His words present her as a powerful force that helps hold the state together and provide the first hint of Gertrude's personal and political aptitude. To fully understand this, however, we have to understand the role of women in early modern society.

Elizabethan England offered very few roles for women and fewer still with any public authority. The *Law's Resolution of Women's Rights*, a 1632 text collating various laws about women's legal rights and duties, acknowledges only three estates: unmarried virgin, wife, and widow. The fourth, with even fewer legal protections, was the whore. Belonging to their fathers before they were married and their husbands after, women were property. Confined to the private sphere, their roles were domestic and familial. Actual women, families, and households often deviated, sometimes quite radically, from the ideals prescribed by the Bible, the State, and the extensive range of treatises on household governance and women's responsibilities. Nonetheless, the social disabilities under which women laboured were extensive. Independence was hard to come by. Women were defined only 'vis-à-vis man' and their lives were dominated by their subjectivity to male family members.[31]

In this context, we may quickly realise why Gertrude chose to remarry. The play does not specify her exact legal position: it is not clear whether she was already 'jointress' in Old Hamlet's lifetime or whether it is a new status as Claudius' wife. If the former, she may have already had a significant degree of financial independence, assured of being maintained in a reasonable quality of life after her first husband's death. If the latter, she has entered into an arrangement designed to ensure her financial security now and later, in potential second widowhood, by securing a joint interest in Elsinore and its

---

[31] Belsey, *Subject of Tragedy*.

territories – a greater level of personal protection than could be assured simply by her dowry [the payment in money or property made by her family to her husband at the point of marriage].

Claudius' specification of the warlike nature of the Danish state is also important. Gertrude is not a commoner but a queen and, prior to her first marriage, either a princess or high-ranking noblewoman to be worthy of a king's hand. Although even royal women were discouraged from meddling in  commonwealth affairs [the queenships of Mary I and Elizabeth I were tricky territory in the sixteenth century!], the associations of her with weaponry and warfare suggests that Claudius, at least, sees her as a political ally. We do not know enough about Gertrude to know whether she was married to Old Hamlet as part of a peace treaty with another territory – a role customarily performed by royal women to unite two ruling families – or whether she serves as private counsel to her husband as well as presenting publicly a united front. We do know that marriage was seen as an image of stability and continuity for the commonwealth; in *The True Law of Free Monarchies: And, Basilicon Doron*, Elizabeth I's soon-to-be successor, James VI of Scotland, promotes a common view in his texts on kingship that 'a king must…marry for the weal of his people'. With the Danish state clearly on the cusp of war again as Young Fortinbras has vowed to reclaim the lands his father lost to Old Hamlet, Gertrude may have made a pragmatic decision to marry Claudius and promote the image of a stable, continuous royal house to help stave off any civil unrest from those who might disagree with Claudius' election.

In the first half of the play Gertrude plays the part of the loyal Queen, supporting Claudius in her short speeches. Critics tend to read this behaviour as passive compliance rather than acknowledging that these scenes take place in the public sphere, where it is Gertrude's duty to support her husband. Nonetheless, Shakespeare succinctly showcases her intelligence. As Tamara Tubb on the British Library's excellent *Discovering Shakespeare* website points out, 'her clipped instruction to Polonius to speak '[m]ore matter with less art' demonstrates her ability to see through rambling rhetoric and seek real information – an invaluable skill in politics'. Moreover, Gertrude often offers insights that the male characters have overlooked and 'anticipates, or correctly identifies key moments, themes, or implications within the play as a whole'. Even as she echoes Claudius' appeal to Hamlet to cease his very public mourning for his dead father in Act I, Scene 2, she notes that there is something 'particular' about his grief and, though he rebuffs her, she continues to reflect upon it. By Act II, she has already realised and, in private, speaks more frankly to Claudius about the contribution of 'our o'erhasty marriage' to her son's antic disposition.

Gertrude's capacity for self-reflection reaches a zenith in the closet scene of Act III, Scene 4, when Hamlet reveals that her second husband murdered her first. Her realisation that she has been inadvertently supporting an act of regicide, albeit retrospectively, stains her soul with 'black and grained spots'. While some critics have suggested that the regicide might not be news to her and even that Gertrude may have been somehow complicit in her first husband's death, her 'amazement' – observed by the Ghost – strongly suggests her unknowingness. The value of her as a political ally and independent thinker is also reaffirmed when she immediately switches her

allegiance from Claudius to her son, swearing to keep secret until her death Hamlet's performance of insanity and her own knowledge of the fratricide in order to allow Hamlet to enact his retribution.

While Gertrude's own ability to act on what she has discovered remains limited in accordance with the social roles of women – a queen crying murder on her husband would have swiftly found herself locked away if not executed – she turns what power she does have against Claudius in the final scene. Among women's options for commanding their own lives was to take command of their own deaths. A number of early modern plays stage female suicides as acts of resistance against social norms and ideologies. In John

Webster's revenge tragedy, *The Duchess of Malfi*, the titular character's order to her executioners to 'pull and pull strongly, for your able strength/ Must pull heaven down upon me' [IV.2, 175-6] rejects the authority of her brothers to take away her life and turns it instead into one of her final commands. Similarly Gertrude, in ignoring Claudius' orders not to drink, uses her own death to back up her son's attempt to restore justice to Elsinore. Not only does she save Hamlet from the poisoned cup by drinking it herself, her dying cries of 'the drink! the drink! I am poisoned' publicly announce Claudius as her killer and spur Hamlet out of his inaction to execute his uncle.

In addition to being clever, politically aware, and willing to die for a cause, Gertrude also fulfils more conventional roles as a woman in society: providing an heir to the throne in Hamlet, acting as a supportive mother-figure who is plainly concerned for and protective of Hamlet, as well as his predicted fiancée Ophelia. In many ways she is a very modern woman, the kind who 'has it all': as mother, wife, and mentor, and someone who sustains a complex political career in a turbulent patriarchal society.

So, what do you think? Unfairly labelled by some, mostly male, critics as false and lustful and lecherous, is Gertrude a victim of bad press? When you look closer is she, in fact, the strong, smart, self-aware female protagonist we have suggested? Or do you disagree with our argument? You could contend that Gertrude's status as dowager queen was enough to protect her way of life after her husband's death and that, even if she did decide to remarry, she could have waited longer than a month or investigated her husband's death further. You could note too that, according to patriarchal canons, Gertrude fails to protect her son. By entering into a marriage with Claudius, she could potentially give birth to another heir, displace Hamlet from the line of succession, and 'disrupt the patriarchal power structure'[32] You could also say that Gertrude betrays her son by misleading him into believing their meeting in the closet is in private, when she knows Polonius is spying on him on behalf of Claudius.

---

[32] Jardine, *Still Harping on Daughters*, p.93.

And what of her carefully aesthetised description of Ophelia's death? Though sometimes the poetic rendering of the death scene is interpreted by critics as showing Gertrude trying to soften the heavy blow to Laertes while also saving Ophelia's reputation by implying her death was not suicide but an accident, some productions have come to entirely different and less sympathetic conclusions. Indeed, one production had Gertrude glancing at her husband during this suspiciously pretty speech, as if she was checking she's getting the story they have concocted together right. The implication being that Ophelia's death was not suicide, nor an accident, but a murder. Certainly, at least, Gertrude's highly elaborate narrative raises questions both about its veracity and about why no-one attempted to prevent Ophelia's death.

We must surely agree, however, that the Gertrude we see is not the Gertrude that any of the men in the play see: she is 'an independent moral being'[33] who makes her own choices, despite her status as subject to her husbands and son.

[33] Graf, *Gertrude's Role*, p. 40.

Ophelia

Ophelia speaks a mere 4% of the lines in the play, so the fact that many critics have dismissed her as an insignificant minor character is unsurprising. Rather than being explored as a character in her own right, commonly Ophelia has been examined in terms of what she reveals about Hamlet. A difficult character for modern audiences to empathise with, she is often considered to be the archetypal 'disposable woman'; it is Hamlet's and Laertes' reaction to Ophelia and her death that are seen as critically important, both to the play and the audience, rather than her character or her death. As the influential feminist critic, Elain Showalter, pointedly puts it, conventionally Ophelia is seen to be 'touching in her weakness and madness, but chiefly interesting, of course, in what she tells us about Hamlet'.[34]

When the critical focus does turn to Ophelia, a failure to fully appreciate the societal pressures that women of the period faced can lead to overly harsh assessments. Expected to obey their male relatives unquestioningly [failing to do so was considered to be a sin], Elizabethan women of her class had little agency or autonomy. Many women were treated as little more than property, as reflected by Polonius' statement that 'I have a daughter - have while she is mine - who in her duty and obedience, mark, hath given me this' [II,2]. Ophelia's father notes her 'duty and obedience', qualities required both of a daughter and a potential wife. the first two clauses also highlight the societal

---

[34] Quoted in *The Cambridge Student Guide* to *Hamlet*, p.98.

expectations of Ophelia and women in similar positions: Treated as a possession of her father's, on marrying she will be expected to defer similarly to a husband. Male characters instruct Ophelia of these duties: Her brother, Laertes instructs his sister on the importance of protecting her 'chaste

treasure' for marriage, while Polonius instructs her to 'Tender [herself] more dearly/ Or...you'll tender me a fool' [Act 1, Scene 3]. The ambiguity in his words reflects the ambiguity of Ophelia's situation. The verb 'tender' in the imperative can be interpreted to be protective - i.e. that Polonius wants Ophelia to be more kind to herself or not to

give in so easily. But 'to tender' is also to offer goods for sale, implying that she should offer herself at a higher price, acknowledging the transactional nature of marriage in the period. As Laertes' words imply, Ophelia is valued primarily for her chastity. When Hamlet destroys her reputation, he destroys her chance of a future with him or with anyone else.

Ophelia is a challenging character to write about and for modern readers to empathise with as there is little evidence of her 'true' self. In 1558, John Knox wrote that 'woman in her greatest perfection was made to serve and obey man'.[35] In many ways, the fact that Ophelia is an ideal Elizabethan woman - chaste, obedient and subordinate to the men in her life - means that her character is a blank slate for characters, actors, directors and audiences alike. Like many women of the period, her fate is decided by men - not only by Hamlet, Polonius, and Laertes, but Shakespeare and the male actor who would have played her. Ophelia's voice is limited and her words are often discredited, turning her into a blank space for the projection of male suffering. A catalyst for Hamlet's and Laertes' actions, her death is soon forgotten. Many modern audiences also struggle with her passivity and dutifulness, criticising her for being a victim, without acknowledging the irony that the characteristics that a modern audience finds most frustrating [submissiveness, obedience and passivity] were seen as the ideal for women at the time of the play's first

---

[35] Knox, *The First Blast of the Trumpet Against the Monstruous Regiment of Women.*

performance.

In appreciation of Hamlet's tragedy, Ophelia's fate has often been ignored. His suffering is so compelling that hers is eclipsed. Rather than see her as what she is - a victim of the society she lives in, unavenged and unremembered - she has been overlooked, both in life and  death. In Act I, Scene 3, she is told by her father and brother to 'fear' a relationship with Hamlet and obediently rejects him 'as [Polonius] did command'. But even when she has 'repelled his letters, and denied his access to [her]' [Act II, Scene 1], she cannot win: Polonius decides that it is her rejection that 'hath made him mad' and hence prioritises Hamlet's needs over her protection. After Polonius offers to 'loose [his] daughter' to Hamlet, so that the Prince's actions can be observed, and once she has been rejected and humiliated, he speaks to her only to say 'You need not tell us what Lord Hamlet said/ we heard it all'. Even to her father, who should care for and protect her, Ophelia's feelings are less significant than Hamlet's. Polonius does not comfort his daughter. Having exploited her as his spy, he dismisses her and her pain, underlining how she is little more than a pawn in a dangerous game played by men.

This idea is also supported by her interaction with Hamlet in Act III. Famously he commands her to 'Get thee to a nunnery!' [Act III, Scene 1], claiming that 'wise men know well enough what monsters you make of them'. It is easy for an audience to believe Hamlet's insinuations, noting the plural 'men' whom she is claimed to have power over and believing that she has betrayed him. However, it can be argued either that Hamlet feels betrayed, knowing that she has sided with Polonius and Claudius [something that as an obedient daughter she was compelled to do], or that Ophelia is simply a foil for Hamlet's madness and, either knowing that he is being observed, or simply being aware that she will report his comments, his treatment of her is a way of proving his 'antic disposition': Knowing his claims to be untrue, he also knows that attacking the woman he once loved [despite his denials] will be taken as evidence by the two onlookers that 'his noble mind is here o'erthrown'. Alternatively, following the arguments of Freud, Hamlet's hostility could be read as expressing the displaced rage he feels towards Gertrude's sexuality, with Ophelia again merely the innocent victim.

Hamlet instructs Ophelia 'to a nunnery, go' and, on the face of it, these imperatives seem brutal, implying either that she should reform her behaviour and learn from the celibacy of nuns or take precisely the opposite course - in contemporary Elizabethan slang a 'nunnery' referred to a brothel. However, Hamlet can be argued to be genuinely 'cruel to be kind': Rejecting Ophelia for her own safety, he is acknowledging that men 'are arrant knaves all; believe none of us'. Underneath his apparent hostility, maybe there is tenderness and a desire to protect. Hamlet is, after all, correct: Ophelia would indeed be safer in a convent, a solely female sphere, than she can be in Denmark where she is subject to the machinations of powerful men, especially her father, King Claudius and, of course, Hamlet himself.

Ostensibly, these attacks on Ophelia's chastity, reputation and chances of marriage seem unfounded and cruel, especially when Hamlet adds that 'be thou as chaste as ice, as pure as snow, thou shalt not escape calumny'. Despite his choice of similes implying an awareness of Ophelia's chastity and purity, Hamlet seems to be cursing her. But under the guise of madness, he is in fact predicting the truth: She will not escape calumny and her reputation will be irrevocably damaged. Rather than the accident presented by Gertrude, Ophelia's death is often seen as 'doubtful'. Critics cite her death by drowning [a common method of suicide for unmarried pregnant women], Hamlet's lewd comments, her bawdy songs and her mention of 'rue', an abortifacient [as well as a symbol of both bitterness and repentance] as evidence of a sexual relationship with Hamlet being her real motive for suicide.

Critics analyse Hamlet's madness, looking for 'method in't', but even her own brother dismisses Ophelia's words as simply 'a document in madness' and evidence that she has lost her wits [Act IV, Scene 5]. An Elizabethan audience would have believed as much - that she was driven mad by unrequited love as by the death of Polonius - and there is little dissent from Claudius' statement that Ophelia becomes 'divided from herself and her fair judgment' [IV,5], i.e. she appears to them to be acting without reason. However, throughout the play, Ophelia has displayed no true, independent self from which to be divided and she has been afforded no opportunity to exercise her own judgement. Polonius' death 'divided' Ophelia from the influences that had constructed her identity thus far - her father and Hamlet, the man she has loved, who has made their future impossible through his rejection, through his own madness and through his murder of her father. From this moment onwards, Ophelia is no longer bound to the men in her life. Nor to a sense of self, societal norms or, indeed, sanity.

As a mad woman, Ophelia is powerless. She is seen merely as a helpless victim. Again she is a foil for Hamlet and comes off the worse: Whereas Hamlet is a tragic hero, she is merely tragic, feeling too much rather than thinking too much; weak, rather than afflicted with intellectual melancholy. She has been dismissed as lovesick or hysterical by generations of audiences, who minimise her grief for Polonius and abandonment by Hamlet.

Critics are divided about the significance of the flowers that Ophelia gives out. The gentleman who describes her state to Claudius and Gertrude dismisses her words as 'half sense' and 'nothing'. But Elizabethan gentlewomen were educated in the symbolism of flowers and audiences are likely to be tempted to read significance into the choice of flowers. Shakespeare pre-empts this, with the same gentleman describing listeners' responses to her speech: 'they aim at it and botch the words up fit to their own thoughts'. Strewing flowers in picturesque madness, possibly Ophelia is little more than the archetypal madwoman. More likely, Ophelia, who until her father's death was unable to express her own ideas or opinions, has been 'made mad' not simply by her father's death but both by the way she herself is entirely disregarded and her inability to take restorative action, unlike her brother Laertes. The audience must question whether Ophelia's songs and flowers are the sign of an entirely deranged mind, or whether, her 'madness' is the only occasion upon which Ophelia is no longer restrained by propriety and reputation, so is free to make statements that would otherwise be both dangerous and improper to say aloud. For instance, her opening comment in this scene, 'where is the beauteous majesty of Denmark?' implies this quality or personage is currently absent from the court.

Throughout the play, Ophelia lacks a voice and rarely expresses her own views. When she does, any meaning is ignored, as seen again here by the pre-emptive dismissal of the meaning of her flowers. In addition her identity has been controlled and constructed for her by the dominant men in her life. For her brother, for instance, she is delicate and beautiful, like a flower. Hence in this scene, by giving flowers away, Ophelia can be read as rejecting this passive feminine identity and finding a new one that is far more transgressive, unbiddable and disturbing. That said, even if we read her madness as a kind of liberation, formed out of snatches of rhymes, proverbs and songs, even Ophelia's mad words are not entirely her own.

Shakespeare does not give stage directions to clarify to whom she presents the flowers, but it is widely accepted that she presents Laertes 'pansies, for thoughts', with the word 'pansies' deriving from the French 'pensees', directly translated to 'thoughts', encouraging Laertes to think about the fate that has befallen both his father and his sister. It is, however, ironic that she presents

flowers for 'thoughts' when she is considered by others to have lost her wits. The rosemary 'for remembrance', may symbolise not only the desire to remember Polonius, but may memorialise Ophelia herself, encouraging Laertes to remember her innocence and its destruction, or may be for the absent Hamlet, remembering a time before their love was lost.

The fennel and columbine are assumed to be presented to Claudius. Fennel symbolised flattery, deceit and infidelity and was used to cast out evil spirits, perhaps implying Ophelia's awareness of Claudius' evil deeds. It was also believed to be a cure for melancholy, which is ironic considering Claudius' role in causing Hamlet's. Columbine was commonly associated with deception and adultery, highlighting both the way Claudius cuckolded his own brother and Gertrude's own betrayal. Ophelia may often have been sentimentalised and romanticised in productions and by audiences and critics[36], but in these lines, her madness reveals essential and dangerous truths

that no other character dares speak. If this is madness, there appears to be method in it.

Rue, symbolic of bitterness and sorrow is also a symbol of repentance and is generally agreed to be presented to Gertrude, who must 'wear [her] rue with a difference' [IV,5]. Where Ophelia is wearing hers in sorrow for her murdered father and lost love, and will soon herself be mourned by others, the Queen should repent for her betrayal of her husband and her son, hoping that this 'herb of grace' is enough to allow her to be forgiven. The apparently innocuous 'there's a daisy' can also be seen as commentary on the current 'state of Denmark': Symbolic of innocence, purity, and true love, these no longer exist in the world portrayed in the play; hence the daisy goes unpresented. Finally, she refers to violets. In Act I, Laertes compares Hamlet's attentions to her to 'A violet in the youth of primy nature,/ Forward, not permanent, sweet, not lasting', a warning that is recalled here: 'I would give you some violets, but they withered all when my father died'. Symbolic of innocence and everlasting love, both have withered for Ophelia when Hamlet killed Polonius.

Her offstage death leads to further mysteries surrounding Ophelia. Romanticised by Gertrude, Ophelia's death is portrayed as a peaceful, albeit tragic, accident. 'Mermaid-like', she dies under a 'willow', a tree associated with forsaken love, 'incapable of her own distress' [IV,7], no longer aware of her suffering nor able to save herself. Shakespeare personifies nature and her clothing to illustrate the tragedy of her death and to imply her purity - from

---

[36] A comparison of this scene in two productions really highlights the different readings of Ophelia's madness. Compare the fey, delicate and picturesque madness of Jean Simmons in Laurence Olivier's 1948 production with the deranged and provocative lunacy of Kate Winslet in Kenneth Branagh's 1996 production.

the 'weeping brook' suggesting that even nature is grieving for her. 'Her garments, [which] heavy with their drink,/ Pulled the poor wretch from her melodious lay/ To muddy death" [Act IV, Scene 7], highlighting her helplessness and passivity and suggesting a fatal lack of agency. In many ways, Ophelia's death is 'muddy' and confused. We may wonder how Gertrude knows all these details, as she was not there to witness the drowning.

Certainly she has a vested interest in controlling this narrative. Presenting Ophelia's death as a tragic accident Gertrude absolves Hamlet of guilt and, in the most radical reading, could, perhaps, even be covering up another murder by her husband, Claudius. Whichever reading we favour, despite Gertrude's aestheticized account, as a suicide, Ophelia's death is perceived by both the Priest and gravediggers as a sin against God. The tragedy of Ophelia's death is undermined by the gravediggers' jokes and condemnation of her. They question whether she should be 'buried in a Christian burial when she wilfully seeks her own salvation', reasoning that 'she drowned herself wittingly' [Act V, Scene1]. And despite their crude treatment of the issue, their discussion often spurs debate about the extent to which Ophelia has agency at the point of her death. Was she, as Gertrude claims, 'incapable of her own distress' or did she willingly and wittingly make the decision that Hamlet could not – 'not to be'? Or, indeed, was the matter taken entirely out  of her own hand by a murderer? It is possible to read her self-murder as her sole act of free will in the play, choosing to end her own suffering. Even this is undermined and romanticised by the court [and by many audiences], making Ophelia an even more powerless and tragic figure: Just as in life her identity was constructed and constrained by others, so it is too even in death.

Due to her suicide, Ophelia receives 'maimed rites', with the priest arguing that instead of 'charitable prayers/ Shards, flints and pebbles should be thrown on her'. Moreover he opines that 'We should profane the service of the dead/ To sing a requiem and such rest to her/ As to peace-parted souls', leaving the audience in little doubt that he believes Ophelia killed herself. The priest claims that she deserves punishment and highlights the lack of 'requiem' [or 'rest'] and 'peace' she will find. This is the fate feared by Hamlet in his soliloquy in Act III, Scene 1 and this moment should be recalled at the end of the play when, Hamlet, who avenges his father's and his own death, speaks his final words: 'the rest is silence'. Restrained by societal expectations, Ophelia cannot become a tragic heroine. Instead, in both life and death, she is merely tragic: she cannot avenge and must merely remember and be remembered.

There is pathos at her funeral. But, even here, the drama directs our pity towards Hamlet and Laertes. Even here, Ophelia is side-lined: the focus is on the emotions of the men, rather than on her. When she is mentioned the focus is on her purity, rather than her personality, with Laertes hoping that 'from her fair and unpolluted flesh may violets spring!' Even here her virginity is more important than her mind or character. Violets symbolise purity and premature death, highlighting the destruction of innocence. A pure, delicate flower, his 'rose of May', for her brother 'sweet Ophelia' had no chance of survival in the 'unweeded garden' of Denmark.

Ophelia's funeral is an emotional scene, from Laertes' grief and allusions to Pelion and Ossa, to Hamlet's shocking claim that 'I loved Ophelia. Forty thousand brothers/ Could not with all their quantity of love/ Make up my sum'. Although this can be seen as a turning point for Hamlet, it is too late for Ophelia. The hyperbolic grief of both men is emotive, but futile. Although they literally jump into her grave, this scene becomes about Hamlet's competitive grief rather than about Ophelia as he attempts to match and exceed Laertes' feelings. Ophelia's story is pushed aside for Hamlet's, even at her own funeral.

Laertes swore to avenge even before Ophelia's death, telling her that 'Hadst thou thy wits and didst persuade revenge/ It could not move thus'. His grief at Ophelia's death spurs him to ignore Polonius' wise instruction, 'To thine own self be true' and makes him vulnerable to Claudius' manipulation. However, at the climax of the play, Laertes realises he has been manipulated and imploring Hamlet to 'exchange forgiveness', exonerates the Prince: 'Mine and my father's death come not upon thee,/ Nor thine on me" [V,2]. At this crucial moment, in Laertes' last, dying words, Ophelia is not mentioned.

At all turns, Ophelia's life has been controlled and constrained by men. And she cannot even rely on any of them - her brother leaves, her father, 'the fishmonger', uses her to try to solve Hamlet's 'madness' and hence curry favour with the King. Hamlet himself rejects her. She is subordinate as both a character and a plot device. The world of *Hamlet* is a brutally masculine one. Women may be motives, tools or foils, but their own passions and feelings are universally marginalised and ignored.

Polonius

Polonius: pompous, garrulous fool <u>and/or</u> well-meaning, loving father <u>and/or</u> pragmatic politician <u>and/or</u> insignificant pawn? The fact that Polonius can be all these things at different times and in different productions testifies to his fluidity as a dramatic creation. Polonius is a highly interesting character to examine, mainly because each production can use him differently to calibrate the tonal variations of what an audience experiences. He can be played as inherently comic: A pompous, old, bumbling fool, openly ridiculed by Hamlet and too unaware to catch the obvious irony of his providing a 'few precepts' in a long meandering speech full of cliched advice. The BBC film version, with David Tennant as Hamlet, showed Ophelia and Laertes reciting fragments of this speech so as to point out its fusty familiarity, their father a mere broken record of hollow advice.

However, he can also be played as straight, rendering him as a small-scale member of the court, aware of his dispensability in a time of rapid and unpredictable political change. Productions have even shown Polonius as a confident, yet terrible, Jazz Age dancer as the court of Claudius congratulates itself on the defusing of the Fortinbras threat while others have shown a fearful or a fawning Polonius eager to appease the African dictator Claudius and his ruthless whims. Polonius' revelation that he 'was accounted a good actor' [III.2.,96] in his university days can be useful in considering his characterisation: is he really a bumbling, prating knave or does he play this role to glean intelligence for the political regime in which he works? Or, indeed, can he be both a trusted chief councillor and also a fool?

For a character who speaks no more than 86 lines, he is present on stage a lot, appearing in 8 out of the 11 scenes. This suggests a character who watches more than he speaks, which is hardly a surprise given his predilection for secret surveillance of the Danish citizenry. This is certainly the case in his first appearance on stage; he is no more than a witness at the self-congratulating celebration of Claudius' new efficient diplomacy. However, his first significant role in the play is that of well-meaning, yet authoritative father to his son and daughter in Act I, Scene 3. His advice to his son is all common sense and very useful for a young nobleman abroad. However, an audience cannot miss the irony of its structural illogic. At the beginning he seems to promote a shallow performance of the self: unobtrusive, background, watchful but polite: 'give thy thoughts no tongue'; 'reserve thy judgement', avoid extremities of behaviour and then with an oddly contradictory flourish 'above all, to thine own self be true, which is the opposite of keeping your thoughts and opinions hidden. However, this promotion of outward performance, masking hidden realities, is unsurprising in a man who specialises in covert surveillance in the service of the state. So much so that he hires Reynaldo to spy on his own son while in France to ascertain whether Laertes is prone to the antics of a wayward libertine. Presumably it is the same Reynaldo that informs Claudius that Laertes is back in Denmark allegedly 'in secret' and intent on demanding answers about Polonius' suspicious death. The fact that Polonius prioritises state stability over his own family loyalties is telling and this is revealed more explicitly in his dealings with his daughter, who he is also spying upon.

When counselling Ophelia, Polonius' tone shifts from gentle fatherly advice to something far sterner. Ophelia mistakenly continues the easy-going tone of her conversation with Laertes, but is quickly reminded of her daughterly obligations. Full of imperatives, Polonius' language is forceful: 'Give me up the truth', 'tender yourself more dearly', 'Be something scanter...', 'look to't, I charge you'. While this is obviously the consequence of Elizabethan patriarchal gender norms, it also points to a character focused on political survival. The assumption of fatherly authority is clear from his frequent use of dismissive language pointing to Ophelia's unavoidable naivety and unworldliness: 'Pooh, you speak like a green girl', 'think yourself a baby', 'Go to, go to'. The ulterior motive seems to be more connected to his keen awareness of his own standing and reputation: 'You do not understand yourself so clearly as behoves my daughter and your honour' [I.3.,95-6]. The fact that he puts his reputation before Ophelia's through the sentence syntax reveals that his political standing is of the utmost importance. This is hardly surprising as Denmark is in the midst of political upheaval with the sudden accession of Claudius and the threat of Fortinbras. While the play does not make this clear in any way, speculation about Polonius' previous political standing is unavoidable.

Given Old Hamlet's heroic martial leadership, it would seem unlikely that Polonius played as large a part in the old court. But the rise of Claudius and his wilier, more political style of leadership suggests that as Claudius rose, so too did his chief advisor. If this is the case, then his high political status may only be in its infancy and he would not wish to jeopardise this in any way. Negating the precariousness of his status in the Claudian court through shrewd domestic governance, points not to a bumbling buffoon, but a clear-eyed opportunist working at the heart of the political state.

Why exactly does he want to spy on his son? To ensure he does not gain the reputation of a 'puffed and reckless libertine' and stain the family name. Why does he spy on his daughter and insist that she deny Hamlet further access? So she does not gain a reputation as a court strumpet and stain the family name. The reputation of being a noble family is of utmost importance to Polonius and he goes to great lengths to ensure their performance of this role is not compromised from within. Ophelia's apparently meek obedience, 'I shall obey, my lord' reinforces the impression of paternal authority and validates his concerns.

The confident authority that Polonius shows in his domestic affairs is balanced by less sure-footedness is his political dealings. While clearly trusted and valued by Claudius, Polonius is understandably eager to stay on the right side of the King. The authority he wields as *paterfamilias* in the private sphere has no court equivalent: in the public sphere he is the one who obeys orders. Nowhere is this more obvious that in their disagreement about Hamlet's feigned madness. Polonius is convinced that it is an unusually acute case of lovesickness: 'I will go seek the king/ This is the very ecstasy of love' [II.1,98-9]. Claudius disagrees, and this may be driven by Gertrude's more sensible

claim that it is 'his father's death and our hasty marriage' that has driven Hamlet into 'distemper'. Here, Polonius moves into foolish territory. Gertrude's thoughts seem most likely to be true, yet Polonius adheres almost bullheadedly to his lovesickness theory. As revealed in the length of his 21-line justification of his actions,

he seems over-eager to justify the logic of his actions. Why? Is this some fawning attempt to appear useful to the King or is it just foolish tunnel vision? Even after Hamlet's harsh abusive treatment of his daughter in the closet scene, he still clings to the conviction that 'the origin and commencement of his grief/ sprung from neglected love' [III.1,176-7].

Claudius, in contrast, appears much more perceptive: 'Love! His affections do not that way tend'. The fact that Polonius has encountered Hamlet both in his feigned 'antic disposition' and this new, unprecedented emotionally volatile state should put him in a position to compare the two. Yet he does not, or cannot. There is a clear, if dangerously aggressive, logic in Hamlet's treatment of Ophelia compared to his lampooning of Polonius immediately prior to the nunnery scene. The former episode doesn't suggest lovesickness, while the latter episode doesn't suggest madness. Of course, the audience benefits from the dramatic irony working at Polonius' expense, but nevertheless his thinking seems shallow.

Polonius could be interpreted as almost innocent by default; so powerful are Claudius' powers of deception that, ever eager to please, he is as easily hoodwinked as everyone else in the royal court. However, rather than

Claudius, it is Hamlet who most influences the audience's view of Polonius.

Sometimes, drawing a distinction between laughing at and laughing with is useful in drama and so it proves here. Shakespeare certainly encourages the audience to laugh at Polonius in the first encounter, where Hamlet calls him a 'fishmonger and a 'tedious old fool' [II.2,171, 214]. Polonius is bamboozled by Hamlet's ingenious doublespeak, showing a slow wit compared to Hamlet's sharp 'madness.' However, in *The Mousetrap* scene, both before and after the play-within-a-play, Hamlet's mockery and teasing wields a more vicious, cutting edge: While Polonius in still undoubtedly the butt of the protagonist's jokes, Hamlet's ignoble behaviour could, in fact, rebound against the Prince. The audience laughter, if the production plays the scene this way, is uncomfortable rather than free and easy - in fact a production could easily create dismay at Hamlet's cruelty. Additionally, Hamlet's pulling rank towards the end of this scene, where the royal prince forces the old courtier to engage in his feigned mad babble and spout humiliating rubbish about the shape of clouds is strikingly similar to Hamlet's disdainful treatment of Rosencrantz and Guildenstern.

This question of audience forgiveness can also be applied to Polonius' untimely and pathetic end. It is very clear that he becomes no more than an unfortunate inconvenience, an obstacle, in Hamlet's overall journey, but it is the way that Shakespeare presents this end that is intriguing. As mentioned previously, the audience should not give Polonius' demise much thought given his close alliance with a villainous antagonist – it should be noted that Claudius has just openly confessed his evil regicide/fratricide to the audience immediately prior to the closet scene. However, Shakespeare problematises such a simple audience reaction, or certainly allows a production the wriggle room to do so.

In another type of play Polonius' death could be played as slapstick comedy and the nature of his death, hiding behind an arras, as rather pathetic. While doing his darndest to please his royal lord, Polonius is mistakenly skewered and called 'a rat', a telling derogatory description. Ultimately, he dies in royal service, a cowardly, spying foil to Hamlet's more manly, though hardly heroic, hero. Polonius' end is ignominious, like the paltry funeral given to him by Claudius, as Hamlet berates his corpse as 'a wretched, rash, intruding fool'. Again, productions can use Polonius' death to regulate the tonal emphasis of the play: Hamlet's disrespect and complete lack of regret can be seen as justified righteous anger towards a meddling fool, responsible for aggravating his various griefs. Or it can be presented as another example of Hamlet's increasingly wild and dangerous behaviour.

Ultimately, the play is Hamlet's story. Hence the audience is forced to view things overwhelmingly from his perspective. So Polonius is usually considered on some level to be a 'foolish prating knave'. However, Hamlet's description of Polonius' corpse as 'most secret and most grave' reminds the audience of the lengths the King's chief councillor went to fulfil his political duties. Though a seemingly minor character, Polonius' death is the powder keg that explodes the plot into life, driving it towards irreversible tragedy. After his manslaughter there is no turning back for Hamlet. Nor for Claudius. While the King's hand is forced, Hamlet finds his inner revenger, taking away the paralysing choice that has hindered him hitherto. Essentially, Polonius is a dutiful, well-meaning courtier destroyed accidentally by the battle between mighty opposites.

The aftermath of Polonius' death is, however, revealing: Both his children point to an adored, if flawed, father. Ophelia's mental devastation is obviously two-pronged: losing a lover, but also a father; Laertes' emotional reaction is public fury rather than private grief as he rails against the dishonour of Polonius' 'obscure funeral -/ no trophy, sword nor hatchment o'er his bones/ no noble rite, nor formal ostentation' [IV.5,205-7]. There is pity in his end: Polonius compromised his family relations with his children to serve the King, yet the family dishonour that he so guarded against by controlling his children arrives in the end in the underwhelming recognition of his loyal service. Neither privately celebrated by Claudius, nor publicly by the Danish state, the old councillor is buried without ceremony.

You might be thinking we've been a little soft and easy on Polonius. Because, there is another, darker way of reading him, of course. Polonius can be read or played as a much more ominous, sinister and dislikeable character, the hungry spider, in fact, at the heart of Elsinore's tangled web of espionage. Polonius, the spymaster, the Frances Walsingham figure to Claudius' Queen Elizabeth I. Claudius' eyes and ears in the court, not only willingly complicit in the degradations and corruptions of the King's surveillance state, but an active agent in its machinations. As Richard Vardy memorably imagines him, Polonius as the Head of the Secret police, a figure prepared to [ab]use his own daughter to further his political ambitions and curry favour with the King. Polonius the sinister figure who has been and continues to be 'instrumental in the seizure and control of power'[37] by a devious and despotic regime. This version of Polonius is hard, however, to reconcile with the other elements of

his characterisation we have covered. Can Polonius be dangerous and ominous and also foolish; a stern, but essentially well-meaning father and also a corrupt and corrupting spymaster? The answer is probably yes. And this makes Shakespeare's depiction of Polonius also the more audacious, simultaneously showing the dangerous power of spies and spying while also poking satirical fun [at

a time when satire was explicitly banned] at the spymaster. What Walsingham might have made of this depiction, we can only guess. Fortunately for Shakespeare Queen Elizabeth's spymaster was a few years dead before *Hamlet* hit the stage.

Vardy, '*Stewed in Corruption – Polonius and the Politics of Denmark'*.

Horatio

For a character who appears to merely bookend the play in terms of his stage time [most visible in Acts I and V], it may come as a surprise that after Hamlet himself, with his formidable 1480 lines, Horatio speaks the most lines in the play [109]. What is the significance of this, if any? Firstly, compared to Hamlet it highlights Horatio's minor role in the overall action, but, secondly, if examining the league of minor characters alone, he seems to occupy a role of some significance, making him both minor and major. Interestingly, in other ways, Horatio embodies a similar duality: In his beliefs he is both logical and superstitious and he is also an outsider as well as an insider. Horatio is not Danish [Hamlet promises that he will teach him the custom of Danish heavy drinking] but is remarkably au fait with the intricacies of Danish politics, presumably from hours of discussion with Hamlet in Wittenberg. In terms of courtly etiquette, he is neither a sycophantic servant of royalty, like Osric, nor prone to aggressive censure, like Laertes. Unlike Rosencrantz and Guildenstern he is a true friend, Hamlet's only confidante, though intriguingly Horatio remains as part of the Danish court, conversing with the Queen about Ophelia's madness, even when Hamlet has been banished to England. Shakespeare also uses Horatio as a mechanism of exposition, sometimes skilfully, as in Act I, and other times quite clumsily, as in Act IV. In Act I, Scene 1 it is Horatio who informs the audience of Denmark's incessant preparations for foreign invasion by the 'young Fortinbras,/ of unimproved mettle, hot and full' whereas in Act IV, Scene 6 he is the messenger of Hamlet's exciting pirate adventures through the letter-reading scene. However, despite these various roles, by the play's end, he has one unequivocal role: Glorifier of Hamlet's tragic legacy.

In a narrative sense, not only does Horatio occupy the one true, reliable friend and ally role for the protagonist, he also seems to suggest a type of sensible foil to Hamlet's more erratic sensibility. Hamlet himself describes Horatio as essentially the best man he's even known: 'thou art e'en just a man/ as e'er my conversation coped withal' [III.3,50-1], which is some praise. Interestingly, Hamlet particularly praises Horatio's ability to take whatever life throws at him with stoical acceptance: 'Thou hast been [...] a man that Fortune's buffets and rewards/ Hast ta'en with equal thanks' [III.2,61-4]. Hamlet admires how his' blood and judgement are so well co-meddled', how Horatio is a rationalist - 'not passion's slave' - attributes that Hamlet struggles to attain. So in a nutshell, Hamlet's vision of Horatio in their friendship is as the reasonable,

balanced and balancing sidekick, and so it is played out in the play itself. When the two are together on stage, Horatio's default is to offer a more clear-headed and moderate alternative to Hamlet's breathless and often intense musings on Elsinore, in particular, and the world, in general.

This view of Horatio as a steady and calming confidante is best seen in Act V, Scene 2 where Hamlet has managed to calm himself down after his wild proclamations at Ophelia's graveside. Horatio seems to have the ability to draw Hamlet out of his most emotional frenzy and into more contemplative spaces. In fact, the First Folio even has Hamlet explicitly regret his actions to Horatio - 'But I am very sorry, Good Horatio,/ that to Laertes I forgot myself' - something which he can admit in private but not in public. Compare, for example, his appallingly insensitive and insulting 'apology' to Laertes before their duel later in the scene. Hamlet has already made a spectacle of himself in public, but in private he seems to have reached a calm and stoical state of acceptance. Now whether this has anything to do with Horatio is moot, but he certainly appears to facilitate a significant transformation in Hamlet's mentality and brings out the best side of the Prince. Hamlet's ease in Horatio's company immediately makes him an attractive figure for the audience.

Indeed, his personal morality seems to be higher than that of his more powerful friend's, both in his castigation of Claudius' villainy ['Why, what a king is this!' – V.2,62] but also his implied disapproval at Hamlet's seemingly cold-hearted dispatching of Rosencrantz and Guildenstern. Horatio's  euphemistic 'So Guildenstern and Rosencrantz go to't' draws a very defensive response from his more powerful friend: they were merely collateral damage in a war between 'mighty opposites'. Given Horatio's similar pawn status to Rosencrantz and Guildenstern, which makes Hamlet's actions appear callous, his presence at such a remark might encourage the audience to question the morality of absolute powerholders in general. Horatio's steadiness as a bastion of quiet morality is one of his key characteristics. Certainly, Horatio is intelligent enough to know that he ranks not much higher than the 'baser nature' that has been sacrificed to the battle of the greats.

That said, when the audience first sees Horatio he cuts quite a different, much more unstable figure. Initial impressions suggest a logical man, governed by reason, sceptical of the superstitious whinnying of the sentries, Bernardo, Francisco and Marcellus, about ghostly visits to the ramparts of Elsinore. While he begins by dismissing their sightings of Old Hamlet's ghost as mere 'fantasy', the minute he sees it he admits that 'it harrows me with fear and wonder'. In fact, towards the end of this scene Horatio has completely reversed his prior thinking, describing the portentous omens of Julius Caesar's murder, most notably the 'the sheeted dead/ [that] did squeak and gibber in the Roman streets.' The rigour of this man of reason is clearly not incorruptible as he immediately assumes the Ghost is not only real, but also that it is a sign of political turmoil - its appearance 'bodes some strange eruption to our state'. This seems like quite an emotional, almost fantastical response. However, maybe this is the logical reaction in a state which is on the precipice of foreign invasion and where a seismic shift in political regime has just taken place. In a play where most things and characters are not as they seem, maybe Horatio's unstable beliefs are quite moderate by comparison.

This wavering of personal beliefs aside, though, the fact that the sentries consult Horatio about this matter at all signals that he has an authority and trustworthiness about him that is widely known, something reinforced by his role as Hamlet's sympathetic ear throughout the rest of the play. Horatio's courageous [compared to the sentries at any rate!] interrogation of the Ghost and his decision to 'impart what we have seen tonight/ unto young Hamlet' portray him as a decisive, active character and this action also aligns him exclusively with the play's protagonist. Shakespeare makes Horatio and Hamlet 'fellow student[s]' of Wittenberg, and thus implies training in logic and philosophy and perhaps a friendship of intellectual equals.

Hamlet is thirty years old and Horatio appears to be a contemporary at university, suggesting that both characters are committed scholars and that they have freely chosen to be friends. Their first meeting reveals some playwrighting slipperiness, however, on Shakespeare's part: Despite being in Elsinore for Old Hamlet's funeral two months before it is only now in Act I, Scene 2, two months later, that they meet. What has Horatio been up to and where has been hiding these past two months? Doesn't matter really, for now Hamlet has a kindly friend on whom he can lean. That said, Hamlet, already aware of all the pretence around him, does seem to check out Horatio's story before confiding in him, asking his friend three times in rapid succession why he has come to Elsinore. Thereafter the warmth of Hamlet's greeting and the easy intimacy of their interactions suggest a genuine closeness between the two men, as signalled by Hamlet's immediate launching into a favourite bugbear: the 'o'erhasty marriage' of his mother. Horatio's response is striking in its measured diplomacy. Rather than a fawning 'Oh yes, whatever you think with an added sprinkle of scorn' he acknowledges fact without stoking the fires of hyperbole – 'Indeed, my lord, it followed hard upon'. This ability to acknowledge, yet not subscribe entirely to Hamlet's emotional outpourings makes Horatio a trusted figure in the eyes of the audience and the ideal companion for Hamlet himself.

His trustworthiness is also clearly valued by Hamlet, not only in his belief that Horatio will keep his 'antic disposition' a secret, but also in the famous Mousetrap scene where Hamlet exposes Claudius' guilt through dramatic cunning. While Hamlet is embarrassing the royal court of Denmark as *The Mousetrap* is performed, it is Horatio's job to give Claudius 'heedful face'. Even though Hamlet allegedly will his eyes 'rivet to his [stepfather's] face', his emotional instability necessitates that after the play-within-the-play they 'will both our judgements join/ in censure of his seeming'. Famously, the reliability of this test is much debated by critics and even the two characters seem at odds regarding how successful it has been. While Hamlet is flushed with perceived success, Horatio is much more guarded. Singing triumphantly, Hamlet regards his little dramatic production as such a successful lie-detector test that he should be offered 'a fellowship in a cry of players'. Horatio, however, reckons the scheme as only worth 'half a share'. Hamlet seems unwilling or unable to listen to his close friend's caution and should have pursued further, perhaps more convincing, evidence. But, instead, Hamlet is carried away by the strength of his feelings before he and Horatio can discuss the matter properly. Cleverly, Shakespeare engineers that they are interrupted, untimely, by those 'adders fang'd', the false friends, Rosencrantz and Guildenstern, which deprives Hamlet of Horatio's more objective observations and, presumably, more logical deductions. Again, Horatio's steadfast manner contrasts strongly to Hamlet's wilder fancies. [See also his peace-keeping role in Act V, Scene 1 where he must calm the enraged Hamlet by Ophelia's graveside: 'Good my lord, be quiet'.]

This renown for dependability is also evinced when Hamlet is out of the country on his way to England where, curiously, Horatio shows up in Act IV, Scene 5 [in the Second Quarto at least], in Gertrude's close company. It might be understandable that Hamlet's friend stays with Gertrude, given Hamlet and Gertrude's recent reconciliation, but from Claudius' perspective having such a close ally of Hamlet's around the royal court might be uncomfortable. While this scene sees him contribute a mere three lines of dialogue, tellingly they are characteristically full of prudent common sense.

Being informed of Ophelia's dramatic mental unravelling, Horatio wisely advises that "Twere good she was spoken with, for she may stress/ dangerous conjectures in ill-breeding minds'. On the surface this appears to be a pretty obvious thing to say, but it echoes Claudius' earlier statement about Hamlet's madness in Act III, 'Madness in great ones must not unwatched go' and, indeed, his concerns about how Laertes 'wants not buzzers to infect his ear' later in this scene, reveals an anxiety about unhinged individuals endangering state stability. This may not necessarily be Horatio's true opinion [the First Folio has Gertrude say these lines] and may be just Shakespeare indicating a ramping up of dramatic intensity through destabilisation of the state. Nevertheless, Horatio speaks them. Is there any chance that a good man has become infected by the corruption and political intrigue that surrounds him? Or even more intriguingly, is Horatio engaged in some counter-spying for his recently departed friend? Or even more concerning, is he there to keep an eye on Gertrude herself, to ensure that she heeds Hamlet's not-so-subtle warning about keeping the truth of his madness to herself? All are tantalising possibilities and every production can stretch these possibilities to suit their dramatic intentions.

Such ambiguity is dramatically jettisoned in the play's denouement. On the precipice of the great journey into the unknown, Hamlet is touched by Horatio's loyalty and desire to follow him into the afterlife. Horatio's claim that he is 'more an antique Roman than a Dane' reminds us of the Roman origins of his name and bring into focus the very different attitudes to suicide in Elizabethan England and ancient Rome. Hamlet is not touched enough, however, to accept this Roman gesture of friendship. Instead, and rather characteristically, he refuses Horatio's gesture of spiritual companionship and insists that he dedicate himself to 'report me and my cause aright/ to the unsatisfied'. Embodying the Renaissance ideal of friendship, Horatio does as requested, informing opportunistic Fortinbras and shocked English ambassador of the torrid tragedy reverberating around Elsinore's courtly halls.

Characteristically, he reverts to his prudent pragmatism, advising restraint and calm. The bodies of the dead must be displayed 'while men's minds are wild, lest more mischance/ on plots and errors happen'. In a spectacular end to the play with its array of tragic deaths, including maybe the death of Denmark itself, the abiding final image of most productions is of Horatio cradling his dead friend and 'sweet Prince'. Horatio's laudatory words, together with Fortinbras' frankly misinformed opinions on Hamlet, do much to rehabilitate any damage to Hamlet's reputation.

Over the course of a play, where Hamlet's inactions highlight his tragic suffering but his actions reveal, arguably, a self-centred and destructive egotism, it is important for the play's credibility that the tragic hero be redeemed. And what better man to convince the audience of this more sanitised Hamlet than good old dependable, reliable and morally sound Horatio?

There are several critical approaches that might render such actions as rather more self-serving on Horatio's part. A cynical Marxist might throw their eyes heavenward as they see a very pragmatic Horatio wheedling his ways into Fortinbras' favour and positioning himself as the puppet leader of a new Norwegian province, thus denying the voice of the people yet again. He would be a most capable and steadfast candidate for such a role and basically the only man left standing in the Danish court at that point! However, a more controversial reading would build upon A.D. Nuttall's forthright claim that Hamlet is 'incapable, seemingly, of a normal sexual relationship with a loving woman'[38]. While much Freudian energy has been expended upon highlighting the warped Oedipal dysfunction between Hamlet and his mother, it could also be argued that he has no interest in Ophelia, not because of his mother, but because of his soul mate, Horatio. Describing Horatio as 'just a man/ as e'er my conversation coped withal' and impressed by his ability to handle all that life throws at him with calm, it certainly seems as if opposites could really attract in this particular relationship. Together with the potentially intensely romantic possibilities of their death embrace ['Romeo and Juliet'

---

[38] Nuttall, *Shakespeare, The Thinker*, p.196.

becomes 'Horatio and Hamlet'] and Hamlet's misogynistic cruelty towards a highly suitable heterosexual partner, queer possibilities cannot be ruled out.

Maybe this is why Hamlet's outlandish claim that he loved Ophelia with such intensity that 'forty thousand brothers/ could not with all their quantity of love /make up my sum' rings so hollow. For all the time, on the margins of the play,

 away from the dramatic conflict between 'might opposites', may lurk another equally compelling drama: Hamlet's inability to realise his love for Horatio or Horatio's love for him. Laertes, after all, advised that Hamlet's choice of life-partner would be tempered by state concerns. While Denmark might put up with the incestuous oddness of Claudius and Gertrude, it seems likely that it would not entertain the gay power couple Hamlet and Horatio. Maybe that's why Hamlet is so angry with Gertrude: the corruption quota has been filled and there's no room for her son and his prohibited desire. Horatio not so much Hamlet's alter ipsi – his second self - but as an unattainable love object.

Other characters
Laertes & Fortinbras

Alongside Pyrrhus and Lucianus, the main dramatic function of both Laertes and Fortinbras is as foils for Hamlet and particularly for Hamlet as an avenger. If we placed Laertes, Hamlet and Fortinbras on a sliding scale of revenge, Laertes would occupy one pole as the keenest, most hot-headed avenger, the one who demands immediate satisfaction for his father's death. Hamlet would be placed in the middle, characteristically hesitating between thinking and violent action, while Fortinbras would occupy the opposite pole to Laertes, as the calmest, most calculating, the one ready, it seems, to play the long game. Seemingly the least driven by the emotional fires of revenge, Fortinbras, of course, is also the only one of the three to survive the avenging task.

As discussed in our essay on themes in *Hamlet*, Shakespeare doesn't primarily use Hamlet's soliloquies to explore the ethics of revenge nor to untangle the intermeshed relationships between revenge, regicide and justice. Rather Shakespeare creates a hall of mirrors, with multiple versions of the revenger and the play invites us to contrast and compare them. Lucianus, for instance, with his 'thoughts black' blurs the distinction between noble avenger and Machiavellian villain, while Pyrrhus is presented as a brutal, pitiless butcher driven more by rage and bloodlust than desire for justice. Within this frame of reference, Hamlet's delay in seeking vengeance appears more reasonable, more modern and encourages the audience to sympathise more with the Prince.

Laertes

Laertes' interactions with other characters reveal important things both about him, about them and about the Danish state. For example, Polonius sending an agent, Reynaldo, to spy on his son, confirms the chief councillor's role as head of espionage in the Danish court and reveals his fundamental lack of trust, even in his son. After his departure for Paris in Act I, we do not see Laertes again until after Polonius' death. In Act IV, Scene 5 he re-enters Elsinore at the head of a rabble which it appears has all-too-easily broken into the castle. The name Laertes means 'gatherer of the people' so there is a sense here that he is fulfilling his latent potential, or his fate. Not only an avenger, Laertes is presented as a possible usurper. This indicates a secondary function of his character – signalling the weakness of Claudius' grip on power. The rabble demands Laertes be king, even though he has shown few kingly qualities, suggesting a chronic lack of support for Claudius among the populace. Moreover, foreshadowing the ease with which Fortinbras will take the castle at the end of the play, Elsinore's defences are easily breached, even, it seems, by an untrained military force, a mere rabble. Even the King's personal guards, his 'Switzers', seem to have vanished. The ease with which Laertes takes the castle confirms something hinted at the start of the play when the guards did not report the ghost to their superiors - the rottenness at the heart of Claudius' Elsinore.

When, armed, Laertes threatens the King, Gertrude shows surprising physical courage, not only interposing, but actually physically trying to restrain him. Undaunted and composed, Claudius also reacts rather impressively to this potentially mortal threat. Having called him a 'vile king' Laertes demands that Claudius give him his father. Telling the Queen twice to 'let him go', Claudius's response - a long, unruffled speech - begins by shrinking Laertes down to a more manageable size: 'What is the cause, Laertes/ That thy rebellion looks so giant-like?' Claudius' deftness in dealing with and eventually manipulating Laertes is shown here and even more so in Act IV, Scene 7 where the King weaponizes Laertes' anger and re-directs it at Hamlet. Claudius's cleverness also suggests Laertes' foolishness. Isn't Laertes far too easily exploited by the King, far too ready to join a murderous conspiracy, far too willing to corrupt himself by lacing his sword with the Machiavellian villain's favourite weapon, poison?

In some ways Laertes experiences the same traumas as Hamlet, only over a much shorter time frame. Bursting in on the King and Queen, Laertes was propelled by a righteous rage for revenge and justice for his dead father. But, rather than immediately sweeping to this revenge he is soon side-tracked by grief. Witnessing the madness of his sister, Laertes is driven to tears.

Laertes' protective treatment of his sister, from his seemingly excessive interest in her love life in Act I to his reaction to her madness highlights how Ophelia is described, treated and controlled by the predominant men in her life. Laertes seeks to retain the sense of a 'sweet', 'kind', flower-like Ophelia, even in her madness, an Ophelia who is still the innocent virgin, the 'maid' he calls the 'rose of May'. At her funeral he will 'leap' into her grave, demanding that the mourners hold off throwing more earth onto the coffin until he has 'caught her once more' in his arms. Once again, this action suggests something transgressive and excessive in his love. Certainly Hamlet thinks so. He too leaps into Ophelia's grave and the two men 'grapple' like two rivals fighting over a lover. And, of course, it is as Hamlet's rival and foil that Laertes serves his most important dramatic function.

'I dare damnation' - Laertes and Hamlet

Close parallels and significant contrasts between Laertes and Hamlet are established in Act I. Intentionally slighting Hamlet in a demonstration of power, after his introductory speech in Scene 2 and having established Polonius' permission first, Claudius graciously grants Laertes' request to leave Elsinore for Paris. Hamlet, of course, is not granted his wish to leave Elsinore to return to Wittenberg. Among the key relationships for Hamlet are those between him and his father, his step-father and his lover, Ophelia. In Act I, Scene 3 Hamlet's royal family is paralleled by the Polonius family, with the focus shifting to Laertes' relationships with his sister, Ophelia, and with his father. So, both Hamlet and Laertes love Ophelia and both characters are also presented, even defined, in terms of their father-son relationship.

If Hamlet is the over-thinking revenger, then Laertes must be the under-thinking one. In classical literature, Laertes was the father of the Greek hero Odysseus, and hence Laertes adds to the network of allusions to classical culture in the play and to their pre-Christian understanding of revenge. Ostensibly Laertes seems less troubled by doubts and worries about the revenge task than Hamlet. More emotional, impulsive and uncritically dutiful than the Prince, Laertes is so determined to have his revenge that he is prepared to threaten even the King, even when he has no evidence of Claudius' culpability for his father's death. Interestingly, however, Laertes isn't oblivious to the potential direst ramifications in the afterlife, the eternal punishment he may suffer as the cost of revenging his father, it's just that he claims he doesn't care about this consequence, however terrible it may be. His duty to his father trumps every other consideration. Everything, every moral scruple, must be swept away by the tide of revenge: 'To hell, allegiance! Vows, to the blackest devil! Conscience and grace, to the profoundest pit! I dare damnation'. But, if revenge is the righteous, noble and just action, an absolute, undeniable moral imperative, why does Laertes think that it entails disregarding his conscience? Moreover, why does he think that he might be damned for it? Certainly, Laertes' framing of revenge - associating it with hell, the blackest devil, the profoundest pit and with sin [losing his 'grace'] - echoes the earlier descriptions of both Lucianus and Pyrrhus as well as Hamlet's 'Hot blood' soliloquy, amplifying the ethical debate in the play about revenge.

Perhaps this is all bluster, hot-air, just words, words, words, as Hamlet might say, hyperbole carried on the wave of Laertes' fury and soon doused by a combination of Claudius' cunning and Ophelia's madness. Yet, even when he has calmed down in Scene 7, Laertes claims he would be prepared to 'cut' Hamlet's 'throat'. Is this really justice? If becoming a cutthroat doesn't seem villainous in itself, Laertes boasts that he would also be prepared to murder Hamlet in this ignoble fashion within a sacred space, a 'church', adding a further sacrilegious edge to the villainy.

Fundamentally *Hamlet* is a play about the past weighing all too heavily on a present that cannot emerge from its shadow, emblematized by sons burdened, overwhelmed and eventually destroyed by the task of honouring their dead fathers. In this Laertes goes further than any other revenger. He is not just prepared to be consumed and destroyed by this duty; he is willing to damn his immortal soul and suffer the torments of hell, for eternity. That's some price to pay for doing your duty to your father.

Young Fortinbras

With a name meaning 'man of the strong arm', expectations for Fortinbras' martial prowess are immediately established. Like Hamlet, Fortinbras is named after his father, suggesting that, despite his strengths, he too might struggle to forge an identity independent of an overshadowing patriarch. Like Hamlet, Fortinbras begins the play intent on revenging his father's death. Reported in Act I by Horatio to be 'hot' and 'full', recruiting an army to threaten Denmark, more soldierly than Hamlet, Fortinbras initially seems an unreflective avenger. However, it appears that Claudius' diplomatic intervention works and, discovering Fortinbras' hostile intentions, Old Norway rebukes his nephew and make him promise not to attack Denmark. It appears that Fortinbras accepts this rebuke. Cornelius reports that young Fortinbras 'makes vows before his Uncle never more/ To give the assay of arms against your majesty'. Well played Claudius, we might think. And also that perhaps Fortinbras wasn't as calm and calculating as we claimed at the start of this essay. But, hang on a moment, something is not quite right here.

Fortinbras' invasion at the end of the play surely undermines readings of *Hamlet* opining that Claudius was an effective king. While for most of the play it had appeared that Claudius' use of diplomatic tools – ambassadors and letters - rather than military force, had neutralised the Norwegian threat, at the end we realise that either the Norwegian king had less control over Fortinbras than he thought or that he was tricked by his nephew. A third possibility is that the King connived with his nephew to deceive Claudius, with an objective of lowering Danish defences and invading at the most opportune time. Whichever way we read this, Fortinbras emerges from this as a shrewd operator and effective military leader. If he was originally hot-headed and impulsive, like Laertes, unlike Laertes he learnt from this and developed a more calculated and ultimately successful approach. Like Hamlet, Fortinbras does not accede to the throne after the death of his father. Like Hamlet, his uncle appears to usurp him. However, unlike Hamlet, Fortinbras survives and becomes king of another country.

How though did Shakespeare want his audience to feel about Fortinbras taking over the Danish throne? Relief that order has been restored? Concerned that a country has been so easily invaded by a foreign power? And what are we to make of Fortinbras dubious appropriation of Hamlet as a soldier? Will Horatio really be allowed to control the narrative on these events now or will it be the victor's version of history that triumphs?

Different productions, of course, may interpret Fortinbras' arrival in Act V in different ways. Sometimes, indeed, productions cut this section entirely and end instead with Hamlet's dying words. Consider for a moment how that editorial decision might affect the meaning and effect of the play. If you were the director, what arguments could you make in favour of cutting or keeping Fortinbras' entrance? As mentioned earlier in this guide, one production had Fortinbras' soldiers shoot all the remaining Danes. What is clear is that the cycle of history has turned again and turned backwards; with Fortinbras' ascension to the Danish throne, the political power of Claudius has given way to another martial king.

Old Hamlet

Old Hamlet has often been viewed nostalgically as a deceased hero. In Act III, Scene 4, Prince Hamlet depicts his father as a martial conqueror and godlike ruler. The former King, his son tells us, bore 'grace' upon his brow, 'the front of Jove himself/ An eye like Mars to threaten and command' [55-56]. In Old Hamlet's form, his son swears that 'every god did seem to set his seal/ To give the world assurance of a man'. Old Hamlet was also, according to his son, like Hyperion – a god of heavenly light. Such classical allusions give Old Hamlet an immense, timeless stature and a sort of mighty heroism untouched by the sordid corruptions of Claudius' Elsinore. Indeed, as a martial king Old Hamlet is presented as the opposite to his successor, the Machiavellian political king, Claudius, who uses diplomacy, not warfare to settle his disputes with Norway. While the overwhelming, perhaps impossibly overbearing, shadow this mighty father throws upon his son is suggested by their shared name, Hamlet too struggles to live up to his father's example.

Yet the man that Hamlet remembers no longer exists; he is dead before the play begins, killed by his brother's hand. The ghost that looks like Hamlet's father is a more ambiguous character – and the play deliberately leaves us questioning its identity as 'a spirit of health or goblin damned,' as well as whether its intentions are 'wicked or charitable' [I.4,40-42].

In life, Old Hamlet appears to have matched up to his son's memories of him. Horatio likewise recalls him as one 'esteem'd' by 'this side of our known world' and as a 'dar[ing]' warrior-king, whose exploits on the battlefield, such as the single-handed slaying of Old Fortinbras, are still lauded some thirty years later. Yet, unlike many other warrior-kings in the literary tradition whose lust for blood costs their realms dearly in both capital and human life, he is careful to protect his people. '[P]rick'd on by a most emulate pride…to combat', he spared his soldiers from battle by engaging in single-combat to win now Danish lands from Norway in a revered feat of empire-building. Even the usurper Claudius acknowledges his brother's 'valian[ce]'.

The Ghost of Old Hamlet, however, is presented much more guardedly. When it is first spoken of upon the battlements in Act I, Scene 1, it is described as a 'thing' and a 'fantasy', as if the image of the former king is nothing more than a conjuration of his close subjects' collective memories. This wariness does not abate when the Ghost appears again. Horatio is the first to allow that the 'dreaded sight' may be more than a figment of their imaginations, but his move to describe an 'apparition' or 'spirit…[that] walk[s] in death' is coupled with expectations of disaster. He speaks uneasily of 'tenantless' graves and

'sheeted dead' walking the streets in Rome before the fall of Julius Caesar and speculates that the Ghost is 'prologue to the omen coming on', a precursor of 'fear'd events' that may be the 'country's fate'. Horatio and the guards are also sceptical that the 'spirit' is that of Old Hamlet. In contrast to the confident metaphors and similes that Hamlet uses to build a picture of his deceased father *as* Jove, alike to Mercury, Mars and Hyperion, the Ghost is described only as '*like* the King'. Though it seems to wear 'the very armour he had on' and 'frown[s]' as the King did, it remains an 'it', a figure '*like* [Hamlet's] father', a thing that 'assume[s]' the dead King's 'person', not the King himself.

Uncertainty around the Ghost's existence and motivations befits the period in which Shakespeare was writing. What ghosts were and where they came from were concerns profoundly entangled in the social, religious, and political upheavals of the mid-sixteenth century. Traditional Catholic beliefs that had governed the country until Henry VIII's break with Rome between 1532 and 1534 – and returned again with the brief reign of Queen Mary [1553-1558] – encompassed the doctrine of purgatory. This late medieval Catholic eschatology held that there were three possible doorways open to a person after death: Those who were so saintly were saved and went directly to heaven; those who were irreversibly damned went straight to hell. The average person was more likely to spend some time in between the two in a space called purgatory, being punished for any transgressions they had not repented for in life before being granted salvation.

The concept of purgatory was problematic even in Catholic society. 'Accounts of Purgatory,' Stephen Greenblatt explains, 'grappled with the belatedness of the doctrine [which crystalized in the late thirteenth century] and the evident difficulty many people had believing in it'.[39]. Its existence, its location, and what means the living and the dead had to communicate with each other were extensively debated. The concept of purgatorial spirits was plagued by theological doubts; three possibilities were acknowledged to explain the appearance of a ghost: 1) that it was an angel sent from God to deliver a divine message; 2) that it was a devil sent to trick humans into sin; and 3) that it was indeed the spirit of someone recently deceased returning from purgatory to resolve unfinished earthly business. The Ghost's claim that 'I am thy father's spirit' would have been worthy of caution, even before the Reformation.

Hamlet, of course, is neither set nor played in a Catholic society. The Denmark Hamlet inhabits is Protestant, with the young Prince attending University in Wittenberg – the site of the Protestant Reformation. Shakespeare's England

---

[39] Greenblatt, *Hamlet in Purgatory*, p.115.

too, in the twilight years of Elizabeth I's reign, had been Protestant for almost forty years. The Ghost's claim is doubly dubious in this context. The Protestant Church rejected the concept of purgatory as lacking any scriptural basis and suppressed all rituals of living-dead dialogue alongside its iconoclasms. While traditional Catholic beliefs and old folklore undoubtedly continued to infuse society and culture, Protestant theology held that scripture was God's primary lifeline to salvation for humanity and angelic visitations were unlikely. Officially, the most plausible explanation for ghosts was that they were demons playing tricks on humans to fool them into sinful behaviour. Some textual editions, as well as performances of the play, tend towards this interpretation by having the Ghost's interjections in Act I, scene v performed from under the stage: the space traditionally used to represent hell in the early modern theatre.

So, is the dead king's spirit a 'goblin damned'? The play does not encourage an easy answer. Critic David George notes that Horatio, Marcellus, and Barnardo all use language that 'reflect[s] Elizabethan doubts about ghosts'[40]. Their initial anxieties that the Ghost may be a fantasy are reiterated when Horatio wonders if, by talking to the Ghost, Hamlet may be 'deprive[d]…of reason/ And draw[n]…into madness'. This speculation is given some credit by Hamlet's later 'antic disposition', echoing the ideas of Reginald Scot whose treatise on witchcraft asserts that ghosts are neither real nor devils in disguise, but symptoms of insanity: 'seene in the imagination of the weake and diseased'.

For Emma Smith, the Ghost is more benevolent. Real, or imaginary, it is a visualisation of the 'throes of the past'[41]. The two pleas it makes – for Hamlet to revenge and to remember – are part of the play's exploration of memory, how to uphold the obligations and conventions of the past, and to recall those who have died in a culture that has recently lost many of its rites and rituals of remembrance. In this interpretation, the Ghost may be seen as a theatrical

---

[40] George, *Hamlet, the Ghost, and a New Document*, p.2.

[41] Smith, *Hamlet: looking backwards*.

device.

A further possibility is to read the Ghost as performing the stereotypic role within the genre of revenge tragedy. Like other spirits, such as Don Andrea in Thomas Kyd's popular and influential *The Spanish Tragedy*, Old Hamlet calls for his son to 'revenge his foul and most unnatural murder'. As we see in other examples of the genre, such calls to revenge are intended to 'redress injustice[s] caused by abuses of power'[42]. Here, revenge is sought for a crime [the murder of the king] where justice is unobtainable through the normal legal channels [the murderer is now the king]. If the Ghost is simply a plot device, though, its claim to be Old Hamlet is doubtful, since it puts the law he once upheld, as essayist Francis Bacon would say, 'out of Office'. Revenge, as Tanya Pollard tells us, 'invariably exceed[s] the original crime, creating new victims, and the revenger is always eventually punished for taking the law into his and her own hands'. The respected king, Old Hamlet was, it seems, more likely to have accepted it was 'the princes part to pardon', as Bacon suggests, rather than risk multiple lives in a chain of revenge killings.

Initially for Hamlet himself, though, the Ghost seems to be both real and 'honest' – the spirit of his father, visiting from purgatory. After his dialogue with it, he describes it as a 'vision', which Shakespeare tends to use for encounters experienced in a holy state. Despite this, he remains chary of its demands and resolves to find evidence to prove Claudius' guilt before he attempts to take revenge. Even if he initially accepts the Ghost as his father, his soliloquies rigorously question the ethics of revenge and he promises only to 'remember'. After all, little is holy or divine about the cascade of events that the Ghost's appearance and interview set in motion, ultimately leading to the destruction of the royal family and loss of Denmark's crown and lands to Norwegian rule.

---

[42] Pollard [from] *The Cambridge Companion to English Renaissance Tragedy*, p.59.

Reflecting on the range of possibilities the play offers us for the presence of the Ghost, it's time to make up your own mind. Is the Ghost really Old Hamlet returned from the dead to seek revenge for his untimely death? A devilish trickster? A fantasy cooked up by anxious guards in the dead of night that becomes a trigger for Hamlet's madness? Or is it something else? Could an argument be made that it is more than one of these things? One thing we must surely agree on is that, whatever the Ghost may be, its presence in the play proves to be the very portent of doom that Horatio predicts.

Rosencrantz & Guildenstern

In our experience, students often feel that Hamlet's trick of re-writing Claudius' letter to the English King and sending Rosencrantz and Guildenstern off to their deaths instead of him and the lack of remorse the Prince expresses about this – just a casual, off-hand, 'they are not near my conscience' – confirms that Hamlet is fundamentally a self-centred, callous character, a character who cruelly mistreats those around him and is, consequently, undeserving of our sympathy. These students are, of course, entirely wrong, about Rosencrantz and Guildenstern at least. For there is no doubt that these two self-serving 'adders fang'd' entirely deserve their brutal comeuppance.

It's no coincidence, of course, that Shakespeare and Hamlet chose the image of snakes to describe Rosencrantz and Guildenstern. The imagery links them to that other prime snake in the fallen garden of Elsinore, Claudius, and of course to the greatest of evildoer of them all, Satan. And, indeed, Rosencrantz and Guildenstern have been ordered to Denmark by Claudius to spy on Hamlet, exploiting the cover of their school friendship to try and deceive the Prince. In their first interaction with Hamlet, after the jokey double entrendres about fortune, the twosome are given ample opportunity to come clean and level with him about why they have come to Elsinore. In fact, Hamlet gives them several opportunities to tell the truth and redeem

themselves in his and our eyes. Not only do they fail this test, but when Hamlet generously offers them an olive branch, they do not take it: Even when Hamlet appeals to the 'rights' of their 'fellowship' and tells them that he has already worked out that they are not making a 'free visitation' and that they were, in fact, 'sent for' and gives them a chance to at least admit as much, they still hesitate. Only when they have no option do they finally confess, that 'My lord, we were sent for'. Too late, by far. Whereas Hamlet can be candid with Horatio, trusting him with his true thoughts and taking him into the plan to expose Claudius' guilt, these two are the reverse. Hamlet and the audience have already established that Rosencrantz and Guildenstern are false friends, snakes in the grass, the malign, corrupted double to Horatio's genuine, singular friendship.

But, at this point, there's still plenty of time left in the play for Rosencrantz and Guildenstern to prove our impressions wrong, or for them to have a change of heart or to perform some sort of redemptive act. If they decided to switch allegiances and help their friend Hamlet, for instance, they could be highly useful double agents. Of course, easy, pliable tools – like hand saws - for Claudius' use, acting out of their own self-interest, obsequiously flattering the King, ever anxious to keep in his favour, keeping tabs on Hamlet as part of Elsinore's network of surveillance, eventually becoming his guards, they do not change. Nor do they show the slightest inclination to do so. As Hamlet dismissively tells them, the pair are like a sponge 'that soaks up the king's countenance, his rewards, his authorities'. Hamlet even warns them that they will be kept 'in the corner' of the King's 'jaw' to be 'swallowed', or that eventually they will be squeezed out, cast aside and left 'dry' by Claudius. It is not a warning they are able or willing to heed.

If, at first, the thinnest mask of friendship hides their true purpose in Elsinore as Claudius' spies, it is not too long before their role becomes utterly transparent. After Hamlet has accidentally killed Polonius and Gertrude has informed Claudius of the murder, it is Rosencrantz and Guildenstern the King turns to. Their task is to find Hamlet, who is somewhere at large in the castle. Claudius tells them to make 'haste' and to 'join you with some further aid'. Often the language of power cloaks itself in euphemism, in this play and elsewhere. That casual sounding 'further aid' is often taken by directors to really mean with armed guards. Their first attempt to bring Hamlet to the King fails, however, with Hamlet's exiting line implying they are like a pack of hounds chasing a fox: 'bring me to him. Hide fox, and all after'. A wily, cunning, evasive fox, who having initially seemed to submit to his 'arrest' ['bring me to him'] then suddenly turns tail and is off. In the Kenneth Branagh film the seeking of Hamlet turns into a full-blown chase through the corridors of the castle, a pursuit that only comes to a halt when a soldier's gun is pointed directly at Hamlet's head.

Act IV, Scene 3 confirms that Hamlet has, indeed, been arrested. Rosencrantz tells Claudius that they have found Hamlet and that he is being held outside 'guarded'. Acting like a guard, it is Guildenstern who brings Hamlet in to see his uncle-father. The next and last time we see them, Rosencrantz and Guildenstern ['with others' who we presume to be soldiers] are accompanying Hamlet as he is taken out of Denmark to board ship for England. Although they are not party to Claudius's conspiracy to have Hamlet immediately executed on arrival, clearly they have been entrusted with guarding Hamlet and ensuring that he endured his banishment. Though the script doesn't explicitly say that these two are carrying Claudius' letter to the English king, they are his henchmen, the people Claudius has increasingly depended on to carry out his business and no other character on stage is a  suitable candidate for this task. Unwittingly, perhaps, but Rosencrantz and Guildenstern carry on their persons Hamlet's death warrant and are escorting him to certain death.

Still, you might argue, that although they are disloyal, despicable, self-serving characters who have readily betrayed their childhood friend, the eager lackeys of a murderous Machiavellian villain, another example of the all-pervasive corruption of the Danish court, Rosencrantz and Guildenstern do not deserve to die. Or that Hamlet should still have shown some remorse for sending them to their deaths. If you think this, as Katy Limmer explains in an article for the English and Media Centre, Elizabethans would have been unlikely to agree. Limmer writes that the 'Intensity of male friendships in the Renaissance explains how shocking and bitter Rosencrantz and Guildenstern's betrayal would appear to a contemporary audience'[43]. For Elizabethans, Rosencrantz and Guildenstern's death are just because they willingly betray one of the most important bastions on which society was built, the true, trusting friendship between men.

So, this double act is not just a pair of comic clowns, helplessly caught up and eventually destroyed, collateral damage in the clash of mighty opposites. Instead they are truly 'adders fang'd', conniving with a corrupt, despotic regime and themselves corrupt.

---

[43] Limmer, *'Male Friendship in Hamlet'*.

The Gravediggers

Act V, Scene 1 is set in a graveyard. Despite its sombre location, it is a scene of seeming mirth. Two clowns, forming a familiar comic double-act, dig Ophelia's grave, their funereal work in stark contrast to their chattering, drinking, singing and their gallows humour. Skulls fly up from their spades and tumble around in the dirt. In the midst of their labour, Hamlet and Horatio enter. Hamlet is appalled by their careless irreverence, exclaiming, 'Has this fellow no feeling of his business, that he sings at grave-making?' He watches the flights of the skulls uncomfortably, speculating that they may be politicians, courtiers, ladies, and lawyers slung around as though they are common criminals, like Cain 'that did the first murder'. For all their seeming

disrespect, however, the gravediggers recognise some among the dismembered dead. One points out the skull of Yorick, 'the king's jester'. Hamlet is distracted from his discomfort, takes the skull, and recreates the clown from memory in almost as much detail as he does when he recollects his father. His perspective on death seems to shift

here and he, like the clowns, muses on the social levelling that takes place in the grave. The arrival of Ophelia's funeral party returns the play to its former sobriety.

Like many of Shakespeare's scenes featuring commoners, the episode with the gravediggers or clowns is not merely a moment of comic relief. Clowning scenes are timed for moments when 'the shock or trauma level of the play has reached a point when…audience members become desensitised' to 'give spectators a chance to catch their breath and mentally prepare themselves for what follows'[44]. Rather than simply distracting from the main themes of the play, however, they reiterate, familiarize and universalise them, often simplified and using contemporary references. As Culwell writes, 'what cannot be understood when expressed by the Prince of Denmark makes logical sense when simply outlined by the gravedigger and put into contemporary terms'.

Among the key topics that the clowns discuss, which are threaded through the play as a whole, are: the rites of memory, social class, justice, political corruption, and identity. Hamlet's speculations on the legitimacy of self-murder in Act I, Scene 2 is explored in the Clowns discussion of whether Ophelia's death is self-defence or self-offense ['se offendendo' – a comic mistranslation of the Latin]. The apparently playful question of whether the man goes to the water or the water comes to the man examines the legal tensions between ecclesiastical and state law regarding possible suicides, where the former denied the victim a Christian burial while the latter excused someone deemed insane from such social rejection on the grounds that they could not be held responsible for their decision. The same theme is continued in Laertes' and the priest's disagreement over what rituals should be performed for one whose 'death was doubtful' in the second half of the scene. The way Ophelia is buried provides a contrast to the ceremonial burial of Hamlet, who died nobly in combat, and the deliberate forgetting that will be Claudius' reward for his treachery.

The corrupt politics of Elsinore emerge too in the clowns' parodies of legal language. Coupled with Hamlet's tirade against the 'skull of a lawyer', 'full of quiddities…quillets… cases…tenures…tricks', the law becomes a prime example of all that is manipulative and deceptive in Elsinore. As portrayed in this scene the law is a paradigm for Claudius' court, with the King himself exemplifying a scheming politician and manipulator of the justice system, one who forces Hamlet to seek wild justice through revenge.

---

[44] Culwell, 'The Role of the Clown'.

The pun on 'plot' as meaning both political scheming and the space in the graveyard – which echoes an earlier one about Fortinbras' attack on an area of Polish ground too small to inter the soldiers who will die fighting over it [V.4,62], and a later one [V.2,9-10] – serves as a forewarning of the play's ultimate end.[45]

Finally, the clowning scene further investigates the concept of performativity that Hamlet first raised in Act I, Scene 2. In their interrogation of Ophelia's suicide, the Clowns suggest that deliberately drowning oneself 'argues an act, and an act hath three branches: it is to act, to do, to perform'. Similar, yet  subtly distinct, as Christie outlines, each of the Sexton's alternatives are 'a repertory of human action' that reminds us that the 'whole play turns on various meanings of act'. There is the supposed performance of grief by the royal couple that Hamlet contrasts with his own authentic turmoil in Act I, Scene 2, and later Hamlet's performance of madness. Both expose the potential for one's outer presentation to differ from one's inner feelings – reinforced here in the disjointed body parts divorced from their former lives. There is Hamlet's *inaction* upon the Ghost's dread command' [III.4.109], where act and deed are set in opposition to his extensive thoughts. And there is his use of players *acting out* the Ghost's tale to affirm his need to seek revenge in remembrance of his father. There is also, of course, the fact that the whole play is itself an act, performed on a stage, and aware of its own theatricality – alluded to in this scene where Hamlet, in the company of Clowns, speaks to the skull of Yorick, the royal Clown, and waiting for him to 'mock [his] own grinning'. Far from being simply a light-hearted scene to break the tension in the play before returning and escalating it, the gravediggers' episode revisits, reimagines, and reinforces the play's principal recurring themes.

---

[45] Christie, *Being and Acting in Hamlet*, pp.3-4.

Minor characters

A note on the names in this play. The setting is meant to be Denmark and yet the names appear to be more Roman and Greek. Laertes, for example, is the name of the father of Odysseus, while even the guards, Bernardo, Marcellus and Francisco sound more Roman than Danish. Claudius and Horatio are also Roman, with the former the name of an emperor who came to power after an assassination. As discussed elsewhere in this guide, this indicates both the thinness of the Danish setting – clearly these events could be happening in Rome or England – and also the pervasive influence of classical literature on Shakespeare. Classical literature provides a sounding board on which contemporary issues such as revenge, regicide and suicide can be tested.

The Guards: Marcellus, Barnardo and Francisco

What is the function of guards? It sounds obvious, but, surely these guards should be protecting the castle from potential external threats. Yet, in Act I, Scene 1 they seem more concerned about potential attack from within Elsinore. Where were they too when Laertes so easily swept into the castle with a rag-tag rabble, a warning surely that should have been heeded before Fortinbras invaded at the end of the play? Where do the guards' loyalties lie? At the start of the play they have witnessed a potential threat, a supernatural armed figure. Their duty is to report this to their superiors. Ultimately, they are the King's guards, so why do they not pass news of this potential peril up the line to Claudius? Instead they inform Horatio and Hamlet. The functions of the court are degraded by Claudius' rule; so too it seems is the proper function of the guards - to protect the country from external dangers.

Cornelius and Voltemand

These two characters are Claudius' ambassadors sent to Norway to ensure that young Fortinbras does not attack Denmark. They exemplify the way Claudius conducts affairs of state, using diplomatic channels rather than military force to deal with external threats to the realm. While from a modern perspective we may be more sympathetic to Claudius' peaceful, political approach, despite initial appearances, his strategy doesn't work. In the end, of course, a foreign force easily takes Elsinore, suggesting that the King had taken his eye off this existential threat.

Reynaldo

With a name signalling slyness and cunning, Reynaldo is more than a spy. Polonius employs him as an agent provocateur, a role in which he has to deliberately spread false rumours about Laertes in order to discover whether he is up to no good in Paris. Polonius had sent his son off with his permission and issued a long list of advice to him. Their relationship had seemed to be close and affectionate. The fact that Polonius follows this with sending Reynaldo to shadow Laertes reveals his fundamental lack of trust and Polonius' habitual use of subterfuge and espionage. If we are tempted to read Polonius as an essentially comic character – a harmless old windbag – his spying even on his own son should give us serious pause for thought.

Osric

Insulted variously as a 'water-fly', 'chough' and 'lapwing', treated with disdain as a comic figure by both Hamlet and Horatio, Osric is like a second, more minor Polonius. Like Polonius, he embodies the sort of character benefitting from Claudius' court; as the King's messenger and judge in the duel he is an integral part of its corruption. However, whereas Polonius was an active agent in spreading corruption, corrupting friendships, parent-child relationships among other things, Osric is a symptom. As Andrew Hadfield writes, Claudius' court is an unstable one in which 'the proper functions of advice, counsel and debate have degenerated to flattery, espionage and silence'[46] The foppish flatterer Osric exemplifies that degeneration; hence Hamlet's hostility and ridicule.

Claudio

When a messenger arrives in Act IV, Scene 7 with a letter informing the King of Hamlet's unexpected return to Denmark, he tells Claudius that the letters were given to him by Claudio. Who the hell is Claudio? Why include him in this exchange? Probably this name is a transcription error. Or maybe not.

---

[46] Hadfield, *Shakespeare and Renaissance Politics*, p.88.

Critical reception

We haven't the time or space here to go into a lot of detail about how different critics have responded to the play since it was produced over four hundred years ago and, in any case, this sort of material is touched upon throughout out guide. It is useful for students to know, however, how the general focus of criticism of this play and Shakespeare's plays as a whole, has changed over time.

Broadly speaking, though it is a highly varied field, what are now called traditional critical approaches tended to be preoccupied with issues to do with characters. As we mentioned in our section on the nature of the play, Aristotle has had, and continues to have, a huge influence on literary criticism, particularly criticism of tragedies. Aristotle's description of the central protagonist as being a high-born character who destroys himself because of a tragic, or fatal, flaw in his character or via a calamitous decision he makes encouraged critics to focus on the titular characters of Shakespeare's tragedies. Examining Macbeth, Lear, Hamlet and Othello, critics suggested a range of different possible fatal flaws, or 'hamartias', for each of these tragic heroes.

Historically, the figure of Hamlet himself has certainly preoccupied critics. For the Romantic poets, Hamlet was the embodiment of the Romantic outsider, the sensitive poetic thinker unable to cope with a brutal world. While Victorian critics saw Hamlet in similar light as a poetic soul, often they were less sympathetic towards his apparent inability to do his duty to his father. One very influential, traditional critic has been A.C. Bradley. In the book of his lectures, *Shakespearian Tragedy*, first published in 1904 and still in print, Bradley focuses mainly on the major characters in each tragedy, exploring what he takes to be their individual psychologies as a means of discovering their true hamartias. Generally Bradley treated Shakespeare's characters as if they were really living, breathing people and even speculated about their lives beyond the world of the plays. As you will have read elsewhere in this book, Bradley identified Hamlet's melancholia, a state of morbidity produced by both his father's death and, in particular, his mother's overhasty marriage as the Prince's hamartia.

Beginning after WWII, modern criticism sought to re-focus critical attention. Feminist criticism, for instance, challenged the general critical valorisation of Hamlet and kindled new interest in the hitherto under-explored characters of Gertrude and Ophelia. Generally modern critics aimed to correct the traditional over-focus on characters alone by re-directing critical attention on the ways in which wider contexts which shaped these characters, particularly history, society, politics and power.

Modern criticism is highly sceptical about the idea that human beings operate in the world entirely as free agents, making all their own choices and decisions without influence from culture or society. Modern critics point out that just as a text is shaped by the time it was written in and the time in which it is read, so too are the characters within it. In a nutshell, these critics relocate the hamartia in Shakespeare's plays away from the protagonists to the societies and the times in which the plays are set. For Jan Kott, for instance, writing shortly after WW II in *Shakespeare our Contemporary* [1961] Denmark is a prison camp, a sort of totalitarian state and Hamlet is the alienated victim of its tyranny. Hence a typical modern critical approach might examine how Hamlet is destroyed not by faults within his own psyche but by contradictory forces within his society. As we have discussed earlier in this guide, these forces might be contradictory notions of the ethics of revenge and regicide.

For modern critics, characters in Shakespeare's tragedies struggle to navigate paths through the treacherous landscape of a period in a liminal state, a period in transition from the late medieval to the early modern period. In the case of many of the characters, not being able to follow the same old familiar paths through this profoundly uncertain landscape leads inevitably to their destruction.

Teaching & revision ideas

Whichever board's exams you'll be taking, a fundamental part of the test will be your knowledge of the play. Check this by trying to write out a summary of the play, scene by scene, without using the script. Try to write no more than a couple of sentences for any one scene. Once you're done, compare it to other versions. Now choose a memorable title for each scene, as if were a chapter from a novel. The first scene, for example, could be called 'The Guards and the Ghost'.

How many scenes are there in the play overall? Twenty. Work out how many there are in each Act and then check against our tally on p. 221.

Now try to write out the narrative of the play in continuous prose using only about one side of A4.

A few pages on is our list of chapter-style titles for each scene of the play. However, there's been some strange eruption to their state and the order has been scrambled. How quickly can you put them back in the right sequence? How do our suggested titles compare to yours? [If you wish to check the correct sequence for these scenes is on p.226]

Write out each scene title on a separate piece of paper and arrange in a pile, face down. Mix them together. Pick up one piece of paper and explain either to yourself or a partner in as much detail as possible exactly what happens in this scene. If you're a bit hazy, go back to the play and remind yourself. Take another piece of paper and repeat the process nineteen times.

Mix the pieces of paper together and turn them over again. Now arrange them in the correct sequence as quickly as you can. Write out the sequence as a timeline. Add extra details, such as where the soliloquies fall. Use a different colour for Hamlet, Claudius and Gertrud and for Polonius and his family.

A similar exercise can be done to consolidate your knowledge of characters and their relationships to each other. Write out the name of every character who appears in the play on a separate piece of paper, turn face down and place in a pile. Now pick up any three pieces of paper at random. Put two of the characters together and separate the third, giving as many reasons for your pairing as you can. Then try to make a different pairing using the same three characters. Once you've exhausted what you have to say, place the pieces in the pile and start again. 10-15 minutes of this exercise, completed regularly will really help secure your knowledge of all the play's dramatis personae.

For each of the play's main characters complete a character circle. This is a diagram in the form of concentric circles. Using a page of A4 paper write the character's name in the middle and around that write words they would use to describe themselves. Draw a circle around that and write down words other characters might use to describe them. Draw a circle around that and write in words critics have written or might write about the character. Draw a final circle and add different 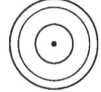 interpretations of the character in various productions you've seen. In the remaining space write down any further thoughts you have about the character.

Minor, unnamed characters can slip under the radar of our critical attention. Tracking them, however, can often be a useful and incisive way of re-reading the text, one that can open up new perspectives. Albeit always rather out of the spot-light of dramatic attention, in the background are various unnamed characters, such as various messengers, players, sailors and gravediggers. Make a list of all the play's unnamed characters and check exactly which scenes they appear and what they say. What would be lost if all these characters were cut from the play?

As you may have noticed, *Hamlet* is a very long play. Imagine you have been asked to direct a slightly abridged version. Which scenes, or sections within scenes, could you cut and why? Once you've decided on these cuts to the play, try to make a strong counterargument about why they must be retained. For example, does the play really need Act I Scene 1? If *Hamlet* started, as some productions have, with Claudius's speech in Scene 2 nothing much would be lost in terms of the plot and we're going to see the Ghost quite soon at the end of this Act. Couldn't you also safely cut the start Act IV Scene 5 - the dialogue between Horatio, Gertrude and a doctor or gentleman – and start the scene more dramatically with Ophelia's entrance? As discussed elsewhere in this guide, wouldn't it be more dramatically powerful to end the play with Hamlet's dying words, rather than with the superfluous Fortinbras?

All narratives feature characters being frustrated in their pursuit of something they think they really want or need. Consider character motivations and objectives in this play. Pick any scene from the play and write down all the characters within it. Then for each character decide on what you consider to be their overall, most important objective for the whole play. Next write down their objective in this scene. Now zoom further in and consider what might be motivating their behaviour in each interaction they have with other characters. Notice the points at which it is easier and harder to decide what is motivating a character. To what extent are these motivations hidden from the other characters? Which characters are the most transparent and which are the most opaque?

Focus on the inner Hamlet, how his thoughts are presented, by reading his soliloquies in a sequence. How do his thoughts and his thinking change and in what ways do they stay constant? What are his major preoccupations and his typical manner of self-expression? Now flip this process on its head and focus on Hamlet's outer life. List all the characters Hamlet interacts with during the play, such as Hamlet & Claudius; Hamlet & Gertrude, but also Hamlet & the pirates. For each pairing, write down what the interaction reveals about Hamlet and about the other characters.

Thought-tracking: Pick a scene and imagine you can freeze the action at any five points. Once the action is frozen you can look into any of the characters' thoughts. Either you could focus on one character's thoughts or range more widely. It might also be interesting to speculate on the thoughts of characters listening rather than speaking.

Probe, hook, deflect, block. This exercise involves thinking about how characters use words to try to influence each other. Pick a scene or section of a scene featuring only two of three characters. Hamlet's interactions with Rosencrantz and Guildenstern when they first arrive in Act II or the nunnery scene between Hamlet and Ophelia in Act III should work well. For each exchange of the dialogue decide whether the words are intended to ask questions of the other character [probe], intrigue and draw them in [hook], avoid answering their question by switching topic [deflect] or outright refuse to engage [block].

Walking out a soliloquy. You'll need a bit of space for this exercise and ideally more than one person. One person needs to get up and begin reading a soliloquy. As they read they should walk forward slowly in a straight line until they reach a piece of punctuation. At this point, decide whether to carry on walking in the same direction, to deviate a little, turn ninety degrees in one direction or even turn volte face. The exercise will help you to map out the pattern of Hamlet or Claudius' thoughts and make the abstract more tangible. After completing the exercise, watch the soliloquy in a couple of different productions. What do these performances share with your interpretation and how are they different from each other and from your own mapping? [One common physical characteristic in many performances of Hamlet's soliloquies is to have the Prince walking forwards and then turning back, forwards and back, for obvious reasons.]

Who's most to blame? This one works best in a classroom setting. The teacher puts names of the principle characters on different tables. When the class enters the room they have to walk around the tables and then choose to stand next to the one showing the character they think is most to blame. Once everyone has decided, going around the tables each in turn, the pupils should try to persuade other pupils to come to their table.

Repeat the exercise above, but add another possible culprit. The pupils who pick another element as the main cause of the tragedy should each write down who or what they consider this other to be [perhaps Fortinbras or the socio-historical context or uncertainty about the ethics of revenge]. Replace the characters' names with this new set of possible culprits on the tables and repeat the exercise for a final time. Now all the pupils should be ready to tackle an essay based on this question.

The same exercise can be repeated with different questions. For example, who is the best king in *Hamlet*? Again, once pupils have chosen their table and their king they should try to both justify their decision and persuade other pupils to join their table.

Chapter-style titles for scenes, scrambled.

The poison plot and death by drowning

Claudius' conscience

The graveyard

Polonius' wise advice

The spymaster

Enter Rosencrantz & Guildenstern and other actors

The grief of Ophelia and Laertes

Get thee to a nunnery!

The Mousetrap

The Norwegians are coming! [My thoughts be bloody]

The guards and the ghost

Revenge at last!

Ghostly grievances

Pirate adventure!

Gertrude's dilemma

Finding Hamlet

Conflict in court

An imminent apparition

Gertrude's closet

To England he must go

Total: 20

GLOSSARY

ALIENATION EFFECT – coined by German playwright, Berthold Brecht, it reverses the conventional idea that audiences suspend their disbelief when watching a play

ANTITHESIS – the use of balanced opposites, at sentence or text level

APOSTROPHE – a figure of speech addressing a person, object or idea

ASIDE – words spoken for only the audience to hear

CADENCE – the rise and fall of sounds in a line

CATHARSIS – a feeling of release an audience supposedly feels at the end of a tragedy

CONCEIT – an extended metaphor

DRAMATIC IRONY – when the audience knows things the on-stage characters do not

FIGURATIVE LANGUAGE – language that is not literal, but employs figures of speech, such as metaphor, simile and personification

FOURTH WALL – the term for the invisible wall separating the audience and the actors on the stage

GOTHIC – a style of literature characterised by psychological horror, dark deeds and uncanny events

HAMARTIA – a tragic or fatal flaw in the protagonist of a tragedy that contributes significantly to their downfall

HEROIC COUPLETS – pairs of rhymed lines in iambic pentameter

HYPERBOLE – extreme exaggeration

IAMBIC – a metrical pattern of a weak followed by a strong stress, ti-TUM, like a heart beat

IMAGERY – the umbrella term for description in poetry. Sensory imagery refers to descriptions that appeal to sight, sound and so forth; figurative imagery refers to the use of devices such as metaphor, simile and personification

JUXTAPOSITION – two things placed together to create a strong contrast

METAPHOR – an implicit comparison in which one thing is said to be another

METONYM – when something closely associated with a thing stands in for that thing, such as a book representing education

METRE – the regular pattern organising sound and rhythm in a poem

MONOLOGUE – extended speech by a single character

MOTIF – a repeated image or pattern of language, often carrying thematic significance

ONOMATOPOEIA – bang, crash, wallop

PENTAMETER – a poetic line consisting of fives stressed beats

PERSONIFICATION – giving human characteristics to inanimate things

PLOSIVE – a type of alliteration using 'p' and 'b' sounds

ROMANTIC – a type of poetry characterised by a love of nature, by strong emotion and heightened tone

SIMILE – an explicit comparison of two different things

SOLILOQUY – a speech by a single character alone on stage revealing their innermost thoughts

STAGECRAFT – a term for all the stage devices used by a playwright, encompassing lighting, costume, music, directions and so forth

STICHOMYTHIA – quick, choppy exchanges of dialogue between characters

SUSPENSION OF DISBELIEF – the idea that the audience willingly treats the events on stage as if they were real

SYMBOL – something that stands in for something else. Often a concrete representation of an idea.

SYNECDOCHE – when the part of something represents the whole, such as the crown for the British monarchy.

SYNTAX – the word order in a sentence. Syntax is crucial to sense: For example, though it uses all the same words, 'the man eats the fish' is not the same as 'the fish eats the man'

TRAGEDY – a play that ends with the deaths of the main characters

UNITIES – A description of a play's tragic structure by Aristotle that relates to three elements of time, place and action

WELL-MADE PLAY – a type of play that follows specific conventions so that its action looks and feels realistic.

Chapter-style titles for scenes; correct order

Act I
1. The guards and the ghost
2. Conflict in court
3. Polonius' wise advice
4. An imminent apparition
5. Ghostly grievances

Act II
1. The spymaster
2. Enter Rosencrantz & Guildenstern and other actors

Act III
1. Get thee to a nunnery!
2. The Mousetrap
3. Claudius' conscience
4. Gertrude's closet

Act IV
1. Gertrude's dilemma
2. Finding Hamlet
3. To England he must go
4. The Norwegians are coming! [My thoughts be bloody]
5. The grief of Ophelia and Laertes
6. Pirate adventure!
7. The poison plot and death by drowning

Act V
1. The graveyard
2. Revenge at last!

Recommended reading

Bradshaw, G. *Hamlet*. Connell, 2016.

Gibson, R. *Hamlet*. CUP, 2002.

Maguire, L. *Studying Shakespeare*. Wiley & Sons, 2013.

McEachern, C. *The Cambridge Companion to Shakespearian Tragedy*. CUP, 2013.

McEvoy, S. *Shakespeare the Basics*. Routledge, 2006.

Palfrey, S. *Doing Shakespeare*. Arden, 2005.

Smith, E. *This is Shakespeare*. Pelican, 2019.

Websites

The British Library, *Discovering Shakespeare*

The English & Media Centre have many great articles on *Hamlet*.

Peripeteia.webs.com

About the authors

Head of English and freelance writer, Neil Bowen has a Master's Degree in Literature & Education from the University of Cambridge and is a member of Ofqual's experts panel for English. He is the author of *The Art of Writing English Essays for GCSE*, co-author and editor of *The Art of Writing English Essays for A-level*, *The Art of Poetry* and *The Art of Drama* series. Neil runs the peripeteia project, bridging the gap between A-level and degree level English courses www.peripeteia.webs.com and delivers talks at GCSE & A-level student conferences for The Training Partnership.

Having taught in the UK and Bermuda, Freya Crofton is now Head of English at Harrow International School, Hong Kong. She has a BA in English Language and Literature from the University of Leeds and is particularly interested in Literary Criticism, C20th American fiction and, obviously, Shakespeare.

Having been awarded a first-class honours with a Dean's Commendation from the University of Exeter, Dr Briony Frost completed her PhD thesis on Jacobean Drama and politics. A regular seminar leader for the peripeteia project, Briony has lectured in English Literature at Plymouth and Exeter Universities and is currently working at the University of Bath.

A music specialist and academic scholar during her school career, Susanna Mackay is currently studying for an MA in English Literature at Trinity College, Cambridge.

An Irish English teacher, Michael Meally holds an MA in American Literature as well as first class degrees in English Literature and Engineering. Michael is the co-author of *The Art of Writing English Literature Essays* and has contributed to several of the *Art of Poetry* books.

Printed in Great Britain
by Amazon

21198173R00133